The European Court of Justice

The Politics of Judicial Integration

Renaud Dehousse

Foreword by William E. Paterson

Part of this book was first published
in French in 1994 by Montchrestien
as *La Cour de justice des Communautés européennes*

This edition first published 1998 by
MACMILLAN PRESS LTD
Houndmills, Basingstoke, Hampshire RG21 6XS
and London
Companies and representatives throughout the world

ISBN 0–333–69316–7 hardcover
ISBN 0–333–69317–5 paperback

A catalogue record for this book is available
from the British Library.

This book is printed on paper suitable for recycling and made from fully managed and sustained forest sources.

10 9 8 7 6 5 4 3 2 1
07 06 05 04 03 02 01 00 99 98

Printed in Malaysia

Published in the United of America 1998 by
ST. MARTIN's PRESS, INC.,
Scholarly and Reference Division,
175 Fifth Avenue, New York, N.Y. 10010

ISBN 0–312–21510–X

THE EUROPEAN UNION SERI...

General Editors: Neill Nugent, ...

The E... European Union, ran... al introductory texts to ...initive assessments of key institutions and ac... and policy processes, ... the role of member states.

Books in the series are written by leading scholars in their fields and reflect the most up-to-date research and debate. Particular attention is paid to accessibility and clear presentation for a wide audience of students, practitioners and interested general readers.

The series consists of four major strands:

- general textbooks
- the major institutions and actors
- the main areas of policy
- the member states and the Union

Published titles

Michelle Cini and Lee McGowan
Competition Policy in the European Union

Renaud Dehousse
The European Court of Justice

Desmond Dinan
Ever Closer Union? An Introduction to the European Community

Wyn Grant
The Common Agricultural Policy

Justin Greenwood
Representing Interests in the European Union

Alain Guyomarch, Howard Machin and Ella Ritchie
France in the European Union

Fiona Hayes-Renshaw and Helen Wallace
The Council of Ministers

Simon Hix and Christopher Lord
Political Parties in the European Union

Brigid Laffan
The Finances of the European Union

Janne Haaland Matlàry
Energy Policy in the European Union

Neill Nugent
The Government and Politics of the European Union (Third Edition)

John Peterson and Margaret Sharp
Technology Policy in the European Union

European Union Series
Series Standing Order
ISBN 0–333–71695–7 hardcover
ISBN 0–333–69352–3 paperback
(*outside North America only*)

You can receive future titles in this series as they are published by placing a standing order. Please contact your bookseller or, in the case of difficulty, write to us at the address below with your name and address, the title of the series and the ISBN quotes above.

Customer Services Department, Macmillan Distribution Ltd
Houndmills, Basingstoke, Hampshire RG21 6XS, England

Forthcoming

Simon Bulmer and Drew Scott
European Union: Economics, Policy and Politics

Simon Hix
The Political System of the European Union

John Peterson and Elizabeth Bomberg
Decision-Making in the European Union

Ben Rosamond
Theories of European Integration

Richard Sinnott
Understanding European Integration

• • • •

Simon Bulmer and Wolfgang Wessels
The European Council (Second Edition)

David Earnshaw and David Judge
The European Parliament

Neill Nugent
The European Commission

Anne Stevens
The Administration of the European Union

• • • •

David Allen and Geoffrey Edwards
The External Economic Relations of the European Union

Laura Cram
Social Policy in the European Union

Wyn Grant, Duncan Mathews and Peter Newell
The Greening of the European Union?

Martin Holland
The European Union and the Third World

Malcolm Levitt and Christopher Lord
The Political Economy of Monetary Union

Anand Menon
Defence Policy and the European Union

James Mitchell and Paul McAleavey
Regionalism and Regional Policy in the European Union

Jörg Monar
Justice and Home Affairs in the European Union

John Redmond, René Schwok and Lee Miles
Enlarging the European Union

Hazel Smith
The Foreign Policy of the European Union

Mark Thatcher
The Politics of European High Technology

Rüdiger Wurzel
Environmental Policy in the European Union

• • • •

Simon Bulmer and William E. Paterson
Germany and the European Union

Phil Daniels and Ella Ritchie
Britain and the European Union

Other titles planned include

European Union: A Brief Introduction
The History of the European Union
The European Union Source Book
The European Union Reader
The Political Economy of the European Union

• • • •

Political Union
The USA and the European Union

• • • •

The European Union and its Member States
Reshaping the States of the Union
Italy and the European Union
Spain and the European Union

Contents

List of Tables, Boxes and Figures

Tables

Boxes

Figures

For **Marc-Antoine** and **Aurore**

Foreword

The European Court of Justice has only gradually attracted the wider attention that has accompanied the Commission and the European Parliament since their inception. The Court was, of course, always of interest to lawyers, and its decisions were subject to exhaustive analysis by a new breed of Euro-lawyers which developed in parallel with the Court. From the beginning, the Court, like the Parliament and the Commission, had seen the value of positive scholarly commentary as flanking support for its own efforts to extend and develop its jurisdiction through interpretive judgments. In this effort, the Court was probably more successful than either the Commission or the Parliament, and a rich legal literature grew up around its jurisprudence and the implications of the creation of what was proclaimed as a new European legal order.

In this literature the scope of legal integration was contrasted very favourably with the economic and more especially the political dimensions where progress had been painfully slow, and a key role was allotted to the Court, which was held to have transformed the Treaty of Rome into a kind of constitution for the European Community. The regard in which the Court was held in the legal world was reinforced by the increasing recourse of national courts to Article 177, whereby they could seek its preliminary opinion on cases involving a European law dimension. The increased centrality of the European Court of Justice for lawyers, however, contrasted with its neglect by other students of the European Community who failed to read the legal commentaries and often felt excluded by the technicality of the judgments. The lack of consistent reporting of the Court by newspapers, contrasted to their coverage of other institutions – partly associated with its location in Luxembourg rather than Brussels – was also a handicap in this regard.

In this important study Renaud Dehousse succeeds brilliantly in making the European Court of Justice accessible to non-legal scholars, but he also does much more. His two central achievements are, first, to analyse the way in which the Court became subject to marked political turbulence in the 1990s and how it has responded to this politicization; arguably, however, his most important and novel contribution is to analyse the role of the Court in the policy process. This analysis was long overdue and provides not only a much sharper lens with which to view the activities of the Court, but changes established views of the relative importance of all the other actors in the European policy process. No student of the European Union can afford to neglect Professor Dehousse's work.

University of Birmingham WILLIAM E. PATERSON

Preface

This book is an attempt to make a balance sheet of the contribution of the European Court of Justice (ECJ) to the integration process. One easy way to describe it is to say that it is more a book about the law and its role in the integration process than a law book. As such, it has been greatly influenced by work undertaken jointly with colleagues from the European University Institute in Florence with whom I share the belief that legal issues can only be fully understood by reference to their broader societal context.

This book is an expanded version of my work *La Cour de Justice des Communautés européennes*, first published in 1994. With respect to the French version, the text has been expanded; it includes two additional chapters covering the juridification of the European policy process (Chapter 4) as well as the recent move away from the activist line of the first decades (Chapter 6). As a result, the text has almost doubled in length.

My gratitude goes first to Yves Mény, who convinced me that a book of this kind was needed at a time when academic debate on the ECJ was still non-existent. I am also grateful to Antonio Cassese, Carol Harlow, William Paterson, Peter Russell, Martin Shapiro, Mary Volcansek and Joseph Weiler for their comments on various parts of the manuscript. My long-standing intellectual partnership with Joseph Weiler has exerted more influence on this work than citations will ever tell. I also wish to thank Vincent Wright, who encouraged me to write an English-language version of my earlier book, and my publisher, Steven Kennedy, for his advice and patience.

Rewriting a book is a complex task. I could not have made it without the support of a number of people: Anny Bremner, Claire Kilpatrick and Eugene McNamee helped me to produce a book in a language which is not my own; Mimmo Monda and Ellen Vos provided first-class research assistance; and Annick Bulckaen and Evelyne Dourel went patiently through many versions of the manuscript. I am most grateful to all of them.

The reader might be puzzled by my insistence on referring to the European Community (EC), rather than to the European Union (EU), as is now almost universally done in English-language publications. There are two reasons for this seemingly old-fashioned choice. First, the book covers the role of the ECJ since its establishment in 1951, long before the creation of the EU by the Maastricht Treaty in 1993. Secondly, the drafters of that treaty conceived of the European Union as a complex structure based on three pillars: the European Communities, together with two intergovernmental pillars (the common foreign and security policy and justice and home affairs). In their wisdom, they chose to confine the jurisdiction of the ECJ to the first (Community) pillar – a decision to which we shall return in Chapter 6. As a result, the European Court is an institution of the European Community, not of the European Union, notwithstanding the minor changes introduced by the Treaty of Amsterdam in 1997. To reflect their choice, I have therefore decided to stick to the traditional usage of terms. Unless otherwise indicated, 'the Treaty' refers to the Treaty of Rome (EC Treaty) and the Treaty provisions that are cited are EC Treaty provisions.

A last-minute problem was caused by the signing of the Treaty of Amsterdam, which introduced a new numbering of the EC and EU Treaties. As the new numbering will come into force only with the ratification of the treaty, the pre-treaty Article numbers are given in the text throughout, with the new Article numbers following immediately in square brackets the first time each Article is cited in a paragraph or series of paragraphs. Tables of equivalence between old and new numbers appear in Appendices A and B. I hope this concern for legal correctness will not deter too many readers.

RENAUD DEHOUSSE

Introduction

The relationships between law and society have always been complex. Law, although often produced in response to social phenomena and thus shaped by them, also tries to regulate these phenomena. It therefore acquires the status of an independent variable in relation to them. This latter characteristic is particularly marked in the European Community. European integration was primarily conceived of in the hope of breaking with a bloody past. Rather than reacting to the evolution in relations between European societies, it was supposed to shape them. In the view of the drafters of the Treaty of Rome, the 'ever-closer union between the peoples of Europe' evoked in the preamble of the Treaty was to be brought about by the decisions of the European institutions.

Thus law is at the same time a cause and an effect, the product of social pressure for some, and instrument of social change for others. This mixed nature makes it difficult to study. Lawyers take its importance for granted, and tend to ignore the broader societal elements that account for its evolution. In contrast, non-lawyers, often disconcerted by its somewhat esoteric traditions, generally assume that the impact of legal developments is confined to the legal sphere.

European Community law has been no exception to this rule. Lawyers have stressed that the European Court of Justice (ECJ) has played a considerable role in the integration process, mainly by transforming the Treaty of Rome into some kind of constitution. Innumerable books have been dedicated to a systematic examination of its jurisprudence. Yet, as has been noted,

> [m]ost of the European legal literature begins and ends with law, describing a legalist world that is hermetically closed to considerations of power and self-interest. (Burley and Mattli, 1993, p. 45)

Moreover, leaving aside a few notable – mostly recent – exceptions, European legal scholarship has been characterized by the uncritical acceptance of the Court's performance. Martin Shapiro's often cited comments well capture the dominant trend:

> The Community [is presented] as a juristic idea; written constitution as a sacred text; the professional commentary as a legal truth; the case law as the inevitable working out of the correct implications of the constitutional text; and the constitutional court as the disembodied voice of right reason and constitutional teleology. (Shapiro, 1980, p. 538)

To a large extent, lawyers' indifference to the broader context in which legal integration was taking place has for long been paralleled by social scientists' lack of interest in Community law in general and the ECJ in particular. The grand theories of the 1960s and 1970s paid only scant attention to the Court, whose role was perceived essentially as that of a 'technical servant' (Weiler, 1982). International relations analyses of the integration process often exclude the possibility of supranational institutions like the ECJ forcing states to adopt a behaviour that would not be consonant with their national interests.

Things have, however, started to change in the wake of the integration revival launched by the Single European Act in 1986. Accounts of the new Euro-dynamism have led to a (partial) rediscovery of the role of supranational actors, including the Court of Justice. Relying mostly on the pioneering works of authors such as Eric Stein (1981) or Joseph Weiler (1981), political scientists have acknowledged, that through its 'constitutionalization' of the EC Treaty,

> of all Community institutions, the Court has gone furthest in limiting national autonomy, by asserting the principles of superiority of Community law and of the obligation of Member States to implement building acts consistent with Community Directives. (Keohane and Hoffmann, 1991, p. 278)

The emergence of the ECJ from the obscurity in which it had been previously confined has generated what Caporaso and Keeler have labelled 'one of the more interesting debates within the new wave's "segmented" (as opposed to "grand") integration theory literature' (1993, p. 40). Contrasting views have been offered to explain the development of legal integration, and the part played by the ECJ in this process (see, for example, Garrett, 1992 and 1995; Burley and Mattli, 1993; Mattli and Slaughter, 1995).

Notwithstanding this recent upsurge of interest in the ECJ, the standard perception of its role remains limited. While it is now generally recognized that 'the Community legal process has a dynamic of its own' (Keohane and Hoffmann, 1991, p. 278), law is often still treated as if it were a separate field, clearly distinct from the economic or political spheres. True, sectoral studies have highlighted the crucial impact of some ECJ rulings over the policy-making process (see, for example, Allen, 1996 or Leibfried and Pierson, 1996 for recent examples), but their findings have failed to be incorporated in a general analysis of the Court's role in the integration process. However, apart from the path-breaking work of Carol Harlow and Richard Rawlings (Harlow and Rawlings, 1992; Rawlings, 1993), there has been little reflection on the ways in which the legal battleground has been used by private actors and public institutions.

In short, much remains to be done to assimilate fully the legal sphere into the analysis of the integration process. This book should be seen as a step in that direction. It attempts to sketch the contribution of ECJ jurisprudence to European integration, and to bridge the gap between lawyers' and political scientists' standard perceptions of the Court.

The first two chapters give an overview of the structures and functions of the Court, and of the way it has shaped the basic elements of the Community's legal order in what is now known as the process of 'constitutionalization' of the EC Treaty. Most of this will be already familiar to those who have studied Community law, who might therefore want to proceed directly to the following chapters.

Chapter 3 discusses the impact of ECJ jurisprudence over the dynamics of European integration apart from the constitutionalization process. It shows that the Court's influence is felt at various levels, and affects all stages of the policy process. It also suggests that Court decisions, though clearly influenced by the context in which they intervene, are more than the translation of states' preferences into legal language: the ECJ has clearly made an autonomous contribution to the integration process. Chapter 4 shows that its influence has not been limited to the substance of Community law, but that it has also transformed the way in which integration has evolved, as legal parameters and judicial disputes have become an important element in the policy process.

If this analysis is correct, then the very magnitude of the Court's role needs to be explained. How has it been able to acquire such an important position when European political tradition, inherited from the philosophers of the Enlightenment, is in principle opposed to government by judges? Chapter 5 tries to answer that question by looking at the environment in which the ECJ has operated. It shows that, for a series of reasons, the activism of the Court has not come up against similar resistance to that which national courts generally have had to face.

However, that era might well be over. Chapter 6 discusses the elements that may have prompted the Court to adopt a more cautious line from the late 1980s onwards. European integration, because of its dynamism, is now provoking increasing resistance, which tends to limit the Court's margin of manoeuvre. Thus, the ECJ, which has promoted a pro-integration line for several decades, might end up being a victim of its own success. Be that as it may, this evolution can also be seen as a confirmation of one of the basic methodological premises of this book: developments in the legal sphere cannot be understood without reference to the broader context in which they take place.

1

The Court in the European Institutional System

The prominent place occupied by the Court of Justice (ECJ) in the European institutional system, finds no parallel in the international system where courts are generally confined to a marginal role. However, it can also be argued that the Court's importance is merely a corollary of the role of law in European integration. In a system where integration is largely dependent on the decisions of the European institutions, it was not possible to endow these institutions with unlimited discretionary powers. Guarantees had to be provided for those – states or individuals – that would be affected by their decisions; avenues of legal redress had to be available. The activities of European institutions were thus subjected to relatively precise conditions of substance, form and competence. Furthermore, given the importance of the concept of the rule of law in European legal culture, mechanisms of control were laid down.

The Treaty of Paris, which instituted the European Coal and Steel Community in 1951, established the European Court of Justice, with its seat in Luxembourg. Subsequently, following the creation of the European Economic Community and EURATOM by the Treaties of Rome (1957), it was decided that a single court would deal with legal disputes arising under all three Communities, though the methods of taking legal action differed in each.

As the years passed, it became clear that the Court was to play its most important role in the context of the EEC Treaty. At the end of 1995, 4024 judgments had been given on the EEC Treaty, compared with 359 on the ECSC Treaty and 19 on the EURATOM Treaty

(General Report of Activities of the EC, 1990–5). Undoubtedly, the dominance of the EEC Treaty is in part attributable to the purpose of this treaty, which covers all the principal areas of economic activity. Traders have indeed played a central role in the development of litigation before the ECJ, particularly in the framework of the preliminary rulings procedure established by Article 177 (Golub, 1996; Stone Sweet and Caporaso, 1997). They benefited from specific features of the Treaty: first, the open-textured character of many of its provisions, and second, the way in which the ECJ defined its own powers, particularly in the framework of the preliminary ruling procedure established by Article 177. Before addressing these two points, the structure of the Court should be briefly examined. However, the purpose of this chapter is not to study at length the inside functioning of the ECJ, for which there already exist detailed reviews (see, for example, Brown and Kennedy, 1995; March Hunnings, 1996). Rather, it will try to outline a number of elements which are indispensible for a proper understanding of its role in the European institutional system and its relationships with the various actors at work in that system.

Composition and functioning

The independence of judicial organs constitutes an essential element of dispute-settlement mechanisms in most legal systems. For the plaintiffs, submitting a case to a judge is to call on an arbiter, who can perform his social function only in so far as he is untainted by any suspicion of collusion with either of the parties and in particular with the government of the day. When this independence is found wanting, the judge's authority is weakened (Shapiro, 1981).

Conversely, with regard to international jurisdictions, there is no shortage of arguments of a functional nature to justify the need for these courts to weave a certain number of links with national societies. The presence within the ECJ of personalities who are familiar with the idiosyncracies of national legal systems is an undeniable advantage for a jurisdiction which has to take into account the laws of the member states in its day-to-day work. Similarly, the impact of the Court's jurisprudence is largely dependent on the quality of the relations it has with national courts. More generally, with the European Community being deprived of any coercive power of its own, it is reasonable to assume that the Court's authority is largely dependent on its representative nature. No matter how great their respect for the rule of law, European citizens would be little inclined to follow the decisions of an organ which did not seem to be sufficiently attuned to their national specificities.

These somewhat contradictory requirements – independence on the one hand and representativity on the other – appear to have influenced the authors of the Treaty of Rome, as traces of both can be found in the provisions setting out the composition of the Court.

A representative jurisdiction?

At present, following several incremental enlargements, the Court is comprised of 15 judges. Article 167 EEC [223] states that they shall 'be appointed by common accord of the Governments of the Member States for a term of six years'. These appointments are made each three years, for a group of six or seven judges, in order not to disturb unduly the functioning of the institution. Unlike the rules for the Commission and the Council, there is no explicit nationality requirement. The Treaty does not require the sharing out of judicial offices between the member states, nor does it prohibit the appointment of judges from non-member states. In practice, however, there is an unwritten rule that one judge will come from each member state. Until the latest enlargement, the big member states (France, Germany, Italy, Spain, the UK) benefited in turn from an extra judge so that the Court would always have an uneven number of judges. The requirement of unanimity for the appointment of a member of the Court makes exceptions to this principle of representativity unlikely.

Legally, the appointment of Court members 'by common accord' prevents the judges being considered as mere representatives of their states; thereafter they are supposed to act completely independently. However, the reality is that each judge is in fact 'proposed' by his or her country of origin, and the choice of each national government is, generally speaking, never disputed. This has permitted a certain politicization of the recruitment of the members of the Court: in several member states, where a tradition of representation of the main political parties exists, the appointment of a judge to the ECJ is included within the general process of balancing out posts of responsibility, such as ambassadorial, ministerial or European Commissioner nominations. However, in contrast to the Commission, it is the judges themselves, and not the governments, who elect the President of the Court. The period of office is three years; the President is renewed following each partial change in the Court's composition (Article 167 [223]).

While the member states' margin of manoeuvre may be considerable, it is not unlimited. The Treaty of Rome put an end to the ECSC system, which did not require judges at the ECJ to have any legal qualification and thus allowed Dutch labour leader Joseph Serrarens or French economist Jacques Rueff to sit as judges in Luxembourg in the 1950s. Following the example of the International Court of Justice, only those who are qualified to hold the highest judicial positions in their respective countries or 'juriconsults of recognised competence' can be called upon to sit in Luxembourg (Article 167). In practice, the ECJ has always had quite a diverse composition. It includes a number of former judges and high-ranking public servants, while UK and Irish appointees, in contrast with their colleagues, have often had experience in private practice. Several members have also had a political career prior to their nomination to the Court (Brown and Kennedy, 1995; Rasmussen, 1986). Advocate General Lenz had been a member of the German *Bundestag*, while his colleague La Pergola had been a member of the Italian cabinet, and later of the European Parliament. The Belgian judge, Melchior Whatelet, stepped down from his position as justice minister and deputy prime minister in the Belgian federal cabinet in order to take office in Luxembourg. Such a shift from political office to a judicial position triggered a protest from members of the legal profession in his country, who argued that it could undermine the authority of the ECJ (see *Agence Europe* of 15 and 18–19 September 1995). The university milieu has always been a favoured recruitment ground. Former university professors have long been the largest group in the ECJ, and several of them had only had limited judicial experience before their appointment to it. As we shall see later, this atypical career pattern may arguably have had a certain influence on the way in which the Court carried out its judicial task in its first decades of activity. However, with the latest enlargement, academics have been outnumbered by former members of the judiciary among the ECJ members.

This general survey of the ECJ would not be complete without referring to other categories of personnel which contribute to the life of this institution.

The presence of *Advocates General* is one of the original features of the ECJ. This new role, unknown in several European judicial systems, was inspired by the *Commissaires du gouvernement* who appear before the French *Conseil d'Etat*. Like them, the Advocates General's task is 'to make, in open court, reasoned submissions on cases brought before the Court of Justice, in order to assist the Court in the performance of the task assigned to it' (Article 166 [222]). Subject to the same conditions of recruitment and appointed in the same way as the judges, the nine Advocates General have the same status as the judges. They rank with them in order of seniority, are subject to the same rules, and receive the same salaries. Each of the 'big' member states has been given one post, while the others are passed in turn to one of the small members. This system is clearly meant to compensate for the fact that each state has been assigned one judge, which shows the degree of importance which has been attached to the representativeness of the ECJ.

While they do not participate in the Court's deliberations, in a certain sense the Advocates General have more autonomy than the judges. They are called upon to give their opinions after the oral hearing on questions of both fact and law, the applicable texts and precedents; in short, all of the elements which may help the Court in arriving at its decision. Their opinions always end with a proposed disposition of the case. As it is delivered under their own responsibility, they have greater latitude to take radical positions than judges, who must reach a compromise with their peers. Advocates General's opinions therefore often provide a useful auxiliary tool in the interpretation of sometimes laconic Court decisions.

Judges and Advocates General of the ECJ are each assisted by three legal secretaries. Legal secretaries are chosen by their principal, normally (but not always) from among lawyers from the same country, and stay at the Court for a few years. In addition to research on the points of law raised by the cases, they often play an important role in the drafting of opinions and judgments, somewhat like the law clerks attached to a Justice of the US Supreme Court.

The registrar of the Court plays a key role as link between judicial personnel and administration. Appointed by the Court for six years (renewable), he or she has a twofold task. As head of the Registry, the registrar is in charge of the ECJ record and of the traffic of cases. In addition to these judicial functions, he or she is also responsible for the administration of the Court, its financial management and its accounts (Article 23 of the Rules of Procedure). This is no meagre task: the administration does not have a classical pyramidal structure, but instead a series of parallel departments, several of which (languages services, research and documentation) provide direct assistance to the judicial component of the ECJ (see March Hunnings, 1996, pp. 62–9 for more details) as well as to the Court of First Instance, which is organizationally dependent on the ECJ, and has its office in the same building.

The somewhat prickly language question, the source of discontent in many international institutions, has been resolved in an ingenious manner. A choice of twelve languages is offered to litigants before the Court, as Gaelic, the official language of the Republic of Ireland, has been added to the eleven official languages of the Community. However, French, the only common language of all the members of the Court when it was founded, has imposed itself as the working language. Irrespective of the official language of the proceedings, all the internal documents relating to the case are circulated in French. As noted by two insiders, the resort to a common language has significant advantages:

> Some . . . are of a practical nature and are obvious: a decision-making process devoid of interpreters and translators is clearly more efficient or, in any event, less cumbersome, than one which must rely on them. Other effects are less obvious, but probably more important. In a microcosm whose inhabitants have such diverse roots the use of the same language, bringing with it shared access to the culture which finds expression in that language, facilitates the formation of an *esprit de corps*: in short, it promotes that sense of togetherness without which an institution which is obliged to take several new members on board every three years and which acquires detractors in direct proportion to its increasing visibility could not function effectively. Or even survive. (Mancini and Keeling, 1995, p. 398)

This wise compromise between functional requirements and the need for representativity provides an excellent illustration of the

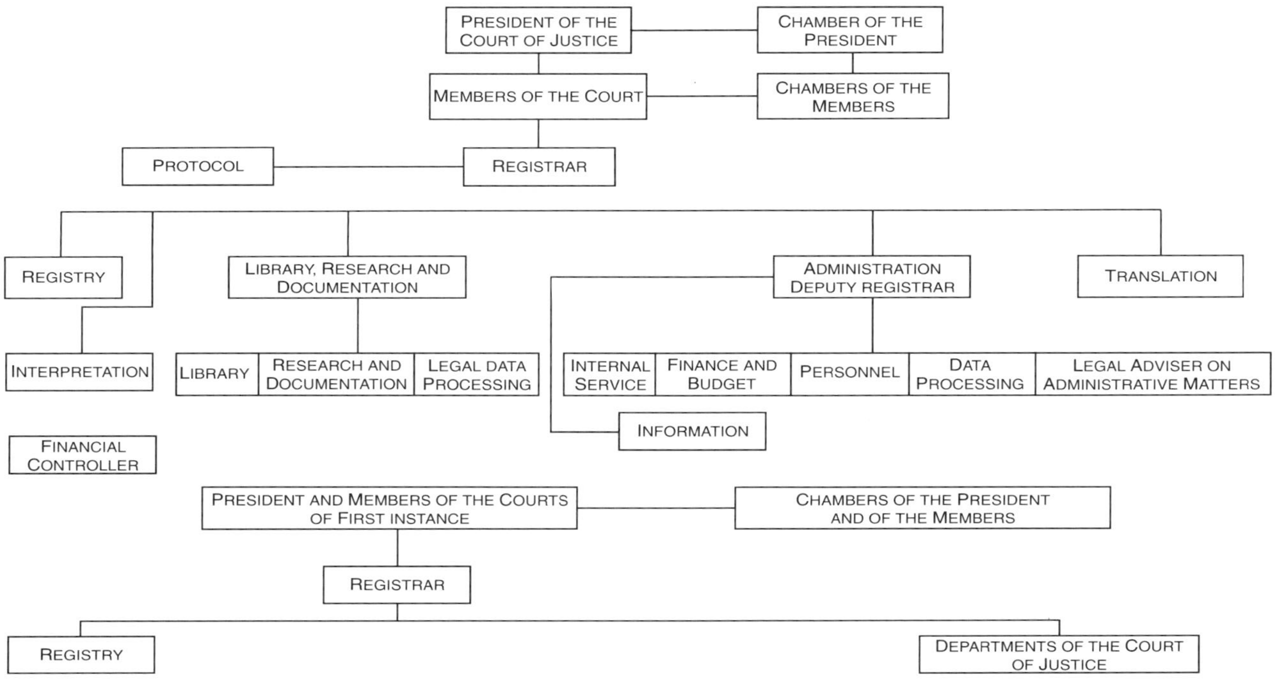

FIGURE 1.1 Abridged organization chart of the Court of the Justice and Court of First Instance

importance which is attached to contacts with individuals in member states. However, the enlargement of the Community is a source of growing difficulties. Multilingualism is costly: to mention but one element, translators and interpreters represent more than 25 per cent of the ECJ's administrative staff. Moreover, French is today less central than it used to be, and the increase in the number of official languages gives rise to a huge workload, which tends to slow down judicial proceedings (Rodriguez Iglesias, 1996). Reforms might therefore prove to be necessary in the not too distant future.

An autonomous jurisdiction

Chosen by the member states, the members of the Court are furthermore deprived of the guarantee of non-removal which, at national level, constitutes the best guarantee of their independence. Of course, their mandate can be limitlessly renewed. However, by allowing governments to decide each six years whether to renew their judicial term of office, this system gives national authorities a means of applying pressure – and it is difficult to believe they do not avail themselves of this means. Thus, when in 1990 Chancellor Kohl publicly criticized the ECJ rulings in relation to social security for migrant workers (*Agence Europe*, 14 October 1992, no. 5835), it was clear that his remarks placed some pressure on the German judge, Manfred Zuleeg. And these public criticisms may well have been only the tip of the iceberg. Be that as it may, Judge Zuleeg, who had also been targeted by the German Constitutional Court (see Chapter 6) was not renewed in 1994.

At the very least this system casts a shadow over the independence of the ECJ's members. Faced with pressures from the national authorities, the guarantees laid down by the texts – the exhortations to the 'independence' and the impartiality of the judges (Article 167 [223] and Article 6 of the Statute of the Court); the stated incompatibility of a position on the Court's bench with a political mandate, administrative or other functions; the judges' undertaking not to accept certain positions or benefits during the term of their mandate (Article 4 of the Statute of the Court) – appear to carry little weight. It is already clear from those countries where the rule of irremovability prevails that career considerations are often used to exert pressure on the judiciary.

However, several structural elements combine to counterbalance the grip of governments on the Court. Decisions are taken collegiately, generally by consensus or, if need be, on a simple majority vote. Moreover, although Article 165 [221] has been amended by the Maastricht Treaty to enable the ECJ to assign any case to chambers composed of three, five or seven judges, a vast majority of cases is still decided by the Court sitting in plenary, or by the larger chamber. Its work therefore retains a strong collegiate character.

Moreover, the Statute of the ECJ requires that judges' deliberations remain secret (Article 32). Judgments contain no indications either of votes taken or dissident opinions. Unlike the situation in the USA, for example, where the behaviour of the members of the Supreme Court and their influence within it have long been the subject of detailed analysis, the contribution of each individual judge to the final decisions of the ECJ cannot be discerned easily. All these elements make it difficult for the national authorities to control how 'their' judge behaves with the deliberations room.

Admittedly, individual judges can at times play a central role in the Court's decisions. The rules of procedure give the President the power to designate a member of the Court to act as rapporteur in each case (Article 10). The judge rapporteur's task is twofold: to produce a report for the hearing in which the facts of the case and the arguments used in parties and interveners' submissions are summarized; and to submit draft judgments which will serve as a basis for the Court's deliberations. The rapporteur is therefore in a position to exert considerable influence upon his or her colleagues. However, to avoid any risk of tension with national authorities, a non-written rule prevents a case coming from a member state being given to a judge from the same country (Brown and Kennedy, 1995, p. 54). The same desire for impartiality also means that preliminary references from a particular member state are generally not given to the judge from that country. In limiting the points of contact between the activities of the members of the Court and the interests of their state, all of these elements erect a barrier against potential attempts by national governments to acquire too direct an influence over the ECJ decisions. The facts suggest that the system is fairly effective: the Court's case law, rightly renowned for its expansive interpretation of the Treaty of Rome, offers a striking refutation to those who wish to see it as a mere puppet in the hands of the member states (see, for example, Garrett, 1992).

What can be concluded from this brief overview? Three elements emerge which are important for our analysis.

The first concerns the tension between representativeness and impartiality which was discussed earlier. The argument can be made that the authors of the Treaty were more concerned with the former than the latter. The delicate equilibrium between member states in the ECJ composition, the role played by national governments in the nomination of judges, even the language policy, all of these combine to give the impression that great care was taken to ensure a certain pluralism in the Court's composition and to maintain its links with national societies. While this has scarcely been commented on, it is an important factor to take into account. The social legitimacy of judicial decisions is largely dependent on the way in which the courts are perceived. The experience of Canada, for example, demonstrates that a court within which different social groups do not feel themselves to be represented has less chance of having its rulings accepted as just. There are ample grounds for maintaining that the link between representativeness and legitimacy is at least as important for an international court as for a national one. At the same time, there are limits to what can be achieved in terms of judicial representativeness. A court cannot encompass within its own ranks representatives of all segments of the European polity. Moreover, the more representative courts are, the less persuasive is the whole idea of judicial review (Mandel, 1994). A court is less likely to be perceived as neutral if national origins or party affiliation play a crucial role in the appointment of judges.

Secondly, the discretion which surrounds judicial selection is worth noting. This is completely unlike the situation in the United States, where the procedure for confirming new members of the Supreme Court by the Senate focuses – sometimes very dramatically – the attention of the media and the general public on the choice made by the President. It is in the muffled atmosphere of ministerial cabinets and diplomatic meetings, sheltered from the public gaze, that the members of the ECJ are appointed. There is no doubt that this unostentatious stance has contributed to the lack of controversy surrounding the Court's activities for many years. We shall return to this later (see Chapter 5).

Finally, it appears that the desire for representativeness has led to certain choices which could endanger the independence of the institution. The almost unlimited power of governments in judicial selection, combined with the brevity of the judicial mandate, could allow national authorities to exercise some control over the Court's activities.

It must be said, however, that the member states do not appear to have abused their power of appointment. Although the ECJ has at times made rather generous interpretations of the Treaty of Rome, which did not follow member state preferences, these audacious interpretations have never led to attempts at 'packing' the Court with more docile characters. It is unlikely that governments wishing to privilege docility as a criterion for judicial selection would turn to the universities as a selection ground, academics not being renowned for their discipline and restraint. Moreover, the US Supreme Court illustrates how difficult it is to predict safely the responses of individuals called upon to serve in a judicial capacity. Several judges nominated by Democrat Presidents have revealed themselves to be relatively conservative, while it was a judge appointed by Richard Nixon who drafted the opinion by which the Court liberalized abortion!

It is thus the brevity of the term of office rather than the governmental power of appointment which is a cause for concern. Of course, the requirements of representativity advise against the creation of irremovable mandates – there is too great a risk of seeing the Court's members, exiled in the fairy-tale duchy of Luxembourg, as elegantly described by an American commentator (Stein, 1981), losing all contact with their country of origin. But the solution currently adopted – a relatively short and renewable term of office – leaves too much room for member states to exercise undue pressure on the judges. It is moreover symptomatic that, in the course of the negotiations leading to the Maastricht Treaty, the member states rejected a proposal by the European Parliament which would have had the effect of providing a 12-year non-renewable mandate for ECJ members. Such a system, inspired by rules governing appointments to constitutional courts in many West European states, would undoubtedly have strengthened the independence of the ECJ's judges. In rejecting this proposal, the member states have demonstrated their unwillingness to give up the advantages which the current system offers them.

From international to constitutional justice

The ECJ can be distinguished in more than one way from other international jurisdictions. Some of its competences are redolent of those of a constitutional court, while others are more like those of an administrative court. These specificities can only be understood by considering the process of integration put into motion by the creation of the European Community. At the same time, however, there has been an evolution in the Court's missions, not least since a substantial share of its functions has been transferred to the Court of First Instance, which was 'attached to the Court of Justice' by the Single European Act of 1986 (Article 168a [225]).

An atypical institutional environment

Most international jurisdictions play a relatively modest role in international life. The most important of these, the International Court of Justice, considers only actions between states. Its very intervention is heavily dependent on the will of states, since the parties to the case must consent to be brought before the Court. The activities of international organizations have very rarely been subjected to judicial control.

This relative weakness is principally due to the decentralized nature of international society, at the heart of which real power rests in the hands of states. To entrust conflict resolution to an independent organ means that states would have to give up part of their sovereignty, something which is repugnant to most of them. Furthermore, the objective needs for judicial control are less acute than in a more organized society. The institutional weakness of the majority of international organizations, for example, means that there is little interest in legally controlling their actions. Why go to the trouble of asking for the annulment of a resolution if it is deprived of binding force? Similarly, when binding decisions are taken, unanimity is often the rule, which allows a state to protect its interests much more effectively than it could do by having recourse to a judicial organ where the outcome is always more uncertain.

The unusual role played by the ECJ stems from the fact that it operates in a very different institutional environment from that inhabited by traditional international jurisdictions. The Treaties of Paris and Rome contained, from the very outset, a number of institutional innovations. The pooling of coal and steel production, evinced by Robert Schuman in his declaration on 9 May 1950, notably envisaged the transfer of powers to an autonomous organ, the High Authority, whose decisions would be binding on the member states. These innovative elements, which would subsequently be expanded to give the Council of Ministers the powers to adopt decisions by majority vote, explain why the Court was given powers unparalleled in most international jurisdictions.

The ECSC Treaty, strongly influenced by the French administrative tradition, thus comes equipped with an extensive arsenal of administrative legal actions (Lagrange, 1979, pp.128–9): annulment proceedings (Article 33), the plea of illegality (Article 36), the action for failure to act (Article 35) and the non-contractual liability of the Community (Article 40). Furthermore, given the fact that the application of the treaty was partially incumbent on the member states, a special procedure was provided to determine breaches by member states of their Community obligations (Article 88).

From many perspectives, therefore, the powers of the Court within the framework of the ECSC Treaty are closer to those of national rather than international jurisdictions: control of the legality of the acts of the High Authority, allowing violations of both substance and form to be ascertained, is more similar to the action for excess of power in French administrative law than to the functions traditionally allocated to judicial organs on the international stage. In particular, the action to determine infringements of Community law by the member state is practically without equal on an international level. From the outset, it was clear that the creation of an atypical institutional system to regulate the relations between the member states had to be accompanied by a reinforcement of the role devolved to the judicial organs. This, however, should not be taken to mean that the authors of the treaties anticipated or desired the ECJ to play as active a role as it has done in the integration process (Rasmussen, 1986, p. 206).

The treaty setting up the European Economic Community by and large adopted the mechanisms provided for some years earlier in the Treaty of Paris, though certain modifications were made in order to enlarge the avenues of legal challenge (Pescatore, 1981a). Given their importance in Community case law, however, the provisions of the EEC Treaty merit more detailed investigation.

An international jurisdiction

Like all international jurisdictions, the ECJ has to deal with disputes between member states as well as cases concerning interpretation and application of the EC Treaty. However, the mechanisms set out in the EC Treaty differ in several ways from international judicial conflict resolution models:

1. The Court's competence is obligatory. In joining the Community, the member states accept its authority; no subsequent authorization is necessary to subject them to its jurisdiction.
2. Its competence is exclusive, since Article 219 [292] forbids member states to resort to any other conflict resolution method where the Treaty is at issue (Opinion 1/91 *re the European Economic Area Agreement*).
3. The European Commission, which Article 155 [211] sets up as guardian of the treaties, has been conferred an essential role in pursuing breaches of Community law (see Box 1.1). The power provided for in Article 169 [226] allows the Commission to initiate *infringement proceedings* when it considers that a member state has breached its treaty obligations. This judicial phase proper is preceded by a politico-administrative phase. The Commission opens the procedure by inviting the member state concerned to provide explanations for the alleged breach. When it considers these explanations to be insufficient, it adopts a reasoned opinion, which fixes a time limit within which the member state must take the measures necessary to comply with its Community obligations. It is only as a last resort, if this reasoned opinion is not followed by the appropriate action, that the case is taken before the ECJ.

This two-phase procedure opens the door to political management of the control of application of Community law. The Court has moreover underlined that the decision whether to initiate infringement proceedings lies within the Commission's discretion (case 247/87, *Star Fruit*). In fact, despite the increasing attention paid to the problems of Community law implementation since the beginning of the 1970s, the Commission has only made sporadic use of its right to go before the Court, preferring to guide the member states along the right path by way of bilateral negotiations with the national

BOX 1.1
Infringement proceedings

Article 169 [226]

If the Commission considers that a Member State has failed to fulfil an obligation under this Treaty, it shall deliver a reasoned opinion on the matter after giving the State concerned the opportunity to submit its observations.

If the State concerned does not comply with the opinion within the period laid down by the Commission, the latter may bring the matter before the Court of Justice.

Article 170 [227]

A Member State which considers that another Member State has failed to fulfil an obligation under this Treaty may bring the matter before the Court of Justice.

Before a Member State brings an action against another Member State for an alleged infringement of an obligation under this Treaty, it shall bring the matter before the Commission.

The Commission shall deliver a reasoned opinion after each of the States concerned has been given the opportunity to submit its own case and its observations on the other party's case both orally and in writing.

If the Commission has not delivered an opinion within three months of the date on which the matter was brought before it, the absence of such opinion shall not prevent the matter from being brought before the Court of Justice.

administrations concerned. Only a small percentage of the conflicts between national and Community law is thus brought before the ECJ by way of Article 169 [226] (Rasmussen, 1986, pp. 235–40). In the decade 1980–90, the number of Article 169 references to the ECJ oscillated between 5 and 14 per cent of the volume of breaches ascertained by the services of the Commission or by individuals. When we add to this picture the high number of last-minute adjustments carried out by national governments to ensure conformity with Community obligations, one sees that only a fraction of infringement procedures result in a Court judgment (Snyder, 1993, p. 29).

The central role played by the Commission is equally well illustrated by Article 170 [227], which deals with infringement proceedings introduced by one member state against another. This provision obliges the plaintiff member state to supply the Commission with the relevant dossier before the case can be brought before the ECJ. The Commission acts as arbiter in this situation: the case can be brought before the Court only following the issuance of a reasoned opinion by the Commission or a delay of three months. In practice, there have been only a couple of Article 170 actions, which tends to confirm the reticence of member states to turn to courts to resolve disputes.

Irrespective of their numerical importance, Article 170 infringement proceedings represent a distinct departure from the cardinal principle of international law: that is, that states are free to choose dispute resolution mechanisms, and is more closely allied to a centralized model of the control of the application of law. The Court has moreover held that the existence of these legal avenues in the treaty divests the member states of all possibilities to resort to the arsenal of unilateral countermeasures provided for in international law. The breach of Community law by other countries cannot serve as an excuse for a state to ignore its Community obligations (Joined cases 90 and 91/63, *Commission* v. *Luxembourg and Belgium*).

However, several aspects of the infringement proceedings remain impregnated with traces of the Community's international origins. Thus, Community law tends to consider the state as a single entity, 'whatever the agency whose action or inaction is the cause of the failure to fulfil its obligations even in the case of a constitutionally independent institution' (case 77/69, *Commission* v. *Belgium*). In conformity with the principle of the international responsibility of the state, whether the breach of Community law is attributable to the legislature, the administrative authorities or local authorities, it falls under Article 169 [226]. This last example illustrates the limits of such an approach: on several occasions, a state has been condemned for a breach attributable to regional authorities, even when central government had no legal means to compel these authorities to respect Community law (see, for example, Case 239/85, *Commission* v. Belgium). This gap between legal responsibility and effective control is hardly likely to consolidate the dissuasive effect of a judicial condemnation.

This links in with a second weakness in infringement proceedings, namely their purely declaratory nature. Of course, the ECJ can provide detailed indications of the measures the member state in breach must adopt to place itself in conformity with its obligations (see, for example, the cases 70/72, *Commission* v. *Federal Republic of Germany* and 42/82, *Commission* v. *France*). And the state concerned 'shall take the necessary measures to comply with the judgment of the Court of Justice' (Article 171 [228]). However, as in international law, the Court's judgment is not self-executing. If a state does not comply it will be in breach of Community law, but the ruling will not be effective in its domestic legal system. The absence of a mechanism to compel state compliance is clearly an important lacuna.

Its absence has been increasingly felt in recent years. From the late 1970s on, the Commission has adopted a policy of strict prosecution of the infringements of Community law. However, the growth in the number of cases brought before the Court has resulted in an increasing number of Article 169 [226] rulings remaining unimplemented, which undermines the dissuasive effect of the whole procedure. The Maastricht Treaty has taken a first step towards remedying this situation in providing the possibility for financial sanctions to be imposed on a member state which has failed to respect a judgment of the Court (Article 171 [228] paragraph 2 – see Box 1.2).

Finally, it is worth noting that the Treaty of Rome, like most international instruments, does not grant individuals standing to challenge breaches of Community law before the Court. The only avenue of legal redress open to them is to present their complaint to the Commission in the hope that it will open legal proceedings. But there is no guarantee that it will do so, since this is a discretionary prerogative. This reflects a relatively traditional conception of international relations, in which individuals play a minimal role. In any case, we shall see later that innovative use of the Article 177 [234] preliminary reference procedure has largely compensated for this deficiency.

A constitutional jurisdiction

Several of the ECJ's functions are similar to those of constitutional jurisdictions. Given the general task of ensuring that 'the law is

BOX 1.2

Article 171 [228]

1. If the Court of Justice finds that a Member State has failed to fulfil an obligation under this Treaty, the State shall be required to take the necessary measures to comply with the judgment of the Court of Justice.
2. If the Commission considers that the Member State concerned has not taken such measures it shall, after giving that State the opportunity to submit its observations, issue a reasoned opinion specifying the points on which the Member State concerned has not complied with the judgment of the Court of Justice.

   If the Member State concerned fails to take the necessary measures to comply with the Court's judgments within the time-limit laid down by the Commission, the latter may bring the case before the Court of Justice. In so doing it shall specify the amount of the lump sum or penalty payment to be paid by the Member State concerned which it considers appropriate in the circumstances.

   If the Court of Justice finds that the Member State concerned has not complied with its judgment it may impose a lump sum or penalty payment on it.

   This procedure shall be without prejudice to Article 170.

observed' (Article 164 [220]), it has to ensure the conformity of the acts of the institutions with the Treaty, which it has itself defined as the Community's 'Constitutional Charter' (case 294/83, '*Les Verts*'). In so doing, it has had to arbitrate conflicts between the European institutions. Like the constitutional courts in a federal system, it has also had to adjudicate disputes relating to the division of competences between the Community and the member states, although so far this latter type of conflict has not played a prominent role in judicial politics at Community level.

The main vehicle for referring both sets of disputes to the Court has been the control of legality established by Article 173 [230] (see Box 1.3), which states that annulment actions can be introduced against all acts 'other than recommendations and opinions' – that is, against all acts aiming to produce legal effects taken by the European institutions (case 22/70, *ERTA*). The original wording of Article 173 made explicit reference only to acts adopted by the Commission and the Council. However, the Court has held that in a system based on respect for law, even acts with legal effects

BOX 1.3
Annulment proceedings

Article 173 [230]

The Court of Justice shall review the legality of acts adopted jointly by the European Parliament and the Council, of the Commission and of the ECB, other than recommendations and opinions, and of acts of the European Parliament intended to produce legal effects *vis-à-vis* third parties.

It shall for this purpose have jurisdiction in actions brought by a Member State, the Council or the Commission on grounds of lack of competence, infringement of an essential procedural requirement, infringement of this Treaty or of any rule of law relating to its application, or misuse of powers.

The Court shall have jurisdiction under the same conditions in actions brought by the European Parliament and by the ECB for the purpose of protecting their prerogatives.

Any natural or legal person may, under the same conditions, institute proceedings against a decision addressed to that person or against a decision which, although in the form of a regulation or a decision addressed to another person, is of direct and individual concern to the former.

The proceedings provided for in this Article shall be instituted within two months of the publication of the measure, or of its notification to the plaintiff, or, in the absence thereof, of the day on which it came to the knowledge of the latter, as the case may be.

adopted by other institutions have to be subject to judicial control. It thus ruled admissible an annulment action introduced by the French Green party against a decision of the European Parliament concerning financing of the party political electoral campaign (case 294/83, '*Les Verts*'). This judicial decision has subsequently been implicitly endorsed by the member states, who modified Article 173 accordingly in the Maastricht Treaty.

Acts of the institutions can be challenged on four different grounds:

- lack of competence
- infringement of an essential procedural requirement

- infringement of the treaty or of any rule of law relating to its application
- misuse of powers.

Some of these grounds are more important than others in disputes before the Court. As the Community's objectives are very generally defined, it is difficult to prove misuse of powers. While easier to manage, questions relating to competence and respect of essential procedural requirements can occasionally give rise to eminently political conflicts. Thus, the ECJ annulled for infringement of an essential procedural requirement a regulation which the Council had adopted without waiting for the opinion of the European Parliament (case 138/79, *Roquette*). Likewise, control of the motivation of Community acts, which appears to require merely the respect of the conditions of form set out in the treaty, can sometimes lead to an examination of the arguments used to justify the well-foundedness of a decision: in such a case, the Court is evidently in a position to play a much more active role (Shapiro, 1992).

The first paragraph of Article 173 [230] lists a number of privileged applicants who are authorized to commence legal proceedings against any binding act: member states, the Council and the Commission. After some hesitation, the ECJ, wishing to preserve the institutional equilibrium of the Community, eventually added the European Parliament to this list, now generally considered to be exhaustive. The Parliament can thus take annulment actions 'provided that the action seeks only to safeguard its prerogatives and that it is founded only on submissions alleging their infringement' (case 70/88, *Parliament* v. *Council*). This judicial innovation was subsequently embodied in the Maastricht Treaty; riding on the coat-tails of this reform, a similar right was granted to the European Central Bank envisaged by that treaty.

The *failure to act* provision in Article 175 [232] allows the Court to sanction the situation where an institution has refused to adopt an act when it was legally bound to do so (see Box 1.4). This action is open to member states and the institutions, as well as to individuals who 'complain to the Court of Justice that an institution of the Community has failed to address to that person any act other than a recommendation or an opinion'. Given the relatively strict conditions governing its exercise, this procedure has played a limited role in the development of the Community. However, the Parliament, which had threatened for years to take such an action against the Council or the Commission, used this Article to obtain a declaration that the Council had failed in its obligation to adopt a common transport policy as required by Article 74 *et seq.* of the Treaty of Rome (case 13/83, *Parliament* v. *Council*).

Finally, the use of infringement proceedings gives the Court the opportunity to ensure that the 'constitutional' law of the Community is respected by national authorities. Preliminary references can also be used for the same purpose, as shall be seen below (see Chapter 2). The range of competences conferred on the ECJ thus places it in the position to act as a general arbiter in conflicts among the institutions and to ensure a faithful application of the Community's constitutional charter, like many constitutional courts do at national level. This constitutional role has increased in recent years as a result of the revival the integration process has enjoyed since the mid-1980s, which has affected the position of the Court *vis-à-vis* political actors, as will be seen in Chapter 6.

BOX 1.4
Failure to act

Article 175 [232]

Should the European Parliament, the Council or the Commission, in infringement of this Treaty, fail to act, the Member States and the other institutions of the Community may bring an action before the Court of Justice to have the infringement established.

The action shall be admissible only if the institution concerned has first been called upon to act. If, within two months of being so called upon, the institution concerned has not defined its position, the action may be brought within a further period of two months.

Any natural or legal person may, under the conditions laid down in the preceding paragraphs, complain to the Court of Justice that an institution of the Community has failed to address that person any act other than a recommendation or an opinion.

The Court of Justice shall have jurisdiction, under the same conditions, in actions or proceedings brought by the ECB in the areas falling within the latter's field of competence and in actions or proceedings brought against the latter.

An administrative jurisdiction

Many of the legal avenues of redress laid down in the EC Treaty are, however, inspired by administrative law remedies. We saw earlier that failure to act and annulment actions were laid down in the ECSC Treaty to allow the actions of the High Authority to be controlled. In the EEC system, they also guarantee the legality of acts of European institutions in areas such as competition or anti-dumping policy.

The right to take an annulment action is, however, only open to individuals when certain conditions are met. They can only challenge decisions which are addressed to them, or those which 'although in the form of a regulation or a decision addressed to another person, is of direct and individual concern to [them]' (Article 173 [230]). In other words, private persons, unlike the institutions with special standing, can only take annulment actions in concrete disputes and under relatively strictly defined conditions.

If we compare this provision with the much less restrictive wording of the annulment action laid down in Article 33 of the ECSC Treaty, which was liberally interpreted by the ECJ (joined cases 7 and 9/54, *Groupement des industries sidérurgiques luxembourgeoises*), it appears clearly that the intention of the Treaty of Rome authors was indeed to limit the possibilities for legal redress open to individuals. However, any party to a case in which the legality of a regulation of the Council or the Commission is debated has the right to plead the grounds of nullity specified in Article 173, to justify the inapplicability of the regulation in question, even if it does not meet the standing conditions outlined above (Article 184 [241]). While this will not annul the regulation concerned, this *plea of illegality* means that individual instances of application derived from the regulation can be invalidated.

The treaty also provides other avenues of legal redress which belong to the realm of administrative litigation (Box 1.5). Thus disputes between the Community and its staff fall within the Court's jurisdiction (Article 179 [236]), as do disputes relating to the non-contractual liability of the Community (Articles 215 [288], para. 2 and 178 [235]). Furthermore, it provides for an expansion of the Court's competence when it has to rule on disputes concerning the penalties laid down by Community regulations. Here, the ECJ must not only rule on the legality of the measure in question but must

BOX 1.5
Administrative litigation

Article 172 [229]

Regulations adopted jointly by the European Parliament and the Council, and by the Council, pursuant to the provisions of this Treaty, may give the Court of Justice unlimited jurisdiction with regard to the penalties provided for in such regulations.

Article 178 [235]

The Court of Justice shall have jurisdiction in disputes relating to compensation for damage provided for in the second paragraph of Article 215.

Article 179 [236]

The Court of Justice shall have jurisdiction in any dispute between the Community and its servants within the limits and under the conditions laid down in the Staff Regulations or the Conditions of Employment.

Article 215 [288]

The contractual liability of the Community shall be governed by the law applicable to the contract in question.

In the case of non-contractual liability, the Community shall, in accordance with the general principles common to the laws of the Member States, make good any damage caused by its institutions or by its servants in the performance of their duties.
The preceding paragraph shall apply under the same conditions to damage caused by the ECB or by its servants in the performance of their duties.

also, where necessary, rule on the reasonableness of the penalty in relation to the gravity of the breach (Article 172 [229]). This applies, for instance, to the controls carried out by the Commission in the framework of competition policy: an undertaking found to be abusing a dominant position in breach of Article 86 [82] can, if it fulfils the standing requirements specified in Article 173 [230], challenge the decision of the Commission before the Court.

In all these areas, the treaty confers *unlimited jurisdiction* on the Court. Parties are not confined to specific grounds; the Court may go beyond issues of legality and also consider the expediency of the acts adopted by the institutions. All of these procedures, in particular in competition cases, thus require a detailed examination of frequently complex factual situations. The ECJ, with its growing workload, found it increasingly difficult to carry out the required fact-finding. Moreover, the staff cases represent an important segment – almost one-third – of its case law. These considerations, combined with an ever-increasing judicial backlog, led to the Court of First Instance being set up at the request of the ECJ.

The creation of the Court of First Instance was motivated by two kinds of concerns:

1. It was hoped that the transfer of some of the ECJ's workload to another jurisdiction would allow it to concentrate on its principal task, ensuring uniform application of Community law.
2. The creation of a specialized court was deemed to be beneficial to the protection of litigants: not only would the new body dispose of more time to examine cases which require intensive fact-finding, but as appeals to the ECJ on points of law were made possible, parties would benefit from increased opportunities to assert their rights.

A real European administrative court, the Court of First Instance, has been given the task of dealing with most of the administrative disputes hitherto brought before the ECJ. Article 168a [225] of the Treaty, inserted by the Single European Act (1986) gave the Council the power, at the request of the ECJ, to transfer to the Court of First Instance, which is attached to it, a certain number of competences. As a result of a two-step transfer, the Court of First Instance now has a general competence for all actions brought by private parties against decisions of Community institutions.

Preliminary rulings and the court-to-court dialogue

The extraordinary development of the role of the ECJ is in large part due to a provision which has been scarcely mentioned up to now, Article 177 [234] of the Treaty of Rome (Box 1.6). Such is the importance of this provision that it warrants individual attention.

Article 177 allows national courts, *seised* of a dispute which raises questions concerning Community law, to ask the ECJ which interpretation should be given to relevant EC provisions or to question the validity of acts of the institutions. The preliminary reference procedure thus establishes a real dialogue between the national and

BOX 1.6
Preliminary rulings

Article 177 [234]

The Court of Justice shall have jurisdiction to give preliminary rulings concerning:

(a) the interpretation of this Treaty;
(b) the validity and interpretation of acts of the institutions of the Community and of the European Central Bank;
(c) the interpretation of the statues of bodies established by an act of the Council, where those statutes so provide.

Where such a question is raised before any court or tribunal of a Member State, that court or tribunal may, if it considers that a decision on the question is necessary to enable it to give judgment, request the Court of Justice to give a ruling thereon.

Where any such question is raised in a case pending before a court or tribunal of a Member State against whose decisions there is no judicial remedy under national law, that court or tribunal shall bring the matter before the Court of Justice.

the supranational judge. Parties in the case before the national court only play a secondary role: they are entitled to take part in the proceedings, but they are not obliged, and at times decline, to do so. Likewise, the ECJ does not give a judgment, telling an applicant that it has won or lost; rather, it responds to a 'fraternal request' from another court for clarification on a point of community law (March Hunnings, 1996, p. 75). It is the former, and not the parties, who decides whether or not a reference should be made; again, it falls to the national judge to apply the Court's conclusions in the case referred.

An analogous mechanism already existed in Article 41 ECSC. Its limited field of application – it related only to the validity of acts of the Council and the High Authority – in tandem with the much wider possibilities for individuals to bring annulment actions under this treaty (Article 33) than under the Treaty of Rome (Article 173 [230]) explain why this provision existed only on paper for several years. Suggestions to extend the interpretive reference procedure seem to have been mooted for the first time by the group of legal experts responsible for drafting the institutional clauses of the

Treaty of Rome. The move was inspired by the preliminary ruling procedures contained in the German and Italian Constitutions which enable lower courts to refer to the Constitutional Court questions relating to the conformity of laws with the Constitution. By entrusting interpretation of the fundamental law to a central jurisdiction, these mechanisms aim to ensure uniform interpretation of the Constitution. A similar functional logic underpins Article 177 [234]. This explains why the decision to refer – optional for lower courts – was made obligatory for courts of last instance (Article 177, para. 3). This was intended to prevent the crystallization at national level of interpretations endangering the uniformity or effectiveness of Community law (Pescatore, 1981a, p. 173).

It is doubtful whether those responsible for this procedural innovation realized the effects it would have on the development of Community law. Though it was slow to get off the ground – the first preliminary reference was made to the Court in 1961 and only 26 references were registered in the nine years following the coming into force of the Treaty of Rome – Article 177 has gradually acquired a central importance in the Court. It is now by far the most frequently employed procedure established by the EC Treaty. Of the 9052 cases brought before the ECJ by 31 December 1995, preliminary references (mostly channelled through the Article 177 route) add up to 3144 – that is over one-third of the total. Following the transferral of the numerous staff cases to the Court of First Instance, preliminary references constitute an even greater proportion of the ECJ's work. Thus, of the 2399 cases brought before it from 1990 to 1995, no less than 1147 (almost half) were preliminary references (ECJ, 1996, p. 216). The weight of preliminary rulings is even more important if we look at judgments delivered by the ECJ. Figure 1.2 shows that preliminary rulings have been steadily pushing up the number of cases handled by the ECJ.

The quantitative aspect is not, however, the most important. The pattern of diffusion of preliminary reference procedure provides a remarkable tool for measuring the degree of penetration of Community law into the national legal orders. Figure 1.3 gives a breakdown of the average number of preliminary rulings per member state of the European Community.

It shows that there are huge differences from country to country. What is more, if one examines the number of cases referred to the ECJ in relation to the population of each state, it becomes clear that

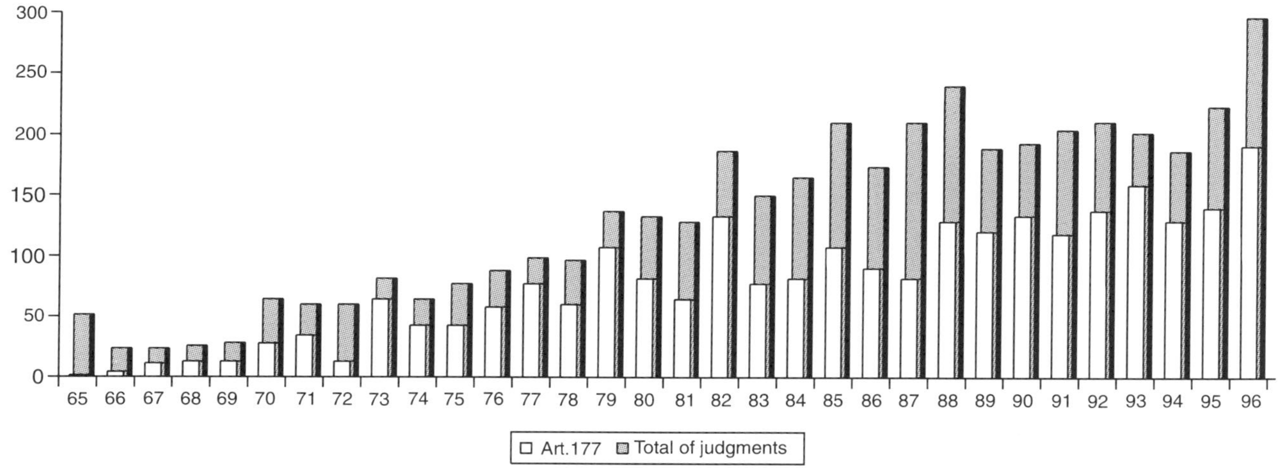

FIGURE 1.2 Judgments delivered, 1965–96
Source: EC General Reports of Activities for Art. 177; ECJ Report of Proceedings and Annual Report of the Court of Justice and the CFI, 1995 for total of judgments.

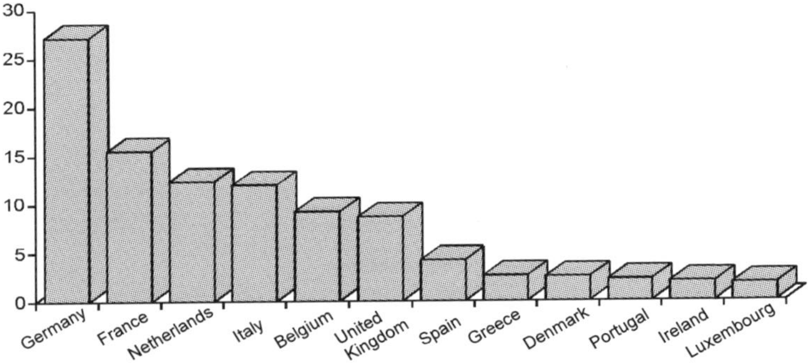

FIGURE 1.3 Average number of prelimininary rulings
(total number of preliminary references from the date of adhesion to the EC to the end of 1995, divided by number of years of membership)
Source: Annual Report 1995 of the Court of Justice and the Court of First Instance of the European Community.

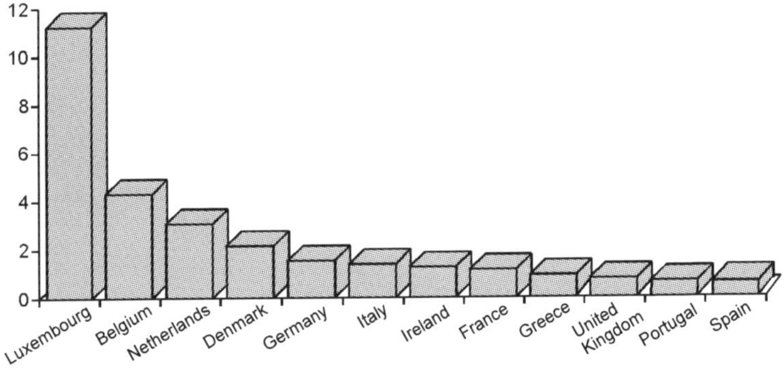

FIGURE 1.4 Propensity to refer questions to the ECJ (no. of preliminary references in 1990–5 per 400 000 inhabitants)
Source: Anual Report 1995 of the Court of Justice and the Court of First Instance of the European Community.

the propensity to refer problems to it varies enormously from one country to another.

Figure 1.4 measures the number of references made in the period 1990–5 in relation to the population of the 12 countries which were members of the EC in 1990 (Austria, Sweden and Finland, which joined later, have been omitted). The resulting ratio gives an idea of national courts' propensity to refer cases to the ECJ. Benelux courts appear to be much more active in the dialogue with the ECJ than their counterparts in other member states. Though the population of Belgium, Greece and Portugal is a comparable size, the Belgian ratio is five times higher than the Greek, and seven times higher than the Portuguese. Similarly, Italian courts have referred twice as many cases as British courts in the period under survey. Recent studies have suggested that these huge variations are linked to the volume of trade: countries that are most active in intra-Community exchanges have played a crucial role in the development of Article 177 [234] litigation (Golub 1996; Stone Sweet and Caporaso, 1996).

In any case, the overall result is impressive. Through this process, as a former President of the Court has remarked, national judges have become ordinary Community judges (Lecourt, 1976). The dialogue with the ECJ seems to have become integrated into judicial customs. Although only courts of last instance are required to refer to the Court when a question of Community law interpretation arises, almost three-quarters of preliminary references come from lower courts (ECJ, 1991, p. 113).

The part played by the latter has been indirectly acknowledged in the Amsterdam Treaty: while the jurisdiction of the ECJ has been extended in a somewhat patchy fashion to areas thus far treated in the framework of the so-called 'Third Pillar' of the EU (essentially immigration and co-operation in criminal matters), the possibility of referring questions to the ECJ has been in various ways restricted to courts of last resort (new Articles K7 [35] of the EU Treaty and 73p [68] of the EC Treaty). Clearly, the drafters of that treaty wanted to avoid the development of a judicial dialogue which might end up eroding governments' authority.

The preliminary reference procedure has also enabled individuals, whose means of direct access to the ECJ are fairly restricted, to bring a significant number of disputes before the Court. The novelty of this is not just of a procedural nature. It also has substantial consequences. As will be seen below (Chapter 2), in about two-thirds of preliminary rulings, the Court has ruled (albeit indirectly) on the compatibility of national provisions with Community law. This has enabled it to wield considerable influence over the application of Community law. The preliminary rulings procedure has also had a significant educational impact. Through their dialogue with the ECJ, national courts have become gradually acquainted with Community law. Conversely, the reference system has enabled them to draw the attention of the ECJ to the practical implications of its rulings, and at times to influence the evolution of its jurisprudence. The partnership that developed between the two levels has led to the development of a positive atmosphere, which has facilitated the reception of EC law by national courts, as will be discussed in Chapter 5.

Conclusion: the birth of a constitutional jurisdiction

The previous pages give a general idea of the hybrid nature of the ECJ's tasks. Like all international jurisdictions, it is called upon to rule on inter-state disputes concerning the application of an international agreement. Like many constitutional courts, the ECJ has the task of ensuring uniform interpretation of the Community's fundamental charter – and to ensure the legality of acts adopted by the European institutions, leading it to act as an umpire in conflicts which pit them against one another. Finally, the treaties establish a certain number of mechanisms to control the acts of public authorities, a role which at national level falls within the competence of administrative jurisdictions.

None of these analogies suffices to explain the multiform nature of this institution. However, the time factor is important here. We have seen how, in several respects, the functions of the ECJ represent a departure from the law governing international jurisdictions. The extent of this departure increased dramatically with the entry of individuals into Community disputes. Disagreements between states do not constitute the core of the Court's activities and, in any case, they are not resolved in the same way as they are before international tribunals. There is no doubt that these specific features have played a major role in the development of Community law. Many of the key judgments – starting with the two most notorious, *Van Gend en Loos* (case 26/62) and *Costa* v. *ENEL* (case 6/64) – originated in legal proceedings brought by a private individual. Add to this the fact that, since 1989, most administrative disputes have been transferred to the Court of First Instance and we are forced to admit that the constitutional element of the ECJ's functions is gradually emerging.

Of course, the treaties establishing the European Communities make up an imperfect constitution. They contain rules which rarely figure in constitutional texts, such as rules on competition law, and do not contain any list of fundamental rights. The avenues of legal redress laid down in these treaties are both more numerous and more diversified than those used to seise more specialized constitutional courts.

It is, however, incontestable that the court has seen itself endowed with a constitutional task: to ensure the uniform interpretation of the treaties. In carrying out its functions, it has had to settle a significant number of issues of a constitutional nature, such as the relationship between Community law and national law, the relations between the institutions and the delimitation of the respective competences of the Community and the Member States. Finally, the very way in which it has exercised its competences, its utilization of preliminary rulings, its expansive interpretation of treaty provisions: all of these factors have undoubtedly contributed to aligning it with constitutional courts.

This statement still needs to be further refined, for the ECJ's role is clearly different from that of the US Supreme Court, for example. The United States possesses a diffuse system of constitutional control within which each federal judge can pronounce on the compatibility of a law with the constitution. This liberal approach is certainly tempered by the presence of the Supreme Court, which can overturn the judgments of lower courts. The Community approach to constitutional control is very different: while the ECJ alone can invalidate acts of Community institutions not in conformity with the treaty (case 314/85, *Foto-Frost*), decisions of national courts cannot be appealed before it. Thus, if it were necessary to pigeon-hole the ECJ into one model, the constitutional court model would clearly have to be chosen. Like West European Constitutional Courts, the primary mission of the ECJ is to provide a uniform interpretation of the Community's constitutional charter, and it does so through a sustained dialogue with lower courts.

2

The Constitutionalization of the Community Legal Order

When the representatives of the member states appended their signatures to the Treaty of Paris on 18 April 1951, they were undoubtedly aware of the importance, not least of which was symbolic, of the act. Were they not, as the preamble of the treaty stated, affirming that the creation of the Coal and Steel Community, the first of the Communities, represented the basis 'for a broader and deeper community among peoples long divided by bloody conflict'? And yet, for the jurist, this revolutionary political development took the rather banal legal form of an international treaty. Clearly, the treaty's content was highly innovative since it eroded, sometimes considerably, national sovereignty. However, its closest resemblance was to a classic international treaty model. Moreover, the treaty was concluded for a period of 50 years, a good indicator that it was not intended to deviate too much from the traditional framework of inter-state relations.

Three decades on, referring to the Treaty of Rome in an important judgment, the ECJ showed no hesitation in presenting it as the 'Constitutional Charter' of the Community (case 294/83, '*Les Verts*'). A couple of years later, it went as far as to suggest that some parts of the treaty were of such importance that they could not be modified at will by the member states (Opinion 1/91). A detached observer of Community life could well have seen this as either a rhetorical device, or the expression of a pious wish. A meticulous lawyer could have pointed out the inappropriateness of such views in relation to what remained an international agreement. In reality, however, none of this happened and there was little criticism.

This lack of reaction is easily explained if one is familiar with Community jurisprudence. Over the years the ECJ has gradually built up a constitutional type structure. It has simultaneously worked to blur the outlines of the components which made the Community most resemble a traditional international order. This is why the Court's declaration was not really surprising. Rather than denoting a revolutionary rupture with the past, it merely stated the logical conclusion of a process dating back to the early 1960s and resting on four pillars: the doctrine of direct effect, the supremacy of Community law, and the case law on both Community competences and 'fundamental rights'. Each of these will be examined in turn.

Direct effect

To grasp the significance of the ECJ's case law, it is important to bear in mind that classic international law principally governs inter-state relations. International treaties are of course binding upon the contracting parties, but their effect in the domestic legal order is primarily determined by the constitutional law rules of the contracting parties. Thus, for instance, Benelux countries generally accept the idea that treaty provisions may, if they meet certain conditions, be directly invoked by individuals before domestic courts. In contrast, in countries like the United Kingdom or Italy, treaties must be 'received' by an Act of Parliament before they can be given effect in the domestic legal order.

What was to happen as regards Community law rules? The question was put to the Court in 1963. A Dutch company, Van Gend en Loos, challenged before the courts a decision which applied a higher customs duty to imported goods than that applicable before the coming into force of the Treaty of Rome, although Article 12 of that treaty prohibited the raising of duties. The Dutch court made a preliminary reference to the ECJ, asking whether this provision had a 'direct application' in the national legal order – in other words if 'nationals of Member States may on the basis of this Article lay claim to rights which the national court must protect…' (case 26/62,

Van Gend & Loos, p. 22). Three member states, supported by the Advocate General, submitted that the wording of Article 12 [25] made it clear that the drafters' intentions were not to create a legal norm of a general nature, but rather simply to place an obligation on member states. At first sight, this was a weighty argument, as in international law the determination of whether the provisions of a treaty are directly effective is essentially carried out by reference to the intention of the parties.

However, the Court did not accept this interpretation. It declared that to determine whether the provisions of a treaty had direct effect in the national legal orders, it was necessary to examine 'the spirit, the general scheme and the wording'. The ordering of this phrase sums up neatly the Court's interpretive method. It clearly demonstrates its unwillingness to stick to a literal interpretation of the treaty (Louis, 1990, p.107). Instead, the Court derived its judgment from the objectives of the treaty, as set out in the preamble and the institutional structure of the Community. Drawing on the fact that individuals from the member states 'are called upon to cooperate in the functioning of this Community through the intermediary of the European Parliament and the Economic and Social Committee' and the existence of preliminary references, which confirms that the plaintiffs are directly concerned by Community law, it concluded that the treaty:

> is more than an agreement which merely creates mutual obligations between the contracting states …
>
> The Community … constitutes a new legal order of international law for the benefit of which the states have limited their sovereign rights, albeit within limited fields, and the subjects of which comprise not only Member States but also their nationals.

Applying these principles to Article 12, it noted that this provision, which sets out a 'clear and unconditional' prohibition, was eminently suitable, by its very nature, to produce legal effects between the member states and their subjects.

The very structure of this judgment is remarkable: the Court, which could have limited itself to a straightforward analysis of Article 12, based its judgment on general considerations on the nature of the Community legal order. The textual arguments offered to justify its conclusion are rather vague: at the time the case was decided, the European Parliament was not directly elected and the members of the Economic and Social Committee were, and still are, appointed by national governments. Yet, the ECJ saw in the establishment of these two bodies an indication that the authors of the treaty somehow wanted to reach out to the individual. This suggests how much it was inspired by 'a certain idea of Europe' – an idea which, in the opinion of one of the heralds of this Praetorian construction, seems to have carried more weight than technical arguments (Pescatore, 1983, p. 157).

On these foundations, the Court would go on to erect a real doctrine of direct effect, according to which not only treaty provisions but also secondary legal norms adopted by the Community institutions could, if they were sufficiently clear, precise and unconditional (that is, if their effectiveness was not dependent on the adoption of positive legal measures at national level), be directly effective in the legal order of the member states.

In identifying treaty provisions enjoying direct effect, the ECJ went beyond the apparent meaning of several provisions. While its first rulings made it clear that it could be read as creating rights that could be invoked by individuals (see, for example, case 6/64, *Costa* v. *ENEL*), it rapidly went further and established that even *positive* obligations to repeal or amend discriminatory provisions by a certain date – generally the end of transitorial periods established by the EC Treaty – turned into a directly effective prohibition after this date (cases 57/65, *Lütticke* and 2/74, *Reyners*). These rulings were of considerable importance, as they made it possible to preserve the integration momentum in spite of the incapacity of European institutions to achieve the legislative harmonization programme set up by the Treaty.

Among the acts adopted by EC institutions, directives posed a particular problem. Directives are, in principle, addressed to the member states, leaving them 'the choice of form and methods' by which they intend to fulfil their obligations (Article 189 [249]). This seems a priori to exclude the possibility that they could create rights and obligations for third parties. The Court, however, held that in certain circumstances, directives could be invoked by private plaintiffs. Having first maintained that the fact that Article 189 provided explicitly for the direct applicability of regulations only did not exclude the possibility that other types of acts could produce analogous effects (case 41/74, *Van Duyn*), it was constrained to refine this position following the hostile reactions of certain national jurisdictions, which rejected the direct effect of directives as a clear violation of the Treaty.

Case 148/78, *Ratti* gave the ECJ the opportunity it had been waiting for to provide a more convincing justification. The facts illustrate perfectly the difficulties inherent in the use of directives. Mr Ratti, a solvents producer, made the grave mistake of conforming with a directive on the labelling of dangerous products before the directive had been implemented in the Italian legal system, resulting in criminal proceedings being taken against him. The Court found itself in the ideal position to argue that, in this case, to deny direct effect to the text in question would seriously compromise its effectiveness. While it was logical to admit that the directive was not directly effective until the deadline for national implementation had expired, the situation changed at the end of that period:

> [A] Member State which has not adopted the implementing measures required by the directive in the prescribed periods may not rely, as against individuals, on its own failure to perform the obligations which the directive entails. It follows that a national court requested by a person who has complied with [a] directive not to apply a national provision incompatible with the directive must uphold that request if the obligation in question is unconditional and sufficiently precise (p. 1642; see also case 8/81, *Becker*).

Of course, this reasoning – inspired by the general principle that one should not profit from one's own wrongs – can only be applied to public authorities, since directives are addressed to states and cannot be a source of obligations for private persons (case 152/84, *Marshall*). However, the ECJ has ruled that even when the plaintiffs cannot plead the direct effect of a directive, national courts are required to interpret national law 'in the light of the wording and the purpose of the directive in order to achieve the result pursued by the latter', which can on occasion lead them to ignore provisions of national law (case C-106/89, *Marleasing*).

It is clear that the doctrine of direct effect constructed by the ECJ has introduced a number of innovative elements. First of all, in its content: aware that contrasting national decisions on the direct effect of Community law would jeopardize the latter's effectiveness, the Court has struggled to impose a uniform interpretation of the relevant provisions. In so doing, unlike in international law, it has paid relatively little attention to the apparent intent of the contracting parties, and more to what it viewed as the functional requirement of the Community legal order. For the ECJ, the very nature and objectives of Community law were the source of this jurisprudential construction. Secondly, in opening the judicial gates to individuals who wished to challenge breaches of Community law, the doctrine of direct effect has altered the dynamics of the integration process. Unlike in the international legal system, overwhelmingly dominated by inter-state elements, individuals, promoted to the status of guardians of the integrity of the Community system, have been able to play a central role in the application of Community law which greatly contributed to the effectiveness of the Community system (see further below).

Supremacy

The rule...

Important as it is, the principle of direct effect is not in itself sufficient to guarantee the effective application of Community law. Even in those states where treaties can, on occasion, be directly applied, without the necessity for internal implementation measures, they often enjoy an identical authority to national law. Thus, where there is a conflict with legislative provisions, it is the most recent provision which prevails. What would happen then in the case of conflict between a Community norm and a piece of subsequent national legislation?

The Treaty of Rome is silent on this point. Article 5 [10] limits itself to stating that the member states shall take 'all appropriate measures, whether general or particular, to ensure fulfilment of the obligations arising out of this Treaty'. It was thus clear that Community law, like international law, required that incompatible national legislation be *set aside*, as treaty commitments have to be honoured. But the real issue was whether this claim to supremacy would convince national courts, which play a crucial role in ensuring the effectiveness of EC law. The issue of the relationship between subsequent national rules and the treaty was first referred to the ECJ by a *giudice conciliatore* from Milan – that is, by a jurisdiction established to adjudicate the most modest disputes among private parties; a good illustration of the importance of the dialogue with lower courts. A shareholder in a nationalized electricity company challenged the nationalization law, notably on the grounds that it breached several treaty provisions. The Italian government claimed the 'absolute inadmissibility' of the reference: according to the government, the Italian judge should simply have applied national law, without referring the problem to the ECJ.

Faced with the treaty's silence, the ECJ once again turned to the 'spirit' of the treaty to answer the question put to it: 'By contrast with ordinary international treaties, the EEC Treaty has created its own legal system which, on the entry into force of the Treaty, became an integral part of the legal systems of the Member States and which their courts are bound to apply.' In establishing a Community of unlimited duration, equipped with its own institutions, and in transferring to these institutions decision-making powers, it continued, the member states 'have limited their sovereign rights, albeit within limited fields'. The Court went on to suggest that the uniform application of Community law represented an 'existential requirement' (Pescatore, 1981b, p. 619): 'the executive force of Community law cannot vary from one state to another in deference to subsequent domestic laws without jeopardising the attainment of the objectives of the Treaty' (case 6/64, *Costa* v. *ENEL*).

Thus, departing from classical visions of sovereignty – which is often held to be indivisible – the Court proposed a new reading of the integration process, centred on the notion of transfer of competences. In conferring on the Community specific attributions, the member states had given up the corresponding competences.

> The transfer by the States from their domestic legal system to the Community legal system of the rights and obligations arising under the Treaty carries with it a *permanent limitation of their sovereign rights*, against which a subsequent unilateral act incompatible with the concept of the Community cannot prevail. (Ibid., p. 594; emphasis added)

The ECJ was most explicit about this proposition in *Simmenthal* (case 106/77):

> [I]n accordance with the principle of the precedence of Community law, the relationship between provisions of the Treaty and directly applicable measures of the institutions on the one hand and the national law of the Member States on the other is such that those provisions and measures not only by their entry into force render automatically inapplicable any conflicting provision of current national law but – in so far as they are an integral part of, and take precedence in, the legal order applicable in the territory of each of the Member States – also preclude the valid adoption of new national legislative measures to the extent to which they would be incompatible with Community provisions.

By virtue of this audacious reasoning, Community law enjoyed absolute supremacy over all national provisions, even those of a constitutional nature. With one stroke of the pen, the ECJ thus conferred on the treaty an authority similar to that of a constitution in a federal system.

The absence of a clear legal basis in the treaty on which to rest this construction could have proved to be a source of weakness. The Community being deprived of any coercive power, the effectiveness of Community law is largely dependent on the dialogue between the ECJ and domestic courts. Thus, supremacy could only be effective if it was accepted by the national courts. Nevertheless, their reaction has by and large been positive. The very principle of supremacy has been accepted by the highest courts of the member states, even if some of them still find it difficult to accept that it is rooted in the specificity of Community law, and prefer to connect it to national provisions – a view more respectful of the concept of national sovereignty, which still holds currency among most lawyers.

This is notably the position adopted by the French *Conseil d'Etat* following a long rearguard battle: it is only in conjunction with Article 55 of the Constitution, which states that treaties have an authority 'superior to that of laws, subject ... to [their] application by the other party', that the chief administrative court found itself able to accept the supremacy of Community law (*Nicolo* case of 20 October 1989). Similarly, in the UK, the authority law is widely held to derive from the European Communities Act 1972, adopted to give effect to the EC Treaty. Should this Act be repealed by

Parliament, it is far from certain that British judges would still accept the supremacy of Community law. Most of them are likely to react in the manner suggested by Lord Denning, a charismatic figure in the British judiciary:

> If the time should come when Parliament deliberately passes an Act with the intention of repudiating the Treaty or any provision of it or intentionally of acting inconsistently with it and says so in express terms, then I should have thought it would be the duty of our courts to follow the statute of our Parliament. (*Macarthys* v. *Smith*, 1979 at 329)

The actual effectiveness of Community law thus depends to a large extent on the attitude of domestic courts – a factor which must be kept in mind in order to understand the evolution of the ECJ's case law.

... and its implications

While the supremacy principle had been laid down very clearly in *Costa* (case 6/64), its procedural implications still needed to be clarified. To ensure complete effectiveness of Community law, national judges, when dealing with a conflict between a national and a Community norm, must be capable of applying the practical consequences of supremacy. This is not always easy, as the judicial function is governed by national law, which may not provide the procedural tools necessary to apply Community law correctly.

Thus, national conceptions of separation of powers frequently prevent courts from reviewing the constitutionality of primary legislation, as is, for instance, the case in the UK. Yet, when they are asked to ensure the supremacy of Community law, are they not being called upon to carry out a similar task? Both seem to involve the legislative will being trumped by a higher-level norm, the Constitution in one case, Community law in the other.

The Italian Constitutional Court, for example, had ruled that a law contrary to Community law had to be regarded as a breach of Article 11 of the Constitution, which authorizes transfers of competence to international organizations. As a consequence of this, any judge faced with a conflict between a Community norm and a subsequent national law had to refer the case to the Constitutional

Court, it being the sole jurisdiction competent under Italian law to rule on constitutional disputes. Such a solution clearly reduced the attractiveness of referring a case to the ECJ. Preliminary rulings normally require over 18 months; and rulings by the constitutional courts even longer. Adding a second set of proceedings was therefore likely to have time and cost implications which would undermine the attractiveness of the Article 177 [234] procedure and therefore the effectiveness of Community law. Asked to rule on the compatibility of this procedure with the treaty, the ECJ made it crystal clear that provisions of national law, irrespective of their constitutional character, could not hinder the application of Community law:

> a national court which is called upon, within the limits of its jurisdiction, to apply provisions of Community law is under a duty to give full effect to those provisions, if necessary refusing of its own motion to apply any conflicting provision of national legislation, even if adopted subsequently, and it is not necessary for the court to request or await the prior setting aside of such provisions by legislative or other constitutional means. (case 106/77, *Simmenthal*)

Similarly, while English law does not authorize courts to suspend the application of laws provisionally, the ECJ, in reply to a question by the House of Lords, considered that this rule could not stand in the way of Community law: if interim relief is necessary to ensure the effectiveness of a judgment to be given as to the existence of rights claimed under Community law, the national judge is obliged to grant it, notwithstanding any national rule to the contrary preventing him or her (case C- 213/89, *Factortame*).

Thus, in the name of the effectiveness (*effet utile*) of Community law and the protection of the rights of individuals, the ECJ placed itself in the position of controlling domestic procedural rules. In so doing, it has, on occasion, significantly modified the role of the judiciary. In the name of application of Community law, the judge has been granted powers which he or she may not enjoy according to domestic law.

This mutation has provoked concern in certain member states, challenging, as it does, seasoned and deeply embedded national traditions. Yet, despite its perturbing effects, it might be argued that the ECJ's broad interpretation of the requirements of supremacy has actually favoured the reception of Community law at national level. In effect, the activism imposed on national courts when they act as agents of Community law application tends to reinforce their position *vis-à-vis* the legislature and the executive. Following the ECJ rulings may thus have provided an excellent justification for some degree of judicial activism. This may have contributed to the generally favourable reception national judges have given to Community law, as will be discussed further in Chapter 5.

Ensuring the effectiveness of EC law

Direct effect and supremacy are two central elements in the EC legal architecture. Thanks to these twin concepts, the ECJ has been able to construct a remarkable enforcement system, which is without precedent on the international plane. The whole edifice rests on three main pillars:

- an interpretation of the EC Treaty as a source of rights which may be invoked by private parties before courts
- a procedural avenue for the dialogue between national courts and the ECJ (Article 177 [234] preliminary rulings) and, more recently,
- a system of state liability for violations of Community law.

The Treaty of Rome as a rights-based constitution

It has been suggested that 'there is hardly anything that has greater potential to foster integration than a common bill of rights, as the constitutional history of the United States has proved' (Cappelletti, 1989, p. 395). Although the European Community has never had a bill of rights, the recognition by the ECJ of the direct effect of a number of treaty provisions has offered a kind of functional equivalent. This was emphasized quite clearly in *Van Gend en Loos*, where the Court stressed that:

> Community law . . . not only imposes obligations on individuals but is also intended to confer upon them rights which become

> part of their legal heritage. These rights arise not only when they are expressly granted by the Treaty, but also by reason of obligations which the Treaty imposes in a clearly defined way upon individuals as well as upon the Member States and upon the institutions of the Community. (case 26/62)

As has been indicated, the ECJ has considerably broadened the range of provisions enjoying direct effect, paying more attention to the 'spirit' of the treaty than to its language. In so doing, it has transformed basic principles which were to guide the action of member states and Community institutions into 'basic freedoms' which private parties can invoke before courts. Workers and providers of services can all claim – and get courts to enforce – a right to free movement. Nationals of EC member states enjoy a right to non-discrimination, and women a right to equal treatment.

This rights-based interpretation of the treaty has not only resulted in a development of judicial review, both at national and at European level; it has also fostered a kind of undeclared alliance between private litigants and pro-integration forces. Through some kind of invisible hand mechanism, individuals trying to vindicate their Community law rights do not only protect their own interests, but also contribute to ensuring the effectiveness of Community law. This transformation was to be of decisive importance for the dynamics of the integration process. Entire parts of the treaty, which might have become a dead letter if their implementation had depended on the goodwill of the member states, can be brought to life at the initiative of private plaintiffs. By bringing the matter before the ECJ, a Belgian air hostess could obtain recognition of a right to equal treatment with her male colleagues that was not recognized by her country's law (case 43/75, *Defrenne* v. *Sabena*); an importer of French spirits was able to gain access to the German market for his products (case 120/78, '*Cassis de Dijon*'); and the rights of football players to transfer to another team without financial restrictions, at the expiry of their contract, could be recognized (case C-415/93, *Bosman* v. *Royal Club Liégeois*). None of these effects could have been produced if the European Court had stuck to a classical, international law like use of the concept of direct effect. European integration and the protection of individual rights (at least those recognized by the treaty) have therefore gone hand in hand (Lecourt, 1976).

Preliminary rulings and decentralized enforcement

This kind of evolution would not have been possible with the enforcement mechanism foreseen by Article 169 [226] of the treaty. As indicated above, infringement proceedings leave little room for private parties. They can of course lodge a complaint with the Commission, but the latter, acting as an independent prosecutor in infringement proceedings, is not obliged to follow suit. Indeed, only a handful of the complaints received by the Commission end up in an ECJ decision.

Construing EC law provisions as granting rights to private parties would have been of little help if the latter were denied any judicial avenue to vindicate these rights (Lecourt, 1991). One could of course bring alleged violations of Community law before domestic courts, but what guarantee was there that they would agree to give effect to treaty law? Even if they did, it was highly unlikely that this would have resulted in a uniform pattern of implementation throughout the Community. One would therefore have had to rely heavily on the infringement procedure, but several elements contribute to weaken the latter's efficiency. The Commission is understaffed to process the complaints it receives. The procedure is lengthy; at most it will yield a ruling declaring the incompatibility of national behaviour with EC law, but nothing guarantees that this will be sufficient to compel national authorities to regularize their behaviour.

In 1976, the Commission, alarmed by allegations of ill-implementation of Community law, decided to initiate systematically infringement proceedings whenever it was aware of a violation of Community law by national authorities. As might have been foreseen, this stricter policy ended up in a larger number of Article 169 rulings. Yet it is far from clear that this has resulted in a more faithful implementation pattern. On the contrary, the multiplication of Article 169 procedures seems to result in a vicious circle that undermines their deterrent effect:

> The greater the number of actions, the less probable it is that the Member States will succeed in executing the resulting judgements; the more cases of non-compliance, the less credible becomes the organ whose decisions are thus disregarded, the weaker those decisions become, the greater is the temptation not to implement them. (Mancini and Keeling, 1991, p. 10)

Indeed the number of infringement rulings disregarded by national authorities has grown steadily in recent years (Commission, 1997).

Set against this background, the ECJ's decision in *Van Gend en Loos* (case 26/62) assumes a truly revolutionary character. It was asked whether a change in the tariff classification of certain products could be considered as an increase in customs duties prohibited by Article 12 [25] of the Treaty when it led to an increase in the tariff applicable to certain products. On the formal level, it was a simple matter of giving an interpretation of what the treaty meant; in practice, however, what the ECJ was being asked to do was to rule on the conformity with Community law of the Dutch authorities' decision to modify their tariff classification.

The consequences of this shift in meaning did not escape the member states. All those who made observations before the ECJ maintained that possible violation of the treaty by member states could only be ascertained in the context of the infringement proceedings laid down in the treaty. By contrast, they argued, in the framework of the preliminary reference procedures, the Court could only rule on the interpretation of the treaty and not on its application in concrete cases.

The ECJ, however, downplayed the difference between these two functions, and held the reference to be admissible. It emphasized that, on the facts of the case, it was not being called upon to rule on the application of the treaty but rather on the meaning of Article 12. To argue that the existence of other legal procedures aimed at sanctioning breaches of Community law precluded recourse to a national judge to ascertain breaches of Community law would, it stated, be equivalent to depriving individuals in the member states from all direct judicial protection. These two legal channels of redress were not mutually exclusive. On the contrary, it added: 'the vigilance of individuals concerned to protect their rights amounts to an effective supervision in addition to that entrusted by Articles 169 [226] and 170 [227] to the diligence of the Commission and of the Member States'.

It would be difficult to exaggerate the importance of this decision. Setting up individuals as agents of a decentralized implementation of Community law not only goes beyond the intentions of the drafters of the treaty, it also breaks free from the tradition of international law, in which individuals play a limited role. Further, it brings the Community closer to the situation which exists in most federal states, where supreme courts have the power to review the compatibility of legislative rules of the member states with federal law.

Of course, the ECJ's powers do not permit it to make explicit pronouncements on the compatibility of national law with Community law. By the Court's own admission, these are issues which it 'must leave ... to be determined by the national courts'. This often leads it to reformulate in an abstract fashion the questions referred by national courts. Asked whether the application of an import duty of 8 per cent by the Dutch customs authorities represented an unlawful increase within the meaning of Article 12 [25] of the Treaty, the ECJ indicated in *Van Gend en Loos* that it could not reply to such a question in the framework of Article 177 [234] proceedings, but that

> the real meaning of the question ... is whether, in law an effective increase in customs duties charged on a given product as a result not of an increase in the rate but of a new classification of the product ... contravenes the prohibition in Article 12 of the Treaty. (*Van Gend en Loos*, p. 14)

In other words, the ECJ has translated the facts of the case into an abstract form, more consonant with its mission as interpreter of the treaty. The difference between the two kinds of approaches was explained by the Court in *Costa* v. *ENEL*. While accepting the Italian government's claim that Article 177 gives no jurisdiction to the Court either to apply the treaty to a specific case or to decide upon validity of a provision of domestic law in relation to the treaty, the ECJ however stressed that it' has power to extract from a question imperfectly formulated by the national courts those questions which alone pertain to the interpretation of the Treaty'. Thus, whereas it could not rule on the compatibility of Italian law with the Treaty, it could interpret the relevant treaty articles 'in the context of the points of law stated by the *Giudice Conciliatore*' (case 6/64, p. 593). But this literal respect for Article 177 should not create any illusions: in almost 60 per cent of the cases where the attitude of national authorities was at issue, the ECJ left no discretion whatsoever to the national judge who was responsible for giving effect to its interpretation (Weiler, 1992, p. 121).

Moving away from a pattern of dialogue between national governments and supranational institutions which characterize international relations, the ECJ has opened the door to private parties. By gaining access to the courtroom, the latter have not only been given power to act as decentralized agents of the implementation of Community law, they have also acquired an opportunity to influence the course of the integration process – an opportunity which at least some of them have seized, as will be seen in more detail in Chapter 4.

Indirect control of the application of Community law via the Article 177 [234] procedure has several advantages over infringement proceedings. Through this channel, individuals, deprived of any direct role in the Article 169 [226] procedure, may compensate for the structural weakness of the Commission, whose limited resources prevent it from being aware of and pursuing all violations of Community law. This decentralization of enforcement procedures allows a more systematic monitoring of the behaviour of national authorities.

Figure 2.1 documents the shift away from the (centralized) Article 169 procedure to the (decentralized) Article 177 procedure in the first 20 years of EC activity. It compares the number of Article 169 rulings rendered each year by the ECJ with the number of preliminary rulings in which one or more questions referred by the national court concern the compatibility of domestic law with EC law. The trend is very clear: the number of Article 177 rulings involving an indirect review of Community law overtook that of Article 169 decisions at the beginning of the 1970s, and has remained higher since. It is worth pointing out that the chart underestimates the volume of Article 177 proceedings, as it only includes the cases which ended with a formal decision taken by domestic courts and not those, for instance, in which the parties settled. The gap between the two procedures is actually higher than is suggested here.

The diffuse control exerted by individuals over national authorities is but one side of the efficiency gain achieved through the transformation of Article 177 proceedings. Unlike judgments given in the framework of Article 169 and 170 [227] proceedings, which have only declaratory effects, the decisions taken subsequent to a preliminary ruling, given by national courts, benefit fully from the authority attaching to judicial decisions in the domestic legal order. All the sanctions available in national law can therefore be applied to national authorities in the enforcement of Community law. States are naturally more inclined to respect the decisions of their own

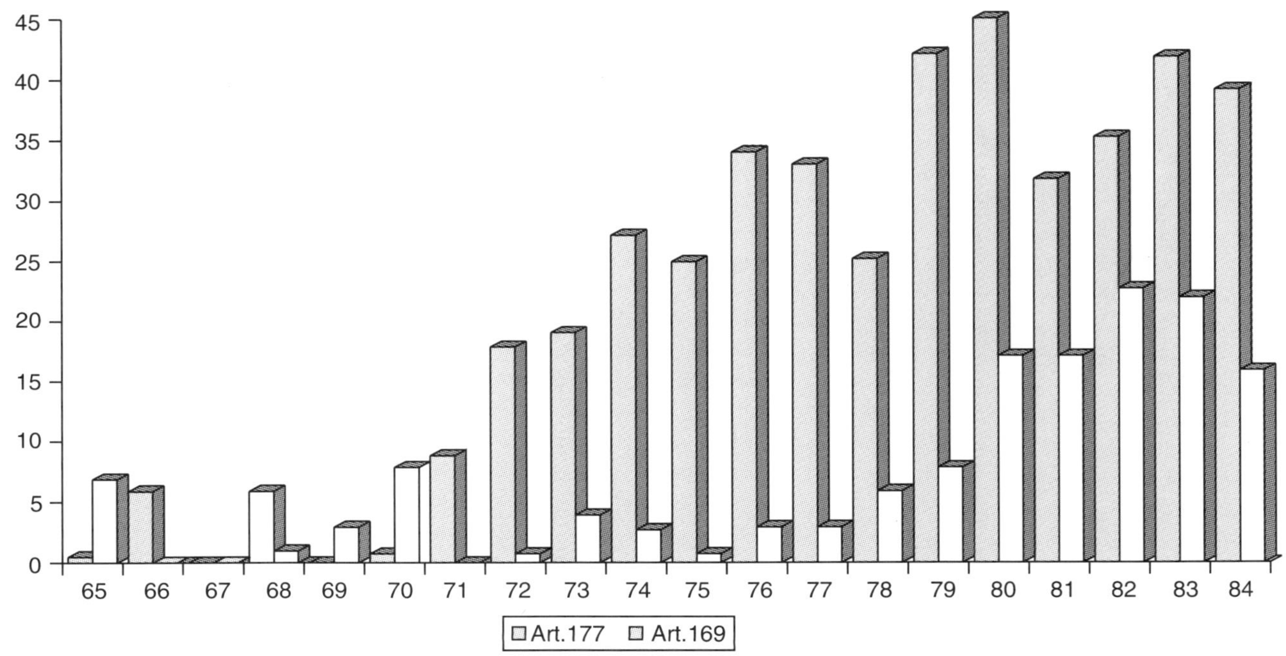

FIGURE 2.1 Judicial review of national law (Article 169 [226] and 177 [234] cases decided in the period 1965–84)

Source: Weiler, 1992, for Article 177 rulings and EC *General Reports of Activities* for Article 169.

courts than those given by international jurisdictions. To the extent that the national judge is content to follow the ECJ's ruling – and we shall see later that this is almost always the case – preliminary rulings have thus greater chances of generating compliance than decisions taken in the framework of infringement proceedings.

The separation of functions established by Article 177 [234], with the ECJ interpreting Community law and domestic courts applying it to the dispute at issue, can thus result in an enhanced effectiveness of EC law. The reverse side of this is obviously that the efficacy of the whole system is heavily dependent on the quality of the relationship between national and supranational judges. This might prove to be a source of problems if the tensions between the two were to develop.

Individual rights and state liability

In spite of the enhanced effectiveness it derives from the ECJ's jurisprudence, there remain limits to the authority enjoyed by Community law in the domestic legal order of the member states. Only those provisions that enjoy direct effect can be invoked directly by private parties before domestic courts. Moreover, the ECJ has repeatedly stressed that directives enjoy no 'horizontal' direct effect – that is, they cannot create obligations against private parties. This turned out to be a source of concern during the implementation of the EC 1992 programme, which was achieved through the passing of some 300 directives. Clearly, such a programme would have made little sense if the decisions adopted at European level remained a dead letter for citizens throughout the Community.

The issue first became a matter of concern in the late 1980s, when a series of Commission reports highlighted the existence of huge bottlenecks in the implementation of Community law (Snyder, 1993). The ECJ, concerned as it has always been with the effectiveness of Community law, could not remain indifferent to this situation.

Its reply came in 1991, in a typical case of non-implementation of Community directives. Remarkably, the case concerned Italy, a country whose record for implementing directives was among the poorest. The *Francovich* ruling (joined cases C-6 and 9/90) concerned a 1980 directive, which established a series of guarantees aimed at protecting employees in the event of employer insolvency. Italy had already been condemned in a prior ruling for its failure to implement the measures laid down by the directive. The plaintiffs, who considered themselves deprived of their rights by this omission, brought proceedings against the national authorities with a view to obtaining the guarantees established by the directive, or alternatively, compensation for the damages they had suffered. Having rejected the direct effect of the directive at issue, the ECJ declared itself in favour of the liability of the Italian state for the damages caused by its failure to fulfil its Community obligations:

> [T]he full effectiveness of Community rules would be impaired and the protection of the rights which they grant would be weakened if individuals were unable to obtain compensation when their rights are infringed by a breach of Community law for which a Member State can be held responsible. The possibility of compensation by the Member State is particularly indispensable where, as in this case, the full effectiveness of Community rules is subject to prior action on the part of the State and consequently individuals cannot, in the absence of such action, enforce the rights granted to them by Community law before the national courts.

Given the silence of the Treaty of Rome on this issue, the ECJ declared the principle of state liability for breach of Community law to be 'inherent in the system of the Treaty'. Anxious to preserve somehow member states' procedural autonomy, it added, however, that the conditions in which such rights could be invoked before national courts remained governed by national law. Be that as it may, through this ruling the Court remained faithful to the rights-based approach it had thus far followed. Once more, private persons were expected to go to court to ensure the effectiveness of Community law (see Harlow, 1996). In later rulings, the ECJ did not hesitate to advertise the possibility of requesting financial compensation when it felt that this could be used as a surrogate to direct effect (see case 91/92, *Faccini Dori*).

This jurisprudence proved to be a source of disruption in national legal orders. In Germany, for instance, there is a clear reluctance to accept liability for decisions taken by the legislature, while in France the *Conseil d'Etat* has accepted that legislation may exclude liability either explicitly or even implicitly. Likewise, domestic rules may limit the obligation to make reparation for damage done to specifically protected interests: German law, for instance, does not recognize loss of profit as a protected asset. As was to be expected, the rather broad principles coined by the ECJ in *Francovich* gave rise to a number of subsequent Article 177 [234] references, in which domestic courts asked for clarification on the compatibility of such restrictions with the *Francovich* principles.

Unsurprisingly, the ECJ did not accept that such restrictions could stand in the way of a uniform implementation of Community law. In a landmark judgment (joined cases C-46/93 and C-48/93, *Brasserie du Pêcheur* v. *Germany and Factortame III*), it laid down in great detail the conditions in which the principle of state liability could be invoked. Although this is not the place to review such conditions, it might be useful to stress that the Court broadened the scope of the principle. In substance, a right to reparation arises when three conditions are met: 'The rule of law infringed must be intended to confer rights on individuals; the breach must be sufficiently serious; and there must be a causal link between the breach of the obligation resting on the State and the damage sustained by private parties' (para. 51). Although it recalled that in the absence of Community provisions, it is for Member States to set the criteria governing reparation, it indicated that such criteria could not make it excessively difficult to obtain reparation, nor could they be less favourable than those applying to similar claims based on domestic law (para. 90).

Whether this will lead to an undesirable development of litigation, as has been argued (Harlow, 1996), remains to be seen. What is clear, however, is that this line of jurisprudence owes much to the ECJ's vision of its own role under the Treaty. In reply to a remark of the German government, suggesting that in the absence of any treaty provision governing the matter a general right to reparation could not be created by judicial decisions, it stressed that

> it is for the Court, in pursuance of the task conferred on it by Article 164 [220] of the Treaty of ensuring that in the interpretation and application of the Treaty the law is observed, to rule on such a question in accordance with generally accepted methods of interpretation, in particular by reference to the fundamental principles of the Community legal system and, where necessary, general principles common to the legal systems of the Member States. (para. 27)

Although this open admission of its law-making role may have surprised more than one reader, still inspired by a vision of courts as mere implementers of law, it perfectly reflects the ECJ's role in the development of the Community legal order. Through an inventive jurisprudence, inspired by the desire to enhance the rights of private litigants in order to foster the judicial enforcement of Community law, the Court has enabled the latter to acquire a remarkable degree of effectiveness.

The delimitation of Community competences

In its case law on direct effect and supremacy – the two central pillars of the Community constitutional architecture – the ECJ has placed great importance on the consolidation of the authority of Community law. Its influence has been equally important as regards Community competences. In this sphere, it has been active in two ways:

- by defending a generous interpretation of Community competences and,
- by subjecting national prerogatives to strict scrutiny.

Like all international organizations, the EC disposes in principle only of those competences expressly conferred upon it by its constitutive treaties. This attribution of competences rule, which is one of the general principles of Community law, has been subsequently expressly consecrated in the Maastricht Treaty (new Article 3b, 1st paragraph of the treaty). Despite its apparent straightforwardness, its practical application can raise some tricky issues. The ambiguous nature of the Community, conceived of as one step on the path towards a union of the peoples of Europe, combined with the complexity of the division of competences, casts some doubt on the consequences which flow from this principle.

It was thus inevitable that the ECJ would have to rule on this question. The opportunity arose in a dispute between the Commission and the Council concerning an international agreement on road transport (case 22/70, *ERTA*). The Commission claimed that the matter fell within Community competences on transport policy: the competence to define a common policy in this area must necessarily include the right to conclude agreements with third states as without this right the effectiveness of measures adopted at Community level risked being seriously compromised. The Council, for its part, could rely on the absence of any explicit provision granting the Community the right to conclude international agreements relating to transport. Furthermore, the very terms of Article 228 [300], which lays out the procedure for concluding international agreements ('where the Treaty provides for the conclusion of agreements') seemed to lean towards a narrow interpretation of Community competence.

And yet, the ECJ showed no hesitation in agreeing with the functional line defended by the Commission. The terms in which it did so leave no doubt whatsoever to its intention to deliver a judgment of principle. With reference to the absence of specific provisions on the matter at issue, it declared that regard must be had to 'the general system of Community law in the sphere of relations with third countries' and not solely to the 'substantive provisions of the Treaty'. Recalling that the Community had been endowed with a legal international personality, it added that:

> the authority to enter into international agreements ... arises not only from an express conferment by the Treaty ... but may equally flow from other provisions of the Treaty and from measures adopted, within the framework of those provisions, by the Community institutions ... in particular, each time the Community, with a view to implementing a common policy envisaged by the Treaty, adopts measures laying down common rules, the Member States no longer have the right, acting individually or even collectively, to undertake obligations with third countries which affect those rules; as and when those rules come into being, the Community alone is in a position to assume and carry out contractual obligations with third countries affecting the whole sphere of application of the Community legal system.

And furthermore, in order to emphasize the general application of this ruling, it added that 'with regard to the implementation of the provisions of the Treaty the system of internal Community measures may not therefore be separated from that of external relations'. This principle of parallel competences would be completed and refined in subsequent decisions (Opinion 1/76, joined cases 3,4 and 6/76,

Kramer). The Court similarly underlined that the logical corollary of the concept of a common policy was the exclusiveness of the Community competence. For example, the notion of a common commercial policy

> is incompatible with the freedom to which Member States could lay claim by invoking a concurrent power, so as to ensure that their own interests were separately satisfied in external relations, at the risk of compromising the effective defense of the common interests of the Community. (Opinion 1/75; *re the Understanding on a Local Cost Standard*)

This was daring jurisprudence both for its method and for its impact. It is true that the notion of implied powers is not unknown in classic international organizations: the International Court of Justice has had recourse to it to interpret the UN Charter. None the less, the way in which the ECJ went about making the aims of the treaty trump the attribution of competences rule is particularly striking. What is more, in the Community context, the parallelism between internal and external competences could have major implications. Unlike the situation prevailing in classic international organizations, the theory of implied powers was used not only to grant the Community a power present embryonically in the treaty but to remove huge swathes of competence from the member states. Even if subsequent practice has attenuated somewhat the effects of this jurisprudential construction, it is understandable that it could have been a cause for concern in some member states.

The ECJ has often been equally bold in interpreting existing heads of competence. In a series of decisions dealing with educational matters, it gave an extremely broad interpretation of the concept of 'vocational training' used in Article 128 [151] of the Treaty of Rome. In *Gravier* (case 293/83), it ruled that

> any form of education which prepares for a qualification for a particular profession, trade or employment or which provides the necessary skills for such a profession, trade or employment is vocational training, whatever the age and the level of training of the pupils or students, even if the training programme includes elements of general education.

A few years later, it added that, in general, university studies fulfil those criteria, with the only exception of some courses of study intended for persons wishing to improve their general knowledge (case 24/86, *Blaizot*). Assuredly, this definition of university studies as 'vocational training' went beyond the common understanding of that latter expression. This notwithstanding, the ECJ relied on this far-fetched definition to rule that the ERASMUS programme, set up by the European Community to enhance the mobility of university students, fell within the sphere of vocational training, except as regards the provisions on scientific research (242/87, *Commission* v. *Council*). Through this ruling, the ECJ opened wide the door to the development of an education policy at European level: not only did it recognize the Community's competence in the field of education, but it greatly facilitated the adoption of ERASMUS type programmes by authorizing their adoption on the basis of Article 128 [151] alone: that is, through a majority vote. If isolated, the opposition of sovereignty-minded governments could therefore be ignored. The risk was clearly perceived by some governments, which pushed in favour of a political response at the time the Maastricht Treaty was being negotiated (see Chapter 6).

This jurisprudence favourable to the expansion of Community competences has quite logically been accompanied by a refusal to recognize in areas of national competence islands of sovereignty protected against all potential Community incursions. The *Casagrande* case (9/74) is a good example of this. The plaintiff, son of an Italian immigrant worker in Germany, was refused an education grant by the Bavarian authorities. He relied on a 1968 regulation which stated that the children of Community nationals resident in another member state should have access to the education system under the same conditions as the national of that state. The Bavarian authorities contended that Articles 48 [39] and 49 [40], the legal basis chosen by the Council for the adoption of the regulation at issue, concerned the free movement of workers and did not authorize the Community to intervene in the education sphere, a matter which remained within member state competences. According to them, the provision in question concerned only social benefits directly related to the employment contract. It could not require equality in education grants.

The ECJ, however, rejected this argument, adopting a much broader reading of the provisions in question. Having examined the aims of the regulation at issue, it stated that to attain its primary objective – to offer children of nationals of another member state access to education under the same conditions as nationals – it was clearly necessary to encompass study grants. True, at that time, education policy as such was not one of the Community policies covered by the treaty. Was that sufficient to invalidate the regulation? No, responded the Court, as even if education was not a Community competence, 'it does not follow that the exercise of powers transferred to the Community is in some way limited if it is of such a nature as to affect the measures taken in the execution of a policy such as that of education and training' (case 9/74, *Casagrande*). The ECJ thus rejected the idea that the member states could have *reserved* competences; namely, areas in which the Community would be completely barred from acting. Of course, this reasoning does not authorize the Community to monopolize education policy. None the less, called upon to choose between the objectives of the measure in question and the defence of member state prerogatives, the Court, in a remarkable example of teleological reasoning, ruled that the former was more important than the latter.

Moreover, it did not stop there. In later decisions, it made it clear that even when the treaty allowed member states to derogate from the free movement provisions for reasons related to public policy, public security and public health, the use made of these derogations remained subject to other treaty rules, and could be subjected to judicial control (case 36/75, *Rutili*). In other words, when the treaty states that national legislation can make exceptions to the principle of free movement, these derogations do not have the effect of reserving certain areas to the competence of the member states (case 35/76, *Simmenthal*).

These various examples can all be understood in the same way. Renouncing the traditional standards of interpretation of international law, according to which an international agreement must be interpreted so as to limit encroachments on state sovereignty, the ECJ preferred to let itself be guided by the ambitious objectives of the treaty, both in interpreting expansively the provisions concerning Community competences and in exercising strict control over the way in which member states utilized their prerogatives. There can be no doubt that this form of teleological interpretation, closer to constitutional traditions than to international habits, contributed to the consolidation of the Community.

Important as rulings of this kind may have been, they should not lead the reader to conclude that the ECJ's jurisprudence was the main force behind the expansion of Community competences that characterized the 1970s and the 1980s. The Court certainly looked favourably on such a development: on more than one occasion, as we have seen, its rulings facilitated action at Community level. We will also see in the following chapter that its rulings have at times prompted the Community legislator to act by opening ways around the stalemate that existed for years in certain areas.

At the same time, however, the importance of these elements should not be exaggerated. Indeed, comparing the ECJ's case law with that of constitutional courts operating in federal systems, one cannot but be struck by a major difference. While litigation on the demarcation of the respective competences of 'central' institutions and of the component units is one of the main activities of federal constitutional courts, it has been relatively scarse at EC level. Undoubtedly, this scarcity is due to structural reasons: in a system where decision-making remains largely consensual, even in areas where majority decisions would in theory be possible, major conflicts between the centre and the periphery over their respective competences are fairly rare. For a 'legislative' decision to be adopted at European level, it must enjoy the support of a large majority of member states, at times their unanimous support. Given this context, it is fairly unlikely that one of them will have the incentive to go to court. This clearly suggests that the main factor behind the expansion of Community competences must be found elsewhere. The fragmentation of decision-making on European issues, both at national and EC level, seems a more plausible cause for that evolution than rulings by the ECJ (Dehousse, 1997).

This may explain why, until recently, the ECJ's rulings on competence issues did not elicit more than occasional criticism from national governments. However, what was acceptable in a Community numbed by the shadow of the veto could become more threatening with the relaunching of the integration process. The Community experienced this in the wake of the Single European Act, which increased the possibilities of majority voting. The new dynamism which followed sufficed to give some credit to the threat of a drift to the centre, thereby contributing to the current infatuation with the concept of subsidiarity. In this new context, the

ECJ's rulings may be viewed with greater concern by national governments; hence, the greater caution displayed by it in recent years (see Chapter 6).

The protection of human rights

Although they proclaim a certain number of rights and freedoms of an economic nature, such as the principles of free movement and the prohibition of discrimination on the basis of nationality against member state nationals, the treaties do not contain a real catalogue of fundamental rights. The judicial control mechanisms established by the Treaty of Rome seem less inspired by the desire to protect the individual rights of the human being than by the desire to preserve the sovereign rights of member states (Weiler, 1986). This omission has been much discussed. Undoubtedly, it is closely connected to the decision to take a sectorial approach to integration. The primary ambition of the treaties was not to set up a new form of society, but, more modestly, to regulate relations between economic agents in a number of areas. Hence, the sentiment that fundamental rights were primarily the concern of national authorities.

The structural limitations inherent in this approach were however to rapidly emerge. The majority of European constitutions do, in fact, enumerate a certain number of rights which individuals can enforce before national courts. It was inevitable that nationals from these states would demand a similar sort of protection from the acts adopted by the European institutions. The ECJ was confronted with this problem fairly quickly. It initially adopted a rather defensive attitude, imprinted with the need to preserve the autonomy of Community law. In *Stork* (case 1/58), it stated that when it had to rule on the legality of Community acts it was not bound to 'ensure the protection of rules of domestic law, be they of constitutional rank'.

This timidity was, however, subsequently called into question by the case law on the 'new legal order', which was examined at the beginning of this chapter. On the one hand, the direct applicability of Community law was bound to multiply the possibilities of contact with national law, simultaneously increasing the possibilities for conflict between constitutional provisions and Community fundamental freedoms. On the other, there was a clear risk that national courts would refuse to apply Community provisions judged incompatible with human rights, to the detriment of the supremacy of Community law. The problem was particularly felt in Germany and in Italy, two countries which had developed a strong sensitivity to human rights issues in the aftermath of the Second World War. The German Constitutional Court had hinted that it might have to examine the compatibility of Community law with the provisions of the German Basic Law setting out fundamental rights (cases 1 BvR 248/63 and 216/67, judgment of 18 October 1967).

The ECJ was therefore forced to reconsider the situation to protect its jurisprudential construction. In *Internationale Handelsgesellschaft* (case 11/70) the defensive considerations which hitherto had informed the Court's position merely adorn rather than determine the ruling:

> Recourse to the legal rules or concepts of national law in order to judge the validity of measures adopted by the institutions of the Community would have an adverse effect on the uniformity and efficacy of Community law. The validity of such measures can only be judged in the light of Community law. In fact, the law stemming from the Treaty, an independent source of law, cannot because of its very nature be overridden by rules of national law, however framed, without being deprived of its character as Community law and without the legal basis of the Community itself being called into question. Therefore the validity of a Community measure or its effect within a Member State cannot be affected by allegations that it runs counter to either fundamental rights as formulated by the constitution of that State or the principles of a national constitutional structure.

Up to this point in the ruling, it has merely recalled – and fully supported – its previous position. On the other hand – and here is the new element – it adds that

> respect for fundamental rights forms an integral part of the general principles of law protected by the Court of Justice... the protection of such rights, whilst inspired by the constitutional traditions common to the Member States, must be ensured within the framework of the structure and the objectives of the Community.

Thus, to get out of the impasse to which its earlier case law had led it, the ECJ explicitly affirmed its resolve to ensure the protection of fundamental rights.

On what legal basis? This was difficult, given the absence of any bill of rights at Community level. In the judgment in question, the Court clearly stated that it did not intend to carry out some kind of straightforward reception of national law – in this particular case German law – but rather to identify possible 'analogous guarantees' specific to Community law, inspired by the common traditions of the member states. In other words, these criteria were designed to leave it a wide margin of discretion. Some national supreme courts – in particular the German and Italian Constitutional Courts – saw in this vagueness a degree of uncertainty so great as to cast doubts on the efficacy of human rights protection at Community level.

To assuage these fears, the ECJ made strenuous efforts to define more precisely the criteria it would employ. In *Nold* (case 4/73), it stated that it was 'bound to draw inspiration from constitutional traditions common to the Member States' – which seems to go further than what it was prepared to concede in *Internationale Handelsgesellschaft* – and that it 'cannot therefore uphold measures which are incompatible with fundamental rights recognised and protected by the constitutions of those states'. This latter formula implies that the violation of a right which is recognized in only one national constitution could suffice to justify the invalidation of a Community measure. The Court also emphasized that 'international treaties for the protection of human rights on which the Member States have collaborated or of which they are signatories, can supply guidelines which should be followed within the framework of Community law'. In this sibylline language, it clearly envisaged the utilization (though not binding) of the European Convention on Human Rights, which was to be explicitly invoked in later judgments (see, for example, cases 36/75, *Rutili* and 44/79, *Hauer*).

Nold had been decided only two weeks before the *Solange I* decision in which the German Constitutional Court declared that as long as (*Solange* in German) the EC did not contain a catalogue of basic rights adopted by a parliament that provided the same guarantees as the German Basic Law, that court reserved the right to ensure that EC law did not violate fundamental rights contained in the Basic law (case 2 BvL 52/71, *Internationale*

Handelsgesellschaft, judgment of 29 May 1974). The threat to the ECJ's authority could hardly be more direct, and it had a substantial influence over the fundamental rights jurisprudence of the ECJ (Rasmussen, 1986, pp. 397–400).

Not only did it annul a number of Community acts for violating 'fundamental rights... the observance of which is ensured by the Court', but it gradually extended its control over the acts of national authorities.

In a first phase, the ECJ had stated that its control would be limited to the acts of Community institutions (see, for example, joined cases 60 and 61/84 *Cinéthèque* v. *Fédération Nationale des Cinémas Français*). This cautious line was clearly inspired by the fear of running into open conflicts with national courts on issues which almost unavoidably involve delicate value judgments. However, there has been a gradual change in position on this issue. Anxious to avoid imbalance in the level of protection afforded to nationals, the ECJ subsequently stated that control could be exercised on national legislation lying within the scope of EC law, whether because it concerns implementation of Community law (case 5/88, *Wachauf*) or because it could hinder the exercise of the principles of free movement set out in the treaty (case C-260/89, *ERT*). It has therefore moved very far from the fainthearted attitude of the first phase.

As a rule, however, it can be said that the ECJ shows a great deference to the political and constitutional sensibilities of national authorities whenever it is alleged that there is a conflict between national rules and fundamental rights protected in the Community legal order. In *SPUC* v. *Grogan* (case C-159/90), for instance, an Irish court had referred a question on the interdiction to advertise commercially available abortions in other member states. It was argued that such an interdiction was a restriction of the freedom to provide services, and that derogations to that principle had to respect fundamental Community principles, including freedom of speech. The ECJ accepted that abortion came under the definition of services within the meaning of Article 60 [50], but it came to the conclusion that as the legislation at issue was primarily applicable to Irish student associations, and not to clinics trying to market their 'services' from abroad, it did not constitute a prohibited restriction. As a result, the ECJ avoided pronouncing itself on the delicate issue of the compatibility with freedom of speech, and was therefore able to stay out of the scorching abortion debate. (See also case C-2/92, *Bostock* and the criticisms in Weiler and Lockhart, 1995.)

Notwithstanding this caution, the development of the ECJ's fundamental rights jurisprudence was sufficient to allay the fears of the German Constitutional Court, which responded in a positive way. In the *Solange II* ruling, taking note of the development on the European plane, the *Bundesverfassungsgericht* argued that it was no longer necessary to control the application of Community secondary law *as long as* the EC, and in particular the ECJ, ensured an effective protection of fundamental rights (Case 2 BvR 197/83 *Wünsche Handelsgesellschaft*, judgment of 22 October 1986). This remarkable judicial dialogue illustrates how important the interaction between the European Court and national courts has been for the development of Community law. Clearly, in this case, the ECJ's human rights jurisprudence was largely developed in response to the concerns and criticism voiced by national courts, either in the cases they referred to Luxembourg or in the positions they adopted in 'domestic' proceedings. Legal values were key elements in this process: constitutional courts insisted on presenting concepts of fundamental importance in the domestic legal order, thereby prompting the ECJ to react in order to protect the supremacy of Community law. But clearly, what was at stake was more than abstract concepts. Both at the national and the EC level, courts were moved by the necessity to protect their own institutional interests. The concern for human rights was clearly symptomatic of some constitutional courts' difficulties to accept the ECJ's claim to the supremacy of Community law. In contrast, accepting the use of domestic law as the yardstick to rule on the validity of Community law would have undermined the authority of the ECJ. In both cases, institutional self-interest appears to have been a primary cause in the court-to-court dialogue.

Conclusion

It is difficult to overemphasize the important contribution the ECJ has made to the integration process. Without the invention of the twin concepts of direct effect and supremacy, where would the Community be today? There can be little doubt that the Treaty of Rome would have remained a set of abstract and distant rules, for the most part unknown, with breaches ascertained only through the rather cumbersome mechanism of infringement proceedings. Given the inefficacy of the system, it is possible that the states would have ended up feeling fully justified in turning to the classic international rule of reciprocity to sanction the breaches of their partners. Counter-measures would have in turn facilitated the progressive fraying of the principles contained in the Treaty.

Nothing like this happened. Through its intricately worked case law, the ECJ established the authority of Community law and conferred upon it a degree of effectiveness unparalleled in international law. Significantly, it laid the first foundations of its case law edifice at a time when, after the momentum of the initial years, integration began to show the first signs of running out of steam and the member states displayed their desire to control the administration and policy machine of the Community (Weiler, 1981). In other respects, however, the development of case law had its own, autonomous dynamic. Direct effect contained the seeds of the Community law supremacy rule; it was to defend the latter, as we have seen, that the ECJ developed Community-level human rights protection.

Is it an abuse of the term to dub this the 'constitutionalization' of the Community legal order? The reference to a constitution will undoubtedly shock meticulous lawyers. Notwithstanding, the analogies are striking, no matter what definition of a constitution one uses.

A constitution is, as we know, the text which defines the conditions of exercise of political power. Yet, is this not precisely what the EC Treaty and its successive amendments, do? It is true that these documents were conceived of as inter-state agreements rather than as the founding text of a new polity. However, a glance at the situation in federal systems is enough to realize that the gap between these two categories is not as great as it might appear at first sight. The idea of a fundamental pact between the different components of the federation has occupied an important position in the constitutional history of these states.

A second distinctive element of constitutions is the supreme nature of the norms therein. At this level, too, the EC parallel is striking. Through its jurisprudence on direct effect and supremacy, the ECJ has set Community law up as a superior-level norm throughout the Community. It is true that international law does not ignore direct effect and that it too claims supremacy over national law (de Witte, 1984; Pellet, 1994). The principal difference between these two claims lies in their respective effectiveness. From this perspective, Community law undoubtedly has the edge. Through the combination of direct effect and Article 177 [234] preliminary reference procedure, supremacy has attained a tangibility in the Community legal order that it has never had in international law.

Moreover, the treaties establishing the Community give individuals, albeit in a roundabout way, the power to demand that a certain number of fundamental principles are respected by the institutions and the member states. This stands in sharp contrast with the international system, where the state's control is largely unchallenged. Because of these structural features, the ECJ has been able to play a significant role in the development of the original agreement. It has not shirked this task as its jurisprudence on the effectiveness of Community law or on Community competences amply testifies. There is a strong argument that this subjection of governments to the rule of law, and the constitutional role played by the Court in the process of constitutional change, aligns the Community system with that of a number of nation-states.

Thanks to the important powers possessed by the ECJ, the treaty has become, like a number of constitutions, 'a living text', not complete on its enactment but rather 'open, and in continuous adaptation' (Rousseau, 1992). This is due in part to the interpretive methods employed by the judges in Luxembourg, who seem to have taken seriously Chief Justice Marshall's comments on the US Constitution: 'We must never forget that it is a constitution we are expounding' (*McCulloch* v. *Maryland*). Community case law, rather than clinging to the real or presumed intentions of the contracting parties – the meat and drink of treaty interpretation – dished up an ambitious reading of the treaties, in which the spirit and aims of these texts were of more importance than their literal wording. Clearly, this construction in turn owes much to the inspired vision of Europe informing the ECJ's judges.

Of course, the treaties do not have the 'constitutive' nature of most fundamental charters, whose stated ambition is to establish a new pact between rulers and ruled in a given society (Diez-Picazo, 1993). The argument is difficult to get around. What is clear is that the Treaties of Paris and Rome mark neither a complete rupture with the past nor the birth of a new polity. Their ambition was of an economic nature and their creation, the Community, merely superimposed itself on the states, without ever staking any claim to replace them. Even now, European society, properly speaking, does not exist.

And yet...the principles developed by the ECJ, all of them closely resembling constitutional principles in many jurisdictions, have spread far beyond the economic sphere, to areas as diverse as education and family law. The unifying influence of Community law has even had repercussions at the level of governmental structures. Suffice it to say that all the national parliaments lament their dispossession of an increasing number of decisions by the Community organs. It would therefore be wrong to claim that relations between rulers and ruled have been unaffected by the integration process.

Above all, to speak of constitutionalization does not necessarily imply the complete assimilation of the Community treaties to a state constitution. More than a state of fact, this term tries to describe a process – a process by which, over time, Community rules have acquired the status of superior legal norms and have had a considerable influence on many societal relations. The legal nature of the Community legal order at the end of that process remains an open question. But there can be no doubt that the ECJ played a primordial role in this evolution. Moreover, its contribution to the integration process did not end there, as we shall see in the next chapter.

3

The Court and the Dynamics of Integration

Many analyses of European integration play down the importance of the role played by the ECJ. Writing in 1971, Stuart Scheingold suggested that the ECJ had thus far made only 'a rather modest contribution to the formulation of Community policy' (p. 16). True, its 'constitutional' role is often acknowledged: it is generally recognized that it has strengthened the federal features of the European Community. Yet its role in the policy process is generally overlooked, when it is not explicitly denied. A widely influential school of thought, intergovernmentalism, maintains that national governments, acting to further their state's interests, determine the rhythm of the integration process (see, for example, Garrett, 1992; Moravcsik, 1993). In this view, progress towards further integration is only possible when there is a convergence of the interests of different states; when these diverge, or when states feel menaced by the development of integration, the movement tends to slow down.

The central role played by national governments in the integration process cannot be denied. None the less, the intergovernmentalist model remains irredeemably reductionist and simplistic. It tends to ignore the breadth of the range of actors who play a role in the integration process: supranational organs, such as the Commission and the ECJ, interest groups and regional authorities. Even ordinary citizens can impinge in various ways – not least by going to court – on policy-making. The complex web of relationships which have formed between these different actors, both at Community and at national level, have made the European political system a different creature from most other international systems. Moreover, the concept of national interest, to which frequent recourse is made, tends to mask the kaleidoscope of interests at play. The 'national interest' of France, repeatedly invoked by the French government during the Uruguay Round negotiations, undoubtedly referred principally to the interests of certain groups like the farmers; it is, however, doubtful that a stalemate in the negotiations would have served the interests of either the export industry or of consumers. Likewise, although the British government presented itself as the defender of the country's supreme interest throughout the 'mad cow' crisis of the first part of 1996, it seemed to be more concerned with beef producers' interests than with those of consumers. In other words, when analysing European policies, the range and diversity of interests and the relationships which develop between all interested actors at various levels must be taken into account (Dehousse and Majone, 1994).

Although the ECJ has long been ignored by integration theory, it has played a role unparalleled by any judicial body in international politics. It has made its influence felt in various ways. The Court has exercised considerable law-making power, which in turn has allowed it to ensure the progressive 'constitutionalization' of the Community Treaties. The ECJ's case law has also acted as a catalyst in the integration process, through the innovations it has introduced in Community policies and through the pressure it has exerted on the legislature. We shall review successively these various contributions to the dynamics of integration.

The Court as a law-maker

It is a commonplace that in most Western European countries the prevailing conception of the judicial role is imbued with the idea of separation of powers. According to this conception, law-making is the function of the legislature. The judge's task is essentially passive: he or she must implement legal rules, and refrain from any creative role. One of the fathers of the separation of powers, Montesquieu, conceived of the judge as an unconscious being, *un être inanimé*, from whose mouth should be uttered only the words of the Law

(*Spirit of the Laws*, bk XI, ch. 6). Even today, Article 5 of the French Civil Code prohibits courts from making general pronouncements about the law. On the face of it, the Treaty of Rome does not derogate from this vision, as it allots the ECJ the task of ensuring 'that in the interpretation and application of this Treaty the law is observed' (Article 164 [220]).

Yet, widespread as it may be, this vision of the judiciary's role is largely fictitious. Firstly, interpreting a rule is by necessity a creative exercise as it requires the judge to choose among the possible meanings of the rule. The broader the rule, the more discretion the interpreter will enjoy. Secondly, while the authority of judicial decisions is in principle limited to the parties in the dispute at hand, they none the less enjoy an indirect law-making effect: in justifying their decisions, judges indicate how they will solve similar disputes in the future.

We have seen in the previous chapter how the ECJ, by interpreting treaty provisions in an expansive manner, has laid down the foundations of a veritable constitutional edifice. But the originality of its contribution does not stop there. The brevity of the treaty has allowed the Court to play an innovative role in a number of areas. The Treaty of Rome in effect possesses the characteristics of what can be termed a 'framework treaty': it sets out very generally a certain number of objectives and puts in place an institutional framework within which the policies intended to attain these objectives are to be generated. In so doing, it makes frequent recourse to legal concepts with fluid contours: Article 30 [28] does not state exactly what is meant by 'measures of equivalent effect' to quantitative restrictions any more than Article 86 [82] indicates under what conditions a 'dominant position' can be abused in competition law. Nor does Article 48 [39] specify the scope of the 'public policy' exceptions to free movement of workers. Finally, Community competences are often defined in a functional manner: Article 100 [94] merely envisages the harmonization of national provisions 'which affect the establishment and the functioning of the common market', while Article 235 [308] confers on the Community in certain cases the power to 'take the necessary measures' to attain 'one of the objectives of the Community'.

The contrast with the texts which national judges have to apply was sharply highlighted by Lord Denning, one of the more colourful figures of the English judiciary:

> The Treaty is quite unlike any of the enactments to which we have become accustomed. The draftsmen of our statutes have striven to express themselves with the utmost exactness. They have tried to foresee all possible circumstances that may arise and to provide for them... In consequence, the judges have followed suit. They interpret a statute as applying only to the circumstances covered by the very words. They give them a very literal interpretation. If the words of the statute do not cover a new situation – which was not foreseen – the judges hold that they have no power to fill the gap...
>
> How different is this Treaty. It lays down general principles. It expresses its aims and purposes. All in sentences of moderate length and commendable style. But it lacks precision. It uses words and phrases without defining what they mean. An English lawyer would look for an interpretation clause, but he would look in vain. There is none. All the way through the Treaty, there are gaps and lacunae. These have to be filled in by the judges, or by regulations and directives. It is the European way. (*H.P. Bulmer Ltd* v. *J. Bollinger S.A.*, 1974)

Indeed, the programmatic nature of the treaty, combined with the relative imprecision of many of its clauses, leaves considerable discretion to the interpreter. Formally, the ECJ would of course be able to maintain that no new rules of law are being created but rather that its work is limited to producing the correct interpretation by extracting it from the bundle of possible interpretations available. Often, however, the margin of manoeuvre at their disposal allows judges to be extremely creative.

The ECJ has not missed its chance to make the most of these interpretative possibilities. On numerous occasions, it has used them to impose an expansive interpretation of Community law. This is particularly evident in its pronouncements on certain basic principles of the treaty.

With regard to the free movement of goods, for example, Article 30 [28] prohibits quantitative restrictions (quotas), on imports as well as on 'all measures of equivalent effect'. This could have been read as a straightforward prohibition on discrimination against imports. However, such an interpretation would have permitted the continuing existence of obstacles to intra-Community exchanges linked to differences between national legislation: a product manufactured in conformity with Italian law may not satisfy the technical requirements of French law. Generally held opinion, both outside and within European institutions, was that when national rules did not discriminate against imported products, harmonization was the only avenue which could be employed to get rid of these obstacles. However, in its judgment in *Dassonville* (case 8/74), the Court considerably enlarged the significance of Article 30 [28], by reading into it a prohibition which covered not only discriminatory measures but 'all commercial rules capable of hindering, directly or indirectly, actually or potentially, intra-community trade . . .'. What matters, in the ECJ's view, is no longer whether or not the national measure at issue discriminates against imported goods, but rather its impact on intra-Community trade. Certainly, Article 36 [30] foresees a series of circumstances in which national rules which fall under this prohibition may be maintained, provided they pursue a public interest protected by the treaty and do not amount to disguised discrimination. None the less, the fact remains that in adopting such a generous interpretation of the Community rule, the Court granted itself the right to review a series of provisions which were believed to be outside its purview. This right to review proved to be so broad that it later reverted to a more restrictive reading of Article 30 in *Keck* (joined cases C-267 and C-268/91, discussed in Chapter 6).

The inventiveness of the Community judiciary did not stop there. For example, Article 119 [141] obliges member states to ensure that for equal work, men and women will receive equal pay. The ECJ has declared that this provision cannot be seen as imposing obligations solely on member states but that it confers a right on affected individuals which can be invoked directly before national courts (case 43/75 *Defrenne*). This ingenious interpretation allowed it to give effect to the principles contained in the treaty, irrespective of the fact that Belgian authorities had failed to take the steps prescribed by the treaty.

More or less contemporaneously, the ECJ resorted to a similar tactic in an equally important judgment on freedom of establishment. Article 52 [43] of the EC Treaty states that access to non-salaried activities and their exercise must be open to nationals of other member states 'under the conditions laid down for its own nationals by the law of the country'. During a transitional period, a general programme established by the Council of Ministers had to harmonize national rules in spheres such as training or access to various professions in order to ensure the progressive elimination of obstacles to freedom of establishment. At first glance therefore, Article 52 [43] *et seq.* seemed limited to setting out an objective and the means for attaining it, without conferring any rights on individuals.

However, the cumbersomeness of the Community decision-making apparatus, combined with the divergent perspectives of the member states, meant that the Community legislature was unable to complete this task within the requisite time limit. Following a petition by a barrister of Dutch nationality, not permitted by Belgian law to practise at the Belgian Bar, the ECJ had to examine the effect of Article 52 in order to decide whether freedom of establishment could be claimed in the absence of the harmonization measures laid down by the treaty. The Court responded in the affirmative, underlining the fact that the shortcomings of the Community legislature could not be allowed to imperil the implementation of the provisions of the treaty. Article 52, it went on to say, imposed on the Council 'an obligation to obtain a precise result, the fulfilment of which had to be made easier by, but not made dependent on, the implementation of a programme of progressive measures'. In the absence of such a programme, the obligation still stood. Thus, the ECJ held that, with regard to self-employed activities, Article 52 contained a prohibition on discrimination on grounds of nationality, which could be directly invoked by individuals after the end of the transitional period (case 2/74, *Reyners*). By this ruling, it actually turned into a negative rule (which better lends itself to direct effect) the positive obligation which everyone had previously read into Article 52.

These examples suffice to give a flavour both of the scope of the ECJ's role and the manner in which it has become one of the principal engines in the integration process. The generous interpretation of the fundamental principles contained in the treaty (the famous 'four freedoms': freedom of circulation of goods, people, services and capital); the tendency to see in these not just negative obligations for the member states, but also sources of rights for individuals; the possibility for these individuals to enforce their rights before a tribunal and obtain their application in the name of the supremacy of Community law – this is the cocktail which the Court has itself concocted to gain its position as one of the principal players in the integration process. It should be stressed that it is the ECJ's *own actions* in forging these concepts which have elevated it to the position of being one of the engines of integration.

The components of this Court-devised cocktail complete and mutually reinforce each other. Thus, the broad interpretation of the treaty provisions would have had little future had individuals not been given a chance to invoke them before courts; direct effect would not have had the same impact if individuals had not been able to challenge those provisions of national law which they considered to be contrary to Community law through the Article 177 [234] procedure, or if the supremacy of Community law had not been recognized. Furthermore, the management of these different components has given the ECJ considerable power. Once the direct effect of a provision has been recognized, it is up to the Court to determine the conditions of its application in cases which come before it concerning the provision in question. In the same way, the exceptions which it has appended to its most audacious decisions confer upon it a considerable margin of appreciation. This is particularly true in the area of the free movement of goods: anxious to compensate for its broad interpretation of Article 30 [28], it added to the exceptions set out in Article 36 [30] a series of 'mandatory requirements' which could justify the maintenance of national rules which would otherwise contravene Article 30 (case 120/78 '*Cassis de Dijon*'). But only the ECJ has the power to decide if and under what conditions a national norm can benefit from these derogations, thus allowing it to arbitrate among the various interests involved. Thus, while promoting the objectives of the treaty, the Court has also furthered its own institutional interests.

Unsurprisingly, this daring case law is often cited as exemplifying the activism of the Court (Rasmussen, 1986, p. 29). Yet, one must keep in mind that its law-making role has been made both easier and more apparent by a combination of features specific to the basic document it had to interpret.

Clearly, the open-textured character of many provisions, together with the purpose-oriented nature of the Treaty, lent itself quite well to the kind of teleological interpretation proposed by the ECJ. Moreover, as indicated above, law-making is to a large degree inherent in the judicial function, although legitimacy concerns often lead people (including of course judges) to downplay this aspect. One of the original features of European litigation is that the law-making side of the judicial process is more *visible* than in other contexts. In part this is due to the way cases came to the Court: about half of its rulings originate in references from national courts, which use the Article 177 [234] procedure to inquire into the compatibility of domestic law with EC law. While recognizing that it has no jurisdiction in such procedures to decide upon this compatibility issue, the ECJ has decided that it could render an (abstract) ruling on the interpretation of the treaty in order to assist domestic courts in deciding the case (case 6/64, *Costa* v. *ENEL*, discussed in Chapter 2). In this context, it often resorts to a general language which is generally associated with legislative law-making. Instead of pronouncing on the compatibility issue, it lays down in broad terms the principles that should guide the domestic court's action.

The *Comet* case provides a good example of this trend. The ECJ was asked to rule that a Dutch law limiting to 30 days the period in which an appeal could be lodged against the decision to raise a levy on exports was incompatible with Community law, as it weakened the direct effect of the relevant treaty provision; that is, Article 16 [repealed]. Instead of discussing explicitly this issue, which it cannot do in the context of a preliminary ruling, the Court laid down in general terms the conditions in which such a rule was acceptable:

> In the absence of any relevant Community rule, it is for the national legal order of each Member State to . . . lay down the procedural rules for proceedings designed to ensure the protection of the rights which individuals acquire through the direct effect of Community law, provided that such rules are not less favourable than those governing the same right of action on an internal matter.
>
> The position would be different only if those rules and time-limits made it impossible in practice to exercise rights which the national courts have a duty to protect.
>
> This does not apply to the fixing of a reasonable period of limitation with which an action must be brought.
>
> The fixing, as regards fiscal proceedings, of such a period is in fact an application of a fundamental principle of legal certainty which protects both the authority concerned and the party from whom payment is claimed. (Case 45/76, *Comet* v. *Produktschap voor Siegerwassen*, p. 2053)

Because of their abstract character, judgments of this kind almost unavoidably resort to a language similar to that of statutory rules. Thus, the oracular tone of such rulings may be seen, in part at least, as a by-product of the indirect manner in which the ECJ came to address compatibility issues. This is not to say that the alleged activism of the Court is merely a matter of style. But this in-built bias in favour of abstract rulings must be kept in mind in any attempt to evaluate the way in which it has fulfilled its task.

Integration through law

The previous section has explained why the judicial component of integration has taken on such considerable importance. However, many integration theories still tend to consider, more or less explicitly, law as a dependent variable, whose evolution reflects – with varying rapidity and precision – changes occurring at other levels. For some, the real reasons for integration are to be sought in technological change or the development of international trade (Sandholz and Zysman, 1989). In contrast, the intergovernmentalist school underlines the role of national governments, whose attitude is said to be the prime factor in determining the rhythm of the integration process (Garrett, 1992; Moravcsik, 1993). Both types of analysis have in common a tendency to regard law as a kind of 'transmission belt', whose primary function is to implement choices made elsewhere. Yet this reductive vision does not do justice to the complexity of the issue.

While the influence of extra-legal variables over the pace of integration process is undeniable, it should not blind us to the fact that, thanks to the presence of an autonomous judicial organ charged with interpreting the treaties, the legal sphere has experienced a dynamic all of its own (Dehousse and Weiler, 1990). This evolution has been determined less by external variables than by the requirements of the Community legal order, as interpreted by the ECJ. Examples to back this up abound: we saw earlier how the concern to ensure uniform application of the treaties pushed it into forging new concepts such as direct effect and the supremacy of Community law, and how threats to the concept of supremacy led it to develop its activity in the field of the protection of human rights; we will see subsequently that, on many occasions, the ECJ has refused to allow the inaction of the organs charged with implementation of the fundamental principles of the treaty to paralyse its application.

This dynamism has had important effects on the way in which the integration process has developed. The Treaty of Rome envisages two main paths for the realization of the common market:

- the first involves the elimination of discrimination based on the origin of factors of production; it is known as *negative integration*, as it is realized largely through prohibitions, generally contained in the Treaty itself
- the second path entails a harmonization programme destined to progressively remove the obstacles to free movement found in the legislation of the member states. As it necessitates intervention of a legislative nature, which determines the response to a common problem, it is often referred to as *positive integration*.

It is widely agreed that, at least until the entry into force of the Single European Act (SEA) in 1986, negative integration held the upper hand and that it still plays a central role today (Scharpf, 1995). While the programme of harmonization of national provisions was hampered by the need for consensus on the minutiae of each and every piece of legislation, the ECJ, through its extensive interpretation of the treaty provisions concerning free movement, has dealt a series of sharp blows to the legislative and administrative apparatus employed by member states to protect their interests (Van Empel, 1992). The prevalence of negative integration is generally attributed to the fact that it is easier to implement clear prohibitions than to jointly determine how a particular problem should be tackled, particularly if this involves unanimous decision-making (Pinder, 1968). This instrumental approach must not, however, mask the importance of the conditions under which each of the institutional actors has had to operate. While the Community legislative process was hindered by the menace of a veto, the ECJ could decide in an autonomous fashion, and thus give precedence to its primary concern – namely to ensure the maximal effectiveness of the treaty provisions. Is it really so surprising that the Court ended up adopting a more trenchant position than the Community legislator in the integration process?

The tension between political and judicial decisions is well illustrated by the *Reyners* case (case 2/74, discussed above). Prior to the ECJ's ruling, it was accepted that Council directives were needed to give effect to the rule that nationals of other member states were to be allowed to set up and carry on business in the same way as a member state's own nationals. The Commission had therefore tabled a number of proposals, many of which were pending at the time *Reyners* was decided. By giving direct effect to Article 62 [repealed], the Court completely modified the situation. A number of draft directives, which had become obsolete overnight, were withdrawn by the Commission, who announced that, where legislative action was still needed, it would henceforth concentrate on the coordination of rules governing the admission to and practice of the professions (Louis, 1990, p. 112). Thanks to the ECJ's far-reaching interpretation of Article 52 [43], the scope of legislative intervention needed to give effect to the treaty had been significantly reduced.

This atypical role constrained the Court to present itself as being particularly attentive to the implications of its decisions. The importance accorded to negative integration risked making it impossible for national authorities to conduct effective policies in fields as diverse as environmental policy, consumer protection and health and safety of workers. Aware of this danger, the Court frequently attenuated the impact of its decisions by multiplying the exceptions to the principle of free movement. In this way, national rules which fell within the scope of treaty prohibitions were redeemed by the ECJ on the grounds that they protected legitimate interests, and that common sense dictated that they should be left in place until such time as a uniform regime had been adopted at Community level (see, for example, cases 110 and 111/78, *Van Wesemael*; case 302/86, *Commission* v. *Denmark*; case 145/88, *Torfaen* v. *B&Q*). Thus, it has, to a large extent, been up to the Court to ensure the equilibrium between positive integration and negative integration.

The dispossession of the legislator has moreover been reinforced by the alliance between the ECJ and individuals. The combination of a broad interpretation of the treaty provisions and an innovative utilization of the Article 177 [234] reference procedure – transforming it into an instrument of control of the actions of national authorities – has had the effect of allowing private individuals to play a role which has no counterpart on the international plane. Mr Costa, in disputing his electricity bill, Mrs Defrenne, in challenging

Sabena's discrimination against its female employees, or the Rewe company, one of the parties involved in the *Cassis de Dijon* case, could all claim the honour of having done more for European integration than many of the national officials who represent their countries in the labyrinth of experts committees which meet in Brussels.

All of these factors combine to explain the atypical dynamics of European integration, at least up to the mid-1980s, and the launching of the single market programme. Not only were state preferences less decisive than in other international fora, but the political process itself was in part overshadowed by the judicial process. A book published shortly before the SEA indicated that progress in the sphere of free movement of goods derived more from the case law of the ECJ than from the work of the Community political organs (Gormley, 1985, p. 249). Readers with only limited knowledge of the reality of the EC might have viewed this argument as yet another example of the myopic perception that lawyers tend to have of reality. The fact is that it neatly sums up more than 25 years of European integration, in which progress towards the ever closer union envisaged by the Treaty of Rome was not only dependent upon the choices of member state representatives, but also on the case law of the ECJ.

Furthermore, the Court's influence is difficult to counter. In many of the cases, it is within the treaty itself that the judge has found the source of his interpretation; these interpretations cannot, therefore, subsequently be put into question by adopting new legislative rules. The ECJ is placed in the same position as a constitutional court: the member states can only force it to change its position by altering the constitutional document: that is, the treaty. That this is not impossible is amply demonstrated by the second protocol attached to the Maastricht Treaty, which limits the retroactive effect of the *Barber* (case 262/88) decision concerning private occupational pension schemes (see Chapter 6). However, this type of 'court reversal' operation is not easy to accomplish, as the unanimity of the member states is required for any modification of the treaty. Moreover, the ECJ has fairly recently hinted that certain fundamental principles of the treaty cannot be revised (Opinion 1/91). Likewise, should the member states want to 'correct' ECJ interpretation of 'legislative' measures adopted by Community institutions, they would be dependent on the Commission's goodwill, as the latter enjoys a near complete monopoly of legislative initiative. That is to say that, in practice, the risk of state intervention to 'correct' the ECJ's case law is relatively limited.

The Court as a policy-maker

Up to this point, we have looked exclusively at the direct influence of EC case law on the integration process in order to show that, through its law-making role, it has had considerable impact on the overall integration process. This must not however allow us to lose sight of the fact that these decisions can equally exercise an *indirect* influence on policy decisions. The ECJ's rulings are significant not only for the rights and obligations which they create, but also for the way in which they can condition – sometimes quite explicitly – the actions of participants in policy debates. Through its innovative interpretations, the Court's influence can be felt at all stages of the policy process:

- it can suggest new avenues to be explored
- it can legitimate certain choices and delegitimate others
- it can provoke Community legislative intervention
- its existence affects the relationships between the various actors involved in policy debates
- it plays a central role in the implementation of common decisions.

While its influence may be difficult to quantify at these various levels, it is often considerable.

The Court as agenda-setter

Policy-making is an uncertain process. For decisions to be taken, various conditions must be met: the problem to be tackled must have acquired sufficient salience, policy entrepreneurs must have identified a potential solution, and they must furthermore be able to convince decision-makers (generally politicians) of the validity of their choice (Kingdon, 1984). Courts may play a significant role in this process, *inter alia* by signalling problems which must be addressed. The ECJ has done so on a number of occasions. One of the most interesting examples is the role it played in the adoption of a European merger control regulation (Bulmer, 1994; Allen, 1996).

The European Commission has been endowed with substantial powers in the field of competition policy: it must ensure that agreements between firms do not distort competition (Article 85 [81]) and that firms that dominate a given market do not abuse their dominant position (Article 86 [82]). Yet, in defining the Community competence, the Treaty of Rome only makes reference to the behaviour of firms, and says nothing of changes in the *structure* of a given market. The Commission rapidly came to the conclusion that if it was to ensure the maintenance of competition in the common market, it should be given the power to control mergers or acquisition of companies.

In 1972, it initiated proceedings against a packaging company, Continental Can, which had acquired its main competitor via a Belgian subsidiary. The Commission argued that in so doing, Continental Can had abused its dominant position. Its decision was challenged before the ECJ, on the grounds that, given its silence on the matter, Article 86 could not be used to introduce merger control into the treaty. Rejecting literal interpretation, the Court argued, much in the same manner as in *Van Gend & Loos*, that it had 'to go back to the spirit, general scheme and wording of Article 86 EEC, as well as to the system and objectives of the Treaty' (case 6/72, *Europemballage and Continental Can* v. *Commission*). Faithful to its tradition of teleological interpretation, it went on to examine that provision in the light of the principles and objectives set out in Articles 2 and 3, and upheld the Commission's broad interpretation of Article 86. In a somewhat Solomon-like fashion, however, the decision was annulled on other grounds.

That victory prompted the Commission to table a draft legislation regulating its powers to control mergers and takeovers. The member states, particularly the UK and Germany, which already had domestic merger control legislation, were reluctant to follow suit. However, their position was undermined by the 1987 *Philip Morris* judgment, in which the ECJ ruled that mergers resulting from agreements entered into by companies could be regarded as a restrictive agreement prohibited by Article 85, and therefore subjected to Commission control (joined cases 142 and 156/84, *British American Tobacco and Reynolds* v. *Commission*). As a result, companies started to notify mergers to the Commission for clearance.

Yet the uncertainties surrounding the scope of Commission powers as well as the implications of a negative decision were such that corporate actors started pushing together with the Commission in favour of a regulation that would clarify the situation. This pressure eventually led to the adoption of the Merger Control Regulation in 1989, barely two years after the *Philip Morris* case.

The Court's role in this story was mostly indirect: it did not grant to the Commission an unfettered right to control mergers and takeovers. Yet, in confirming that some situations at least were covered by Articles 85 [81] and 86 [82], its rulings gave sufficient salience to the issue to allow the Commission to push forward the idea of merger control at European level, which prevailed in the wake of the single market programme. It is also worth pointing out that unlike *Continental Can*, in which the Commission's decision was partly motivated by its desire to establish the principle that it could regulate mergers under Article 86, in the *Philip Morris* case, the ECJ was brought into motion by tobacco firms challenging the Commission's *approval* of the merger between some of their competitors (Bulmer, 1994, p. 432). In this case, the Court can therefore not be presented as a mere agent of some strategy engineered by the Commission. Its rulings, because they are capable of altering the legal situation of all the actors that take part in the policy-making process, can create issues that will have to be addressed by the Community's political institutions.

The Court as policy innovator

The ECJ's innovative capacity has been most markedly evident in the area of free movement of goods. One of the central problems in the implementation of an integrated market lies in the divergences existing between national legislations. National traditions in the fields of consumption and safety of products, the organization of professions, the priority given to environmental protection: all these elements vary – sometimes to a considerable extent – from one country to another. These disparities create inevitable difficulties for imported products, which are often designed and commercially launched according to rules which differ from those prevailing in the country of importation. To eliminate these obstacles to trade, the Treaty of Rome envisages essentially one solution: the 'approximation' of national legislations, better known as harmonization.

However, this legislative avenue is far from straightforward. Harmonization presupposes agreement on the necessity of, and the means by which, Community intervention will take place. Given the treaty unanimity requirement prior to the SEA, agreement was difficult to reach. Years of long and complex negotiations were often necessary to overcome the absence of consensus within the scientific community or to get around the threat of a veto. The rigidity of the process hampered the adaptation of Community directives to technical progress. Finally, the Commission was often criticized for its immoderate fondness for technical detail and its desire to standardize all products placed on the market, without consideration for national and regional traditions which still retain their relevance (Close, 1978).

The limits of this approach were magnified by the protectionist wave which swept across Europe in the 1970s recession. Given its cumbersomeness, the traditional approach was incapable of preventing the proliferation of technical regulations, often inspired by the desire to protect national markets from foreign competition. It is within this context that the Court gave its famous *Cassis de Dijon* judgment. The case arose from a mundane dispute over non-tariff barriers to trade. German legislation forbade the sale of spirits with an alcohol content of less than 25 per cent, which prevented the commercial sale in Germany of Cassis de Dijon, the alcohol content of which is of around 20 per cent.

The importer who brought the case before the national courts claimed that the German law breached Article 30 [28] in creating an obstacle to the free movement of goods. Given the breadth of the all-purpose formula in *Dassonville* (case 8/74) the Court's response was not difficult to predict. The central focus of the debate was shifted to another question: in the absence of a harmonization regime, can a state invoke its legislation to prevent the commercial sale of an imported good? The Court replied in the affirmative, indicating that not only the considerations laid down in Article 36 [30] – morality and public security, protection of health, and so on – but also 'mandatory requirements', such as the fairness of commercial transactions or consumer protection, could legitimately justify derogations from the principle established by Article 30.

However, it added that the legislation in question must actually reflect these legitimate values. The German government advanced as justification the need to protect consumer health and the fact that, being accustomed to finding strong alcohol on the market, consumers could be misled as to the quality of the imported product. Neither of these arguments convinced the ECJ: a norm imposing a *minimum* alcohol content is not necessarily the most effective method of protecting consumer health. As to adequately informing consumers, this could be achieved in a manner less detrimental to free movement, by, for example, imposing adequate labelling requirements. Amplifying somewhat its opinion, it added:

> There is therefore no valid reason why, provided that they have been lawfully produced and marketed in one of the Member States, alcoholic beverages should not be introduced into any other Member State; the sale of such products may not be subject to a legal prohibition on the marketing of beverages with an alcohol content lower than the limit set by the national rules.

Thus, the Court seems to say that if a product satisfies the regulatory requirements of one member state, requirements such as those contained in the German law cannot be used against it. These few words, seemingly anodyne, have had a considerable influence on the development of European integration. One way of understanding this part of the judgment is to say that in the absence of contrary proof, national norms governing the production and marketing of a product in its country of origin must be considered as equivalent to those in the country in which it is to be subsequently imported. The implicit premise of this reasoning was more explicitly elaborated upon in a subsequent 1984 Council document: 'the objectives pursued by the Member States to protect the safety and health of their people as well as the consumer are equally valid in principle even if different techniques are used to achieve them'. It is this convergence of objectives which makes the principle of functional equivalence between national legislations conceivable.

This, however, is merely one possible interpretation of the principle propounded by the ECJ. It was the Commission which, in a much publicized Communication issued to deal with the implications of the *Cassis de Dijon* decision, highlighted the potentialities of this approach. Drawing on the Court's remarks, the Commission developed a general principle of *mutual recognition*: for member states to implement the principle of functional equivalence delineated by the Court, it was not sufficient that they treated imported products in line with national law; rather they had to take into account 'the legitimate requirements of other member states'. In the same vein, Brussels announced its intention to follow up all breaches of this new practice and to redirect the entire harmonization programme: henceforth, all efforts would be concentrated on spheres which remained outside the principle of mutual recognition – evidently the exceptions laid down in Article 36 [30] and the 'mandatory requirements' identified by the ECJ.

This programme was subjected to strong criticism (Alter and Meunier-Aitsahalia, 1994; Nicolaïdis, 1993). The Commission was reproached by many for having gone beyond the ECJ's declaration and for having ignored the numerous exceptions with which it had punctuated its judgment; the Council of Ministers went so far as to commission a counter-interpretation of the significance of the judgment from its own legal service. Despite this resistance, the Commission's efforts proved strikingly successful. Four years after its Communication, the member states accepted its broad approach in announcing a new standardization strategy. One year later, with the *White Paper* on the completion of the internal market, the Commission obtained Council approval for an ambitious programme of measures aimed at eliminating internal borders by 31 December 1992. The notion of mutual recognition occupied a central position in this programme: now the Commission proposed to widen its field of application to apply it not just to the free movement of goods, as *Cassis de Dijon* had done, but also in areas as diverse as the free movement of services or the elimination of fiscal obstacles to free movement.

Thus, the new approach outlined by the ECJ was at the root of the relaunching of European integration, which took place towards the middle of the 1980s. Undoubtedly, the actual concept of mutual recognition was not invented by the Court: it is already contained in Article 57 [47] of the Treaty of Rome concerning recognition of diplomas and qualifications. It is also unquestionable that the concept's extraordinary success owes much to the entrepreneurial political qualities of the Commission, which was capable of grasping the hidden potential of the concept and of finding the means of selling it to national governments (Dehousse and Majone, 1994).

However, the fact remains that it is the ECJ which introduced the concept of mutual recognition – albeit in an embryonic state – into the sphere of the free movement of goods. Moreover, it seems to have done this purely on its own initiative, as there is not the slightest trace of this line of reasoning either in the submissions of the plaintiff, the observations of the Commission, or even in the Advocate-General's opinion. Through a sweeping statement, which could not even be said to have been necessary for the solution of the dispute at hand, the Court implanted in the political debate an idea which was to travel far. It is indisputable that this judicial innovation played an essential role in the causal chain which eventually crystallized in the SEA. In the absence of this catalyst, the relaunching of European integration would undoubtedly have proved a much more arduous task.

The legitimating function of the Court

The capacity to innovate is not in itself sufficient to ensure the successful acceptance of the ideas formulated; the necessity still remains of ensuring that these ideas are adopted by society at large or at least by the policy-makers. Judicial organs are ideally equipped for this task. Their traditional role as interpreters of the law serves to confer on their judgments a unique authority. Courts, unlike policy entrepreneurs, do not propose a range of possible options: they state the law. On occasion, this authority allows them to successfully introduce notions which would be difficult for any other actor to impose.

Cassis de Dijon provides an excellent illustration of this hypothesis. Part of the success of the concept of mutual recognition is directly attributable to its solemn formulation as a legal rule. On a formal level, this interpretation was rooted in the Treaty of Rome and not based on some arbitrary political preference. Undoubtedly, this enhanced legitimacy contributed to the concept's exponential success. The Commission knew how to adeptly exploit this element: it is no coincidence that its first feeler took the modest form of a Communication interpreting the ECJ's judgment. By adopting this slant, the Commission clearly banked on profiting from the legitimacy – legal, but also political – which is inherent to a court judgment.

Recourse to the ECJ can thus become part of the political game. This was clearly demonstrated by developments in the field of insurance law. The Treaty of Rome envisaged the progressive abolition of restrictions on the freedom to provide services within the

Community. However, for more than two decades the problem of insurance regulation has only been tackled as a freedom of establishment issue. The majority of member states had in fact made access to the insurance market conditional on a system of prior authorization, thus allowing them to ensure that insurance companies offered at least a minimal guarantee of financial soundness. The attention of the Community institutions was largely focused on the conditions under which these authorizations were granted, in order to enable companies based in another member state to establish a branch or a subsidiary company elsewhere in the Community. This first wave of harmonization ran into the same structural difficulties as in the free movement of goods area: member states were reluctant to renounce their regulatory traditions, and nothing constrained them to do so. Hence, little or no progress was made.

Once again, it was the ECJ which rang the changes. Weary of the member states' procrastinations, the Commission commenced a series of infringement proceedings against several of them for having failed to fulfil the obligations incumbent upon them by virtue of a co-insurance directive. The most important of these proceedings concerned the Federal Republic of Germany, which the Commission alleged permitted only companies established in Germany to offer their services there (case 205/84, *Commission* v. *Germany*).

The ECJ was careful not to act as the Commission's mouthpiece. It noted that in the absence of Community rules dealing with the conditions of operation of insurance companies, the member states had the right to require and to control respect for their own rules concerning services proffered on their own territory. Given the need to ensure consumer protection, it even conceded the legitimacy of authorization procedures, by which national authorities can make sure that an enterprise fulfils the regulatory conditions laid down for insurance companies.

On the other hand, the judgment contains several concessions to the notion of mutual recognition. It underlines the necessity for the conditions laid down for the approval of an enterprise based in another member state to take into consideration the conditions to which that enterprise is subject in its state of origin. Above all, it rebuts as the 'very negation' of the free provision of services the idea that a stable establishment must already exist for an insurance company to receive authorization to sell its products in another member state. If the principle of free provision of services defined in Article 59 [49] means anything, it permits people who are not established in a member state to offer their services in that country.

Thus, the ECJ has opened the door to a greater utilization of the concept of free provision of services. It can hardly be accused, however, of having pulled away the rug from under the member states' feet: the judgment largely preserves their supervisory powers, thanks notably to the very wide definition of establishment in another member state. The *Commission* v. *Germany* judgment is moreover frequently cited as an example of the new, more prudent path followed by the Court over the past decade (Berlin, 1992, p. 35; Van Empel, 1992, p. 12). And yet, it marks a turning-point in Community insurance market regulation. In the years following this judgment, a veritable explosion of Community activity in this area has been witnessed. Capitalizing on the impetus supplied by the Court's ruling, the Council adopted a series of directives which had existed in a legislative limbo for many years (Everson, 1993, pp. 121–7).

This new tendency owes much to the ECJ. Even if it did not respond entirely to the Commission's expectations, the Court clearly legitimated an alternative approach to that which had previously been followed. A significant proportion of the provisions adopted in the following years endeavoured to delineate the conditions under which the right to free provision of services – brought back into the picture by the ECJ – was to be exercised. Undoubtedly, this legitimation function was not the only influential factor. In particular, the Court's remarks – however moderate – on mutual recognition and their consequent implications for control authorities in the host country must be considered. Was it not better for the member states to construct by agreement a hard core of safety and supervision rules, rather than to run the risk of seeing their national legislations censured by the ECJ? This example provides us with an illustration of another function of Community case law: as a legislative inciter.

ECJ rulings as a catalyst for EC legislation

If case law sometimes acts as a source of inspiration or legitimation for the various participants in the integration process, it can also contain a series of more pressing messages for the attention of the political organs. As I pointed out earlier, the ECJ, by highlighting the importance of a series of provisions in the Treaty of Rome, had to a certain extent filled in the gaps left by the Community legislator. In so doing, it also exerted indirect pressure on the member states, the holders of political power, as the principles consecrated by it went beyond those which the member states had been prepared to concede.

The progressive adoption of the principle of mutual recognition offers an excellent illustration of this process. The initial reactions of the member states to the *Cassis de Dijon* judgment were extremely lukewarm, as it was clear that mutual recognition carried with it a partial erosion of their sovereignty. Furthermore, countries with a high level of economic or social protection feared seeing their producers having to cope with competition from products coming from countries where the legislation was more lax. Despite these reservations, in the space of just a few years, the national governments ended up falling in with the arguments of the Commission and adopting, with the Commission's White Paper, a legislative programme centred on the idea of mutual recognition.

How can this complete u-turn be explained? Changes in the international environment may have played a role in convincing the member states of the necessity of putting in place a single market of continental dimensions the better to resist international competition (Sandholz and Zysman, 1989), but one can also submit that the ECJ's shadow shifted the decisional balance.

Before *Cassis*, the member states subscribed to the opinion that in the absence of a Community harmonizing measure, they remained at liberty to legislate to protect the legitimate interests set out in Article 36 [30], even if at times divergences between national approaches could hinder intra-community trade. This was in effect the interpretation relied upon by the German government before the Court. *Cassis de Dijon* radically altered the contours of the issue. From then on, the member states were vulnerable to proceedings before the ECJ, initiated either by the Commission or private individuals whenever it could be argued that they ignored the requirements of mutual recognition. The final decision on the conflict between free movement and the values underpinning national legislations would therefore have laid in the hands of the Court.

Even if one might think that the ECJ judges would have been concerned to safeguard the legitimate interests of member states, it is understandable that the national governments preferred to avoid dispossessing themselves of an important decisional power. The political avenue offered them more guarantees: by subscribing to the new strategy proposed by the Commission, they held on to the power to decide the exact dosage of harmonization and mutual recognition which they were prepared to accept (Lenaerts, 1992, p. 15).

The same reasoning can be employed to understand why, following *Cassis de Dijon*, the harmonization process accelerated. Unquestionably, this phenomenon owes a great deal to structural change: the SEA provided for a shift to majority voting for two-thirds of the directives envisaged in the Commission's White Paper on the completion of the internal market. However, the impact of this change can also be considered as having been reinforced by the ECJ's case law.

Before *Cassis*, national governments were in a position of strength. As unanimity was required for the adoption of a harmonization directive, they could only be cajoled into relinquishing their national traditions following long and exhaustive negotiations; hence the slowness of the process. At this level too, *Cassis* was to radically change the shaping of the issue, by dangling before the member states the possibility of judicial control of the legitimacy of choices they made at national level. Simultaneously, the significance of deadlock in agreements reached at Community level changed utterly. Far from providing a definite guarantee of the maintenance of national legislation, deadlock now entailed the risk of leading to a form of reverse discrimination in cases where national legislation was condemned by the ECJ. Mutual recognition would lead to national measures being applied to national products only, while goods produced in member states with less stringent requirements would have to be admitted freely. It is hardly necessary to state that this was not a very enticing prospect: no government can lightheartedly accept the idea of placing its own producers at a disadvantage. The sword of Damocles hanging over the member states generated a profound change in the general negotiating context. With one eye on the risks entailed in maintaining the status quo, the incentives to reach agreement were much greater than they had been in the past.

The fear of condemnation by the ECJ is but one of the factors which can modify the conduct of member states. The case law concerning Community competences can also produce a similar effect. Fishing policy provides here a particularly striking illustration. Although the Treaty of Rome envisages the setting up of a common policy on the preservation of marine resources, a matter falling exclusively within Community competence, for several years the Council was unable to reach agreement. Taking advantage of this stalemate, the UK unilaterally adopted a set of conservation measures. The Court, confronted with this in infringement proceedings brought by the Commission, found itself in a difficult situation. While no one disputed the urgent need for intervention by the public authorities, to accept the idea of *force majeure* risked playing into the hands of the most intransigent member states: by blocking all chances of agreement at Council level, they hoped to win back the right to act in a sphere of competence which had been transferred to Community level.

The ECJ, however, managed to avoid this danger (case 804/79, *Commission* v. *United Kingdom*). After restating the rule that exclusive Community competence forbade unilateral action by any member state, it marshalled Article 5 [10], which obliges member states to facilitate all actions by the Community, and Article 155 [211], which confers a general power of initiative and supervision on the Commission. On this basis, it held that member states, set up as 'trustees of the common interest' (p. 1075), could only adopt conservation measures under the control of and with the approval of the Commission. In so doing, it achieved two objectives. Not only was the Commission's right to veto subsequent national measures recognized, but the judgment prompted member states to reach a common position. What was the point of opposing a Commission proposal if the principles inspiring it were to inform the control measures the member states would be obliged to adhere to in the case of further negotiation deadlock? It was infinitely preferable to agree among themselves within the Council, and this is in fact what happened in the two years following the judgment (Lenaerts, 1992, pp. 19–21).

All of the decisions discussed above share the same logic: to goad the Community legislator into action by making it clear that inaction provides no benefits for the member states and may in fact present a number of risks.

Conclusion: the dynamics of legal integration

In this chapter, I have attempted to illustrate the multiple channels through which the ECJ has been able to exercise an influence over the integration process. Its contribution has been important – sometimes even decisive – in shaping the trinity of institutional structures, Community policies and decision-making. This is partially attributable to the competences it possesses, which go beyond those assigned to traditional international tribunals. The fact remains, however, that the use it has made of these powers has allowed it to play a more important role than that generally played by judicial organs at national level.

Of course, this outcome must be looked at in conjunction with the relative sclerosis gripping the European legislature since the 1965 institutional crisis. The armistice which put an end to this crisis – the so-called Luxembourg Accords – complicated considerably the functioning of the Community system by its imposition – factually if not legally – of unanimous decision-making in areas where the Treaty had provided for decision by qualified majority at the end of the transitional period. The resulting legislative inertia placed the Community judge in a tricky position. Each time the ECJ came up against the difficulties created by Council inaction, it was forced to navigate a path between Scylla and Charybdis. Either it concluded that it could not substitute for the political organs when they had failed to act, and refrained from taking any action, thus condoning the stalemate in the integration project, or it tried to offset judicially the failures of the legislature, thus leaving itself wide open to contemptuous critiques of 'government by judges' (Pescatore, 1983, p. 561).

The ECJ tried to steer a path between these two extremes. It endeavoured to extricate from the Treaty of Rome a set of general rules – direct effect and the supremacy of Community law, the principle of non-discrimination, the duty of member states to co-operate, and so on – which enabled it to keep intact the essential values contained in the treaty. At the same time, using a variety of methods, it prodded the political organs into taking action. To be sure, this was facilitated by the important spaces which Community law left for individuals to come before the Court. Legal integration has enjoyed a dynamics of its own: it has developed, in response to the questions put to the ECJ, while political integration was bogged down following the 1965–6 crisis.

What has prompted the ECJ to play such an active role? Clearly, it cannot be ruled out that judges were subject to political pressures; on the contrary, we have seen that their position within the Court exposes them to pressures from national capitals. The member states have not been reluctant to promote their interests, and the Court has shown on several occasions an indisputably political sensitivity. But should one draw from this the conclusion that the ECJ is merely a 'strategic actor', whose rulings are primarily influenced by the anticipated responses of national governments, as suggested by Geoffrey Garrett (1995, p. 180)? There is little evidence to support this view. In a survey of the free movement of goods, Bernadette Kilroy found that in 86 per cent of the cases, the Court followed the Commission submissions, rather than those of member state governments (Kilroy, 1996, p. 23; see also Stein, 1981). From *Cassis de Dijon* to the working time case (discussed in Chapter 6), there was no shortage of judgments in which the ECJ ruled against the declared interests of powerful member states.

Given the secrecy which surrounds the ECJ's deliberations, we are reduced to conjecturing as to the reasons which pushed the judges in one direction rather than another. However, a number of them have made no attempt to conceal their enthusiasm for Europe in their writings. Furthermore, without denying the importance of political factors, it must be stressed that legal values have contributed to moulding Community case law. Supremacy of Community law is in many respects the logical corollary of the doctrine of direct effect developed by the Court; similarly the ECJ developed a closer interest in the protection of human rights in reaction to the dangers facing the doctrine of supremacy. Its activity is also heavily dependent on the way in which its judges conceive of their judicial role. To the concern for judicial independence, deeply embedded in the European tradition, we must add the fear of a legal vacuum. Judge Pescatore, one of the Court's leading minds and one of the chief architects of this judicial edifice, has highlighted that the ECJ, each time that it is seized, has the obligation to give a ruling in accordance with the role assigned to it by Article 164 [220] of the treaty. Unlike political organs, it cannot divest itself of this responsibility, since to do so would be a denial of justice and a breach of one of the fundamental precepts of the judicial ethic. Therefore, where the legislature has not provided the ECJ with appropriate criteria on which to found a solution, it has no choice but to turn to the structural elements of the Community legal system and to forge a solution from what it finds there (Pescatore, 1983, pp. 576–7).

This conception of the judicial role is strongly influenced by the legal tradition prevailing in civil law systems. Community jurisprudence is also characterized by a frequent resort to 'systemic' interpretations of the Treaty of Rome – a standard of interpretation strongly anchored in the academic milieu, from where a majority of judges have come. By focusing on the aims of the treaty and its institutional objectives, the ECJ's case law places itself firmly within the continental legal tradition, where rational and deductive interpretative methods prevail over the empirical and inductive approaches often preferred in common law systems. This method of understanding legal problems has undoubtedly been of central importance in the development of Community case law.

The way in which the legal sphere is structured, with a court endowed with more important powers and greater possibilities of intervention for private parties than in 'classical' international relations, therefore appears to have had a clear impact on the rhythm of legal integration. Values and concerns specific to the legal sphere also played a crucial role in the way the ECJ interpreted its mission as guardian of the rule of law. Of course nothing of this negates the possibility that judges' rulings be influenced by national preferences. But, at the very least, the existence of an autonomous dynamics within the legal sphere should warn us against the dangers of monocausal explanations.

4

The Juridification of the Policy Process

The influence of the ECJ has not only made itself felt on the structures and policies of the Community; it has also affected the behaviour of, and relationship between, the principal actors in the Community political system. Its influence at this level is a natural corollary to what has been examined above. Community institutions, national authorities, interest groups and private parties have all learnt – sometimes to their cost – that the Court is a force to be reckoned with and that legal parameters must form an integral part of their analyses. It is therefore natural for all participants in the European policy process to try to integrate these into their policy strategies. Legal recourse henceforth forms a part of the arsenal by which these groups attempt to promote their particular interests.

Gaining access to the courtroom: the saga of the European Parliament

For those who are used to policy-making in a representative democracy, the idea that a parliamentary assembly would bring another branch of the legislature or the executive before a court seems quite odd. Traditionally, political institutions have other means of promoting their views, and the resort to courts, because of its uncertainty, is not their favourite avenue for solving their disputes. Yet, judicial politics have developed in an unprecedented fashion at the

European level. Even more remarkable is the fact that the European Parliament has had to fight in order to gain access to the Luxembourg Court.

Why the Parliament waged this campaign is easy to understand in view of its position in the law-making process. The Treaty of Rome confined it to a merely advisory function, and did not even formally provide for its involvement in some areas of crucial importance, such as commercial policy. Gaining access to the ECJ to defend its views was therefore more important for the European Parliament than for most legislative assemblies, which have other weapons at their disposal.

This was far from easy, as the original version of the EC Treaty did not mention the European Parliament either as a potential applicant or as a defendant, except in staff matters. However, the Parliament was able to have its standing in various proceedings recognized through a series of ECJ judgments.

The first stage in this quest was the *Isoglucose* case of 1980. The proceedings were initiated by a French firm which challenged the legality of a Council regulation laying down production quotas for isoglucose. One of the arguments used to justify this challenge was that the regulation had been adopted without the opinion of the European Parliament prescribed by Article 43 [37]. The Parliament intervened in the proceedings on the basis of Article 37 of the ECJ's Statute, which allows interventions by 'Member States and institutions of the Community' in pending cases. The Council argued that this power was to be equated with a right of action which the Parliament did not have, but the argument failed to convince the Court, which stressed that such a restrictive interpretation would affect the Community's institutional balance (case 138/79, *Roquette* v. *Council*). This judgment was important in two respects: as far as procedures are concerned, it provided the Parliament with a first channel of access to the courtroom as regards substance, it recognized that the right of the Parliament to be consulted on draft legislation was an 'essential procedural requirement', breach of which would result in the annulment of the legislation at issue.

Although the ECJ hinted in *Isoglucose* that the situation might be different where the Parliament, by its own conduct, made observance of that requirement impossible (an indication which was confirmed later in case C-65/93, *European Parliament* v. *Council)*,

Parliament tried to make the most of this ruling by modifying its rules of procedure. The new rules essentially tried to put pressure on the Commission to incorporate Parliament's amendments in its proposals, modification of which requires unanimity in the Council of Ministers. They provided that when the Commission refused to comply, Parliament could refer the matter back to the competent Committee, thereby delaying its opinion and holding up the procedure. Although the use of this technique has proved to be difficult, it has none the less enabled the Parliament to achieve certain results in urgent matters where delays can cause problems (Jacobs, Corbett and Shackleton, 1995, p. 193).

The right of intervention does not entitle the Parliament to bring matters before the ECJ, but simply gives it the possibility to express its views on pending cases. As such, it did not really allow the development of a real legal policy – that is, a strategy to achieve certain results through the judicial route. Such a strategy would have been possible only if the Parliament's right to initiate proceedings had been recognized. Yet the Court's broad interpretation of the concept of 'institutions' in the *Isoglucose* case represented a real breakthrough, as several treaty provisions enabled 'institutions' to participate in various ways in legal proceedings. This applied, for instance, to Article 175 [232], which enables applicants to challenge the refusal or failure to adopt any acts which the authority is under an obligation to adopt.

Parliament used this opportunity to challenge the Council's failure to introduce a common transport policy as well as to reach a decision on sixteen proposals submitted by the Commission in order to secure freedom to provide transport services. Although the ECJ stuck to its broad interpretation of the term 'institution' in spite of the Council's objection, the Parliament was only partly successful. The Court ruled that there was no legally complete obligation under Article 74 [70] to introduce a common transport policy. In contrast, the Parliament's second claim was upheld: the Court found that the Council was legally required to implement the freedom to provide transport services within the transitional period established by the treaty (case 13/83, *Parliament* v. *Council*). In spite of this partial victory, the transport case clearly confirmed the European Parliament's capacity to use judicial proceedings as an instrument to pursue its own policy – or even political – objectives. Still, its practical scope was limited, as Article 175 [232] actions can only be successful when an institution is under a duty to act. For the Parliament to emerge as a fully-fledged actor in judicial politics, its right to bring annulment proceedings against acts adopted by the Council or the Commission had to be recognized.

A first step in this direction was made in *Les Verts* (case 294/83). It had been decided that a sum of money would be allocated to European political parties, ostensibly for an 'information campaign' but in reality to pay for their campaign in a forthcoming election. The system of allocation clearly favoured those parties already represented in the Parliament, which led the French Green Party to seek the annulment of the decision by the Bureau of the Parliament. Although Article 173 [230] made no mention of the Parliament when listing the institutions whose measures could be contested, its agents before the Court understood they could take advantage of this claim to further their own interests. After some hesitation, they did not object to an extensive interpretation of Article 173 that would allow judicial control over the acts of Parliament, but instead stressed that the same standards of interpretation should lead to a recognition of the Parliament's competence to take annulment proceedings against acts of the Council or the Commission. Although the ECJ did not pick up the last part of the argument, it offered a far-reaching reading of the EC Treaty:

> the European Economic Community is a Community based on the rule of law, in as much as neither its Member States nor its institutions can avoid a review of the question whether the measures adopted by them are in conformity with the basic charter, the Treaty. (p. 1365)

Arguing that the treaty established 'a complete system of legal remedies', it ruled that an 'interpretation of Article 173 . . . which excluded measures adopted by the European Parliament from those which could be contested would lead to a result contrary to both the spirit of the Treaty as expressed in Article 164 and to its system' (p. 1366).

By the same token, the Court granted standing to the Green Party, although the latter clearly did not meet the 'individual concern' test of Article 173, as all parties which might stand in the European elections and were not already represented in the

Parliament were equally affected by the decision at hand. The decision was obviously influenced by the fact that an annulment action was the only avenue open to the plaintiff against what appeared as a biased decision.

While it lost the case on the merits, the European Parliament felt encouraged by this principled interpretation of Article 173 [230]. In a resolution of 9 October 1986, it took the view that the ECJ's ruling implied that it could take proceedings for annulment against acts of other institutions. It decided to test this view by challenging the validity of the Council's framework decision on 'comitology' – that is, the web of expert committees set up to assist the Commission when it acts to implement European legislation. The Parliament argued that this 1987 decision impinged negatively on its prerogatives and brought the Council before the ECJ. Its expectations were confounded: in sharp contrast to the systemic interpretation of *Les Verts*, the Court reverted to a strict literal interpretation and stuck to the text of Article 173, refusing to accept the parallel with either Article 175 [232] or its judgment in *Les Verts*. It further noted that the Parliament's interests were adequately protected by the Commission as guardian of the treaties (case 302/87, *Parliament* v. *Council* [*Comitology*]).

This ruling could have put an end to the Parliament's quest for more complete legitimation before the ECJ. Yet, less than two years later, the Court reviewed its position. While the *Comitology* case was still pending, the Parliament had brought an action against a Council regulation fixing the maximum levels of tolerated pollution in foodstuffs for cattle adopted in the wake of the Chernobyl accident. Parliament argued that this regulation should have been adopted under Article 100a [95], which then foresaw its involvement in the legislative process through what is known as the co-operation procedure, and not under Article 31 Euratom, which only requires its consultation. One would have thought that the *Comitology* judgment of the Court would have led the European Parliament to withdraw its action. Yet it declined to do so. It was known that *Comitology* had been decided by a narrow majority, and that since that ruling new members of the ECJ had been appointed. One could therefore hope that the Court would adopt a more open attitude.

Much of the discussion on the admissibility of the Parliament's claim focused on a weak point in the reasoning followed by the

Court in the *Comitology* decision, namely the argument that the Parliament's rights were sufficiently protected under the existing system, in particular by the Commission acting as guardian of the treaties. The facts of the case at issue proved that this protection was not always effective, as the Commission had taken sides with the Council as regards the choice of the proper legal base for the regulation at issue. Advocate General Van Gerven therefore suggested returning to the view defended by his colleague Darmon (and dismissed by the ECJ) in *Comitology* and thus to grant the Parliament a limited right of action for the defence of its own prerogatives. This line of argumentation, which appealed to the 'rule of law' ethics of *Les Verts* and to the necessity of an effective protection of rights granted by the treaty, ultimately prevailed (case C-70/88, *European Parliament* v. *Council* [*Chernobyl*]).

The ECJ recognized that existing legal remedies were not sufficient to guarantee in all circumstances that a measure adopted in disregard of the Parliament's prerogatives would be reviewed. At the same time, it stressed that, having been entrusted by Article 164 [220] with the task of ensuring that in the application of the treaty the law is observed,

> the Court must therefore be able to maintain the institutional balance and, consequently, review the observance of the Parliament's prerogative when called upon to do so by the Parliament, by means of a legal remedy which is suited to the purpose the Parliament seeks to achieve.

True, it could not by the stroke of a pen include the Parliament among the 'privileged applicants' listed in Article 173 [230]. However,

> [t]he absence in the Treaties of any provision giving the Parliament the right to bring an action for annulment may constitute a procedural gap, but it cannot prevail over the fundamental interest in the maintenance and observance of the institutional balance.

Consequently, it concluded that an action for annulment brought by the Parliament against an act of the Council or the Commission is admissible

> provided that the action seeks only to safeguard its prerogatives and that it is founded only on submissions alleging their infringements. (at pp. 2072–3)

Overruling a precedent is always a delicate operation as it shows the broad margin of appreciation enjoyed by courts in their interpretative mission. The ECJ therefore tried to distinguish the facts of this case from the precedent set in *Comitology*, by stressing that given the divergent views defended by the Commission and the Parliament as regards the proper legal basis in the dispute at issue, the former could not be expected to act in defence of the latter's prerogatives. However, the argument is not very convincing, since already in the previous case there appeared to be a conflict of interests between the Commission and the Parliament, the former having failed to accept a number of amendments put forward by the Parliament to protect its own powers. At any rate, the Court's decision clearly went beyond the intent of the founding fathers of the Community. Interestingly, this remarkable example of judicial creativity was subsequently ratified by the member states who included in the Treaty of Maastricht an amendment incorporating into Article 173 [230] the right of the Parliament (and the European Central Bank) to bring annulment actions 'for the purpose of protecting their prerogatives'.

This lengthy saga teaches us a number of points about judicial politics in the European Community. First, it shows that access to the courtroom was deemed of sufficient importance for an institution like the European Parliament to undertake in a lengthy and exacting litigation strategy in order to have the scope of its rights first recognized and then expanded by the Court of Justice. Secondly, it suggests that judicial politics must be seen in a long-term perspective, rather than on a case-by-case basis. The Parliament's gradual access to litigation featured a succession of stops and starts. Given the number and the variety of actors who played a role in the process within the Parliament – the legal committee, the legal service, at times the President – the Parliament's own policy line was at times uncertain. Had the Parliament failed to persist after *Comitology*, its right to initiate annulment proceedings would probably still not be recognized today. Yet, seen retrospectively, this uncertain process is striking for its overall continuity. Ultimately, the combination of distinct forces resulted in successfully promoting a strategy of development of the Parliament's legal armoury. This reminds us that perseverance is just as much an essential virtue for actors engaged in legal politics as it is for any other political entrepreneur (Kingdon, 1984).

Thirdly, we see once more how decisive the ECJ's vision of its own role has been. Both in *Les Verts* and in *Chernobyl*, appeals to its mission as guarantor of the rule of law have convinced it to go beyond a literal interpretation of the treaty. Stressing the role played by the ECJ in the development of judicial politics might seem tautological. Yet it must be appreciated that also at the level of the Court, the saga which led to the emergence of the Parliament as a litigator was the product of a constellation of circumstances. Had the ECJ adopted a more conservative attitude, or had it simply been more concerned about possible political reactions to its rulings, events would have followed a different course. These are elements worth remembering, given the more hostile environment surrounding decision-making at European level today.

The development of judicial politics

The existence of a court entrusted with the mission to act as an umpire in institutional disputes was bound to have an impact on the decision-making process. Yet, it took some time for this possibility to materialize: in 1969 Andrew Green, referring to, among other things, the agricultural crisis and the Gaullist boycott of European institutions in 1965–6, observed that thus far the most publicized political controversies had not been submitted to the ECJ (Green, 1969, p. 444; see also Scheingold, 1971). However, participants in the policy process have gradually come to realize that they could use the legal sphere to achieve ends that could not be achieved – or at least not so easily – through an exclusive reliance on the ordinary policy process. This has led to the development of various kinds of 'legal strategies'.

Going to court is of course the most obvious, though not the only, way for a political actor to use the legal sphere. We have seen how the Commission used this option to force member states to provide a larger space for the free provision of services in the insurance market. Governments have not been slow to reproach the Commission for utilizing a strategy which short-circuited ongoing debate in the Council of Ministers (case 205/84, *Commission* v. *Germany*, p. 3797). This, however, has not prevented them from following the same course when their own interests are at issue. Member states have realized the advantages of the judicial process in protecting their prerogatives against an unwanted Community competence development. Several governments have, for instance, brought the Commission before the ECJ to obtain the annulment of a decision requiring member states to communicate information regarding their policies on migrant workers from third states. In their view, such a decision could only be adopted by the Council of Ministers. The Court, however, held that Article 118 [137], which gives the Commission the task of 'promoting close cooperation between the Member States in the social field', implicitly authorized it to take steps 'which are indispensable in order to carry out that task', including the adoption of binding decisions (joined cases 281, 283–5 and 287/85, *Germany and Others* v. *Commission*). Likewise, governments hostile to transfers of sovereignty have repeatedly sought the annulment of decisions taken by a qualified majority in the Council of Ministers. Shortly after the coming into force of the SEA, the UK government, which had been outvoted on a directive on hormones adopted by the Council, managed to get the Court to annul it by invoking a breach of the Council's rules of procedure (case 68/86, *United Kingdom* v. *Council*).

More recently, it has tried to convince the ECJ judges that Article 118a [138], which concerns workers' health and safety, did not empower the Community to harmonize legislation regulating working time. The fact that the UK government brought the matter before the ECJ is quite symptomatic of the development of judicial politics. British concerns for national sovereignty had actually played an important role in the drafting of the directive at issue, which only lays down minimum requirements, and leaves ample room for derogations either through legislative interventions or through collective agreements. Yet the very principle of a pan-European regulation of working time, no matter how liberal, was perceived as anathema by the Conservative government in power in London, who saw in it a threat to the flexibility of the labour market, a central plank in its policy platform. A legal challenge provided a good opportunity to invite the ECJ to adopt a restrictive interpretation of Article 118a, which would have protected the British government against the risk of seeing far-reaching measures adopted by qualified majority in the future. In other words, institutional concerns, rather than specific problems related to the substantive content of the litigation, appear to have played a central element in the British decision to go to court. However, the attempt was largely unsuccessful. The Court, adopting a broad interpretation of the concept of 'working environment' in Article 118a [138], upheld most of the directive, with the exception of the provision on Sunday rest (case C-84/94, *United Kingdom* v. *Council*).

These contrasting examples illustrate one of the essential features of judicial politics – their uncertain character. Even courts whose behaviour is regarded as fairly predictable, because they have spelt out in clear terms the vision underlying their decisions, can occasionally change their views. The European Commission learnt this to its cost at the time of the Uruguay Round, an agreement on trade liberalization concluded in the framework of the GATT. The Commission was anxious to gain recognition of the Community's exclusive competence to conclude this agreement, as it wanted to avoid the necessity of a ratification by all member states. Given the reluctance of several governments, it decided to seek an opinion from the ECJ on the basis of Article 228 [300] (para. 6). The Commission clearly expected that in the wake of its bold jurisprudence on external relations (see Chapter 2), the Court would uphold its claims. However, its hopes were belied; the Court ruled that Community external competences did not include the power to conclude agreements liberalizing trade in services or dealing with intellectual property (Opinion 1/94). As a result, the Commission was left in the uncomfortable position of having to convince the member states to revise the treaty in order to enlarge the scope of the Community's commercial policy. Given the lack of enthusiasm displayed by most governments for any extension of Community competences, this was an arduous task. The solution adopted in June 1997 by the Treaty of Amsterdam, which basically defers the final decision on this matter to the decision to the Council, acting unanimously, clearly falls short of the Commission's hopes. No one can tell for sure what would have happened if the ECJ had not been consulted, yet it seems clear that the Commission's initiative has turned out to be detrimental to its own institutional position.

Law suits are not the only way for political actors to pursue their strategy before the ECJ. Proceedings before the ECJ are characterized by a high number of *amicus curiae* briefs, filed by actors with an interest in the issue at stake, ostensively to assist the Court reaching a wise decision, but often to protect their specific interests (March Hunnings, 1996, pp. 73–9). The European Commission is the most regular participant in this exercise; it even makes a point of presenting both written and oral submissions to the Court in all Article 177 [234] proceedings. In contrast, the Council of Ministers, given its position as the upper house of the Community legislature, only appears before the ECJ as a defendant. However, member states can submit observations individually. Some national governments tend to do so when the compatibility of domestic law with Community law is challenged; others will intervene in matters that affect them specifically. The Italian government, for instance, has been traditionally active in cases regarding the social security entitlements of migrant workers.

Even when the ECJ is ultimately not brought into motion, law plays an important role in the policy process. As one Canadian scholar aptly observed, the 'legalization of politics cannot be regarded merely as a change in the *forum* of politics-otherwise-as-usual but also to be appreciated as part of a change in the *form* of politics *whatever the forum*' (Mandel, 1994, p. 81). The prospect or even the sheer possibility, of a court battle leads participants in the policy process to integrate legal concerns in their strategies, since they must make sure to fit their actions into forms that can be endorsed by the ECJ, if need be. Questions such as the competence of the Community to adopt certain acts or the correct procedure to do so and basic values propagated by the Court, such as proportionality, therefore play an important role in the policy debate. *Ad hoc* procedures have been set up by some institutions to ensure that legal matters are given due consideration. Following the *Chernobyl* case and the development of inter-institutional disputes on the legal basis of Community acts, for instance, the European Parliament has modified its rules of procedures to invite its committees 'to ensure that its rights have been fully respected' whenever they examine community legislation (Rule 84).

This in turn explains the prominent role of lawyers in the European policy process. The three political institutions – Parliament, Council of Ministers and Commission – each have their own legal service, which intervenes at various levels of the policy process, be it to advise on procedures or on the legality of decisions which are contemplated, or to handle cases brought before the ECJ. The legal service of the Commission occupies a prominent place within the institution. Its influence is felt throughout the range of Community policies, as it must be consulted at an early stage on each legislative proposal. Its opinions are systematically attached to draft proposals when they are discussed by the Commissioners (Berman, 1995). Significantly, the Director of the Legal Service is one of the few Directors-General to attend all meetings of the Commission. Even in Parliament, where, for the reasons discussed above, the need to establish a legal service was perceived relatively late (towards the mid-1980s) its role is now clearly gaining in importance, reflecting of the growth of the Parliament's legislative powers (Corbett, *et al.*, 1995, p. 183).

Considering the basic uncertainty of judicial politics, why do they form such an important part of the strategy of European institutions? Several factors may explain this; some are technical (legal), others linked to the specific nature of the European policy process.

On the technical side, judicial politics are a by-product of the division of power in the Community both on a vertical plane (between the Community and the member states) and on a horizontal plane (between Community institutions). On the vertical plane, the Community has been endowed with limited competences only (Article 3b [5], first paragraph). On the horizontal plane, each institution must act within the limits of the powers granted to it by the Treaty (Article 4 [7]). Moreover, their powers vary considerably according to the legal base which is used to justify Community intervention. The institutional reforms of the last decade – the SEA and the Maastricht Treaty – have exacerbated this problem: no less than 23 different procedures can currently be used (Piris, 1994), which creates an enormous potential for conflict. As in any divided-power system, an institutional umpire was needed to ensure that each organ does not exceed the limits of its prerogatives. To a large extent, the importance of the role played by the ECJ reflects the rather arcane division of power effected by the EC Treaty.

However, other elements have contributed to enhance the role of judicial politics. In other political systems, where institutional disputes may be decided by constitutional courts, the judicial avenue is but one way of solving such conflicts. Political forums may also be used for this purpose; majority parties often prefer to solve the dispute through bargaining, rather than referring the matter to a court over whose decisions they may enjoy little control. This kind of alternative does not exist within the Community system, where party politics plays a small role. Moreover, even though the Maastricht Treaty has increased parliamentary control over the Commission, the Community system is mostly a system of checks and balances, in which each institution enjoys considerable autonomy. In such a context, there seems to be less room for the settlement of institutional disputes through the party system, even if partisan politics were to develop. One could even argue that if this were to happen, this development might be accompanied by the emergence of a new kind of judicial politics in which the judiciary would have to arbitrate conflicts between the majority and the opposition. The experience of France, where such conflicts have fuelled the growth of the *Conseil constitutionnel*'s policy role (Stone, 1992) is quite suggestive in this respect. Whatever happens, judicial politics seem to be called upon to play an important role at European level in the foreseeable future.

The strategic use of litigation

Political institutions have not been the only actors who have tried to use the legal sphere to enhance their own position or to achieve outcomes that could not be attained through other means. Private actors, be they large corporations, interest groups or simple individuals, have gradually realized that litigation could offer them additional means to pursue their own interests.

Surely such a development was not contemplated at the time the EC Treaty was signed. Reacting to what was perceived as a liberal interpretation of the ECSC Treaty by the ECJ, the drafters of the treaty had opted for a strict formula curtailing the right of private persons to seek the annulment of decisions taken by EC institutions (see Chapter 1). However, two elements have enabled private plaintiffs to be much more active on the vertical axis: that is, in relations between the Community and the member states. The first of these elements was the interpretation given by the Court of the prohibitions of discrimination contained in the treaty. We have seen above that in the wake of *Van Gend & Loos* (case 26/62) the Court has construed many of these provisions as creating rights which private parties could invoke directly before domestic courts. Even provisions such as the equal opportunities clause of Article 119

[141], the language of which suggested that they were addressed to member states only, were declared to enjoy direct effect. This rights-based interpretation of the treaty enabled private parties to rely on a broad range of European law arguments in legal disputes. Access to the ECJ was also made easier by another transformation, of a procedural nature this time, namely the increasing use of the preliminary rulings procedure to refer to the Court disputes where the compatibility of domestic law with EC law is at stake (see Chapter 2).

The combined effect of these two developments has been to significantly increase the possibility for private actors to make a strategic use of European law in order to further their own interests. Whenever they view the Community law rule as more favourable than the national rule, by bringing an action before a domestic court and by convincing the latter to refer the case to Luxembourg, they can hope to achieve results that cannot be achieved through the ordinary policy process. Thus, for instance, large stores have relied on the provisions regulating the free movement of goods (Article 30 [28] and following) to challenge domestic rules prohibiting the opening of shops on Sunday, pharmaceutical firms have done the same with marketing rules that were detrimental to their own interests, women have been able to rely on the equal opportunities clause of Article 119 [141] to secure benefits which were denied to them by national legislation, and so forth.

This 'Eurolaw game', which has become the focus of growing attention (Harlow and Rawlings, 1992; Rawlings, 1993; Barnard, 1995), is by nature complex. From often broad treaty provisions, the ECJ has to derive the rules applicable to the facts of the dispute at hand. Given the collegiate character of the Court's decision-making, the compromises that emerge in its rulings do not always help to dispel the ambiguity inherent in general provisions, the interpretation of which can give rise to many disputes. In addition to this basic uncertainty, the process is often lengthy and cumbersome. Litigation before the Court is a time-consuming exercise: the average length of a preliminary ruling procedure is about 18 months. Furthermore, preliminary references are only interlocutory proceedings in the context of a much longer litigation. Some 13 years elapsed between the dismissal of Mrs Marshall and the ECJ's decision in the *Marshall II* case, in which the Court ruled that EC law required that women who had been forced to retire earlier than men in contravention of Article 119 [141] should receive 'full and adequate compensation' irrespective of national provisions setting a ceiling for such compensation awards (case C-271/91, *Marshall* v. *Southampton Area Health Authority, n. 2*). And this was not even the end of Mrs Marshall's judicial odyssey, as the industrial tribunal had still to rule on the exact amount of the compensation to which she was entitled.

It is therefore hardly surprising to note that the strategic use of European litigation described above is mainly practised by large corporations (Harding, 1992) or lobbies which dispose of sufficient resources to engage in uncertain and costly legal battles, such as the British Equal Opportunities Commission (Barnard, 1995). Both corrrespond to the archetype of the 'repeat player' described in an influential essay by American legal sociologist Marc Galanter (1974) – that is, actors with the necessary resources and experience to engage in lengthy legal battles, and whose strategy is often designed to achieve long-term results through a series of cases. For such actors, the parameters of success and failure are not necessarily identical to those of ordinary litigants. Immaterial benefits achieved through litigation may be of considerable importance. Even if lost, a case can be useful to their long-term strategy because the publicity it entails will help them to put an issue on the political agenda, or simply because it will create uncertainty and delays in the application of rules that are detrimental to their interests. Moreover, being in the fortunate position of being able to play long games, they are often able to pick test cases where their chances of winning are best or that may be used in lobbying campaigns in favour of a change in legislation.

When persistent, such actors can significantly shape the ECJ's case law in a given area. The British Equal Opportunities Commission and its counterpart organization in Northern Ireland have together funded one-third of the references to the ECJ on matters relating to equal pay and equal treatment at work (Barnard, 1995, p. 254), which may explain why UK cases largely dominate in those areas. True, interest groups may at times face difficulties gaining access to the courtroom, as their legal interest in the matter may be deemed insufficient to bring the matter before the Court. The ECJ itself has on the whole been less favourable to the development of public interest litigation – litigation by interest groups – than have American courts (Harlow, 1993). To overcome this difficulty, some groups have resorted to what is known in the US context as a 'test case' strategy, and have tried to identify a plaintiff with strong chances of succeeding in law suits that would promote the group's interest. The *Defrenne* cases, for instance, which marked the beginning of equality litigation before the ECJ, were the product of a campaign launched by a Belgian lawyer who wanted to test the compatibility of Belgian legislation with Article 119 [141] and tried, with the assistance of some lobbies, to identify potential plaintiffs to bring the matter before the ECJ. Mrs Defrenne, an air hostess who had been forced to retire at the age of 40 and was therefore entitled to a pension inferior to that of her male colleagues, was in the right situation to bring a successful test case before the Court, and agreed to lend her name on the condition that she took no active part in the proceedings (Harlow and Rawlings, 1992, p. 283).

The cases on Sunday trading that reached the ECJ in the late 1980s were also part of a larger litigation strategy. In his thorough analysis of this saga, Richard Rawlings has shown how litigation before the European Court has been used by large stores to achieve results which they had been unable to obtain through the political process (Rawlings, 1993). After the failure in the British Parliament of various proposals to remove restrictions on Sunday trading, the offensive moved from the political to the judicial arena. Invoking the turnover losses generated by the prohibition of Sunday trading, retail stores argued that as a significant part of the goods they sell were imported from other EC countries, the ban on Sunday trading was to be regarded as a measure having equivalent effect to a quantitative restriction on imports within the meaning of Article 30 [28]. Although the reasoning might seem far-fetched, the ECJ's sweeping statement on the scope of Article 30 in *Dassonville* (see Chapter 3) made it possible to argue that the British law had a Community dimension.

The Court's response (case 145/88, *Torfaen BC* v. *B&Q*) was remarkably ambiguous. On the one hand, it recognized that the rules at issue were not primarily designed to govern patterns of trade betwwen EC member states, but that they

> reflect certain political and economic choices insofar as their purpose is to ensure that working and non-working hours are arranged as to accord with national or regional socio-cultural

> characteristics, and that, in the present state of Community law, is a matter for the Member States. (p. 364)

At the same time, however, the Court indicated that:

> the prohibition laid down in Article 30 [28] covers national rules governing the marketing of products where the restrictive effects of such measures on the free movement of goods exceeds the effects intrinsic to trade rules.

Whether this proportionality test was actually satisfied by British Sunday trading regulations was deemed to be 'a question of fact to be determined by the national court' (ibid.).

Such an ambiguous ruling is difficult to regard as a courtroom victory for large retail stores. This notwithstanding, the litigation was clearly beneficial for their interests. Throughout the proceedings they were able to continue trading on Sundays. The open-ended character of the ECJ ruling gave them the opportunity to engage in lengthy proceedings before lower courts on the proportionality issue, which acted as a strong deterrent on the local authorities who had to enforce the ban. Moreover, the mushrooming of litigation on this issue generated contradictory judgments across the country: some courts acquitted while others convicted, for the same kind of behaviour (Rawlings, 1993, pp. 317–20).

Confronted with this confusion and with higher courts' reluctance to review policy judgments made by the Parliament, the ECJ gradually moved away from *Torfaen* (see, for example, cases 312/89, *Conforama*; and 332/89, ('*Marchandise*'). In *Stoke-on-Trent* v. *B&Q* (case C-169/91), while reiterating that Sunday rest legislation primarily reflected the socioeconomic characteristics of the member states, it addressed directly the proportionality issue, and ruled that as imports were not discriminated against, but only indirectly affected, the UK legislation was not excessive.

The Sunday trading saga illustrates the potential of litigation at European level for resourceful players. It also shows how the open-ended character of many provisions of the Treaty of Rome, and the ECJ's frequent willingness to interpret them in an expansive fashion, can lead to the development of judicial policy-making: important policy decisions are shifted from the political to the judicial arena. While paying lip service to the legitimacy of policy choices made by the national legislatures in this area, the ECJ clearly indicated that their freedom of action was constrained by Community law, and that courts, both at national and at Community level, were to act as the ultimate umpire in cases of conflict, and rule on the reasonableness of policy decisions made by national authorities.

In areas where Community law's influence is felt, courts are therefore in a position to play a significant role in the policy process. European litigation on free movement of goods or equal opportunities has led to changes in the legislation of a number of countries. The economic impact of some of these rulings has been noteworthy. In the UK, for instance, rulings on equal treatment have generated an avalanche of claims by ex-servicewomen who were discharged by the armed forces on the grounds that pregnancy made them unable to perform their duties. In 1994, the British government indicated that it had already paid a total of £30 million in compensation to some 2700 women, while another 2000 claims were still pending (Barnard, 1995). The Court's *Francovich* jurisprudence has also created financial incentives to litigation whenever plaintiffs deem the rights they derive from Community law to be violated by national authorities. In the *Factortame III* case (C–46 and C–48/93), for instance, Spanish fishermen claimed a total of £30 million for the damage they had allegedly suffered because of the statutory licensing system ruled invalid by the ECJ.

This suggests that judicial policy-making may have a cumulative effect. Well-publicized judgments are viewed as creating opportunities that can be exploited in other areas. The notorious *Cassis de Dijon* (120/78) ruling was clearly a major source of inspiration for lawyers, who started challenging national rules governing the marketing of goods. Litigation on salient political or societal issues such as Sunday trading obviously acts as a catalyst that triggers further claims. The same is true when courts award large sums in compensation for violations of Community law on the basis of the *Francovich* case law.

Conclusion: judicial policy-making and its limits

The development of judicial policy-making and the ensuing juridification of the policy process bear evidence of the existence of some autonomous dynamics within the legal sphere. Developments of this kind were clearly not foreseen, let alone desired, by those who drafted the European Treaties. Their origin must be traced back in decisions of the ECJ: had the judges opted for a classical, international-law type interpretation of treaty provisions, had they declined to review indirectly the compatibility of domestic law with Community law or had they simply regarded themselves strictly bound by the precise wording of some key provisions like Article 173 [230], things would have been different. Through its innovative interpretations of the treaty, the Court has provided more room for political actors, be they national governments or European institutions, to pursue their policy objectives within the legal sphere. It has also provided private actors with both incentives and instruments to use the judicial avenue whenever Community law was more favourable to their interests than national regulations. As a result, an important number of decisions have been shifted from the political to the judicial arena. Moreover, the process appears to have a cumulative effect: the more important decisions are taken by the judiciary, the more potential plaintiffs will be tempted to go to court to protect their interests.

This might of course be a source of difficulty in a system which is often criticized for its weak legitimacy basis. It can already be said that a 'political deficit' currently exists in the European Union, as actors such as political parties, trade unions, or even the media that traditionally dominate the political scene at national level, and therefore provide useful markers to voters, are generally weaker at European level (Dehousse, 1995). In many respects, judicial politics aggravate this situation. By replacing 'conflicts of interests' with 'matters of principle', they clearly contribute to depoliticize the political process (Mandel, 1994, p. 78). Partisan conflict is transformed into allegedly non-partisan questions about the proper interpretation of the treaty. True, in the first decade of existence of the EC, things could be viewed in a more positive light: access to international courts is, after all, rare for private plaintiffs, and the possibility of challenging the authority of national administrations is appealing. As the influence of the European Community is now felt in a larger number of areas, the costs of this system are however becoming more obvious. ECJ rulings can be resented as intrusive and disturbing of well-established traditions.

This may explain the ECJ's more cautious attitude in recent years (see Chapter 6). The Court seems to be aware that an excessive development of judicial policy-making may expose it to more hostile reactions. Already in the past, it has on several occasions limited the temporal effect of its rulings, indicating that as the law was unclear prior to its judgment, its findings would be applicable only to the claims that had been lodged by the time the ruling was rendered (see cases 43/75, *Defrenne* and C-262/88, *Barber* for two notorious examples). By resorting to this technique, which openly recognizes the creative character of some of its rulings, and has therefore been the focus of much criticism (see, for example, Rasmussen, 1986; Hartley, 1996), the ECJ has tried to prevent governments from being submerged by a flood of claims. Likewise, reacting against the tendency of traders to systematically invoke Article 30 [28] against domestic laws on the marketing of goods, even when they do not discriminate against imported goods, the Court partially reversed *Cassis de Dijon* in the *Keck* C–267 and 268/91 decided in 1993 (Joliet, 1995), thereby limiting the possibilities for private plaintiffs to use the European judicial arena to achieve results that they could not achieve through the 'ordinary' political process. However, that the ECJ itself had to react to police this strategic use of litigation is in itself an indicator of the importance of judicial politics in the European Community.

5

The Paradox of Compliance

It is a truism that, in most contemporary legal systems, the primary function of the courts and tribunals is to apply already established rules: to state the law and not to create it. This, however, is largely a fiction: judicial organs, by their very nature, necessarily carry out a creative task, particularly when they have to apply a text of a general nature, which is evidently the case for most constitutions.

Be that as it may, this fiction fulfils an important social function. In a system which sees itself as democratic, it is no easy task to find a justification for judicial creativity. This undoubtedly explains why it is rare to find a court which openly declares its creativity: limiting itself to an apparently much more modest role contributes to the legitimacy of its decisions. There can be little doubt that the fiction of literal interpretation plays an important role in legitimating the role of judges.

Casting an eye over the ECJ's jurisprudence it is difficult to escape the conclusion that it has been capable of playing a much more important role than that played by the majority of supreme courts at national level. Even accepting that the latter have also been increasingly called upon to fill constitutional lacunae, they have not had to create a comprehensive constitutional structure, as the ECJ has done. Its achievement is even more remarkable when we consider that it possessed relatively weak legal foundations upon which to build. The 'constitutional moment' was singularly limited. The Treaty of Rome was not preceded by a real institutional debate on how a would-be integrated Europe should be governed; rather its provisions were inspired by a functionalist strategy which laid emphasis on medium-term objectives and how they should be achieved. Yet, using these meagre resources the Court was to construct its jurisprudential edifice, assuming for itself a role as innovator unparalleled in national supreme courts – not to mention international judicial fora.

This evidently raises a certain number of issues. If it is difficult for national courts to assume a creative role, the same should hold true – if not truer – in a less integrated international grouping such as the European Community. How then did the ECJ manage to pull it off?

The question relates mainly to the reception given to its case law: why was it that its audacious interpretations did not encounter greater resistance from its principal interlocutors? The question relates less to the *formal* legitimacy of the Court's work, which has merely made use of the instruments placed at its disposal in the Treaty of Rome, than to its *social* legitimacy. Given the hostility which greets any tendency to confer a political role on the judiciary, one might have expected the Court's innovative solutions to have been countered with fierce resistance by the majority of the principal institutional actors affected. Yet this has not been the case. Leaving to one side occasional critiques of its work, up to the late 1980s (see, for example, Rasmussen, 1986), the ECJ's case law edifice was given a positive – even enthusiastic – welcome, and, in most cases, its judgments have been faithfully applied. More generally, the institutions which could have had an interest in setting their faces against the Court have not offered any real resistance.

Governments and national parliaments could have rebelled against a discipline which reduced – sometimes considerably – their margin of manoeuvre. True, overruling the ECJ is difficult, as it often requires a treaty amendment, which must be approved by all state parties. Yet, member states, had they wanted to put a curb on judicial activism, were certainly not short of means to apply pressure: they might have decided not to comply with certain rulings, packed the court with appointees more sensitive to states' rights, or even curtailed the Court's powers, to mention but the most widespread techniques used to counter judicial influence (Stone Sweet and Caporaso, 1996, p. 8). However, until the Maastricht Treaty, episodes of resistance were isolated. Sporadic critiques of the ECJ were made by member state representatives, and certain governments exhibited ill-will in complying with some of the Court's judgments (Rasmussen, 1986), but the very fact that these instances of reluctant or half-hearted compliance provoked outcry in informed circles merely confirmed the considerable weight carried by its decisions. Until the late 1980s, no trace of systematic resistance to the ECJ's jurisprudence could be discerned. Nor can it be said that governments responded to bold Court rulings by appointing judges that were more reluctant to engage in judicial activism. What is striking instead is the gradual acceptance by national governments of the new principles carved out by the ECJ. As early as 1976, former ECJ President Robert Lecourt could note that foundational principles such as direct effect and supremacy, the very existence of which had been denied in early cases, were now generally accepted (Lecourt, 1976, p. 307).

It might also have been expected that the national courts would have shown some irritation with their more than slightly intrusive supranational counterpart, which seemed sometimes to lose sight of the reserve expected from judicial bodies. After all, because of their tightly-knit relationship with the ECJ, national courts are often the first to be confronted with its innovations. Furthermore, Community case law has, on occasion, imposed a duty on them to ignore certain essential national constitutional stipulations. There are few countries where the normal courts can adjudicate on the constitutionality of national legislation, and yet these very courts are bound to ensure the conformity of national law with a superior norm – the Community norm. Even if certain constitutions – such as the Italian Constitution – confer a monopoly on a constitutional court to deal with issues of constitutionality, the ECJ has none the less ruled that lower jurisdictions are bound to immediately set aside – without consulting the Constitutional Court – laws that contravene Community law (case 106/77, *Simmenthal*). Moreover, it has also insisted that English courts accept, in certain cases, the setting aside of a national law whose conformity with Community law is doubtful, irrespective of the fact that this kind of interim measure was previously unknown in English law (case C-213/89, *Factortame*). Each of its decisions, wrong-footing as they did national judges with regard to their constitutional obligations, could have given rise to a major institutional conflict. Yet, on the whole, the national jurisdictions have bowed to the ECJ's requirements.

It is true that certain higher national courts fought a long rearguard battle against these innovations. The French *Conseil d'Etat* over a long period refused to accept the direct effect of directives jurisprudence (*Cohn-Bendit* judgment of 22 December 1978) and the supremacy of Community law, while the German Constitutional Court expressed reservations as to the efficacy of human rights protection in the Community order (see Chapter 2). But these are isolated cases, from which we should not therefore extract a general rule, all the more because even these courts have subsequently adopted positions in closer conformity to Community law. Evidence suggests that the ECJ's creative jurisprudence has been detrimental to the development of the dialogue with national judges treating the interaction as an ongoing dialogue: the number of preliminary references to Luxembourg has been growing steadily since the early 1960s. Moreover, in most cases, national courts seem content to adhere to the Court's instructions. A study of the application of preliminary references by national courts in the period 1960–85 has revealed that the level of faithful compliance reached 95 per cent – a figure which many constitutional courts would probably envy (Weiler, 1992, pp. 102–4).

It would therefore appear justified to speak of a widespread acceptance of the ECJ's jurisprudence. True, there have been in recent years signs of erosion of its authority, as will be seen in the following chapter. Yet the question remains: how can the pattern of acquiescence which dominated until the late 1980s, in spite of the considerable innovations introduced by the Court, be explained? This is a huge question which demands a multi-factorial response. Such a response, for want of concrete evidence, must perforce be constructed around a series of hypotheses about the relevant factors involved. Some of these are of a systemic nature: they concern the role the judicial function plays in the European institutional system. Others relate to the manner in which the ECJ itself has carried out its role. Still others relate to the specific motivations of the Court's various institutional interlocutors. These factors combine to explain why its activities have not encountered stronger resistance.

Systemic factors

The first of these pertains to the values conveyed by the ECJ jurisprudence. Judicial activism is perceived as a dangerous phenomenon in all legal systems. Yet, the arguments propounded to denounce it deal less often with pure institutional concerns than with the substance of judicial decisions; what is deplored is not so much the fact that judges arrogate excessive powers but rather that they put these powers in the service of a bad cause. In this perspective, the US example is illuminating: the Supreme Court has been equally castigated for its activism by liberals and conservatives alike, the liberals reproaching the conservatism it displayed towards the ambitious social plans of the Roosevelt administration, the conservatives upbraiding its aggressive racial desegregation policy. These critiques were aimed much more squarely at the goals pursued by the court than at its methods of interpretation.

This line of analysis facilitates comprehension of the favourable reception given to the jurisprudence of the ECJ. It is no secret that it was inspired by the desire to develop the integration process and safeguard it against any risk of political setback. Drawing a parallel with the US experience suggests that if the Court's jurisprudence has not been the object of severe critique it is because far-reaching consensus surrounded the values it espoused.

This hypothesis is supported by several types of empirical observation. First, European integration has incontestably constituted one of the great post-war ideas in Western Europe; in a short space of time, the idea of Europe has received overwhelming support from the population of the member states and in its chief political families. Moreover, the empirical surveys conducted by Gibson and Caldreira have indicated that judicial activism did not seem to exert a decisive influence over the acceptability of ECJ decisions. In contrast, popular acceptance of ECJ decisions seemed directly affected by their substance: only one-fourth of persons surveyed indicated that they would accept a decision with which they strongly disagreed (Gibson and Caldreira, 1995, pp. 476 and 479). The importance of the values advocated by the Court is also confirmed *a contrario* by the fact that the rare voices raised to criticize its activism can be traced to those who found the movement towards integration either too fast or too slow. Rasmussen's *On Law and Policy in the European Court of Justice* (1986), is a good example: while blaming the ECJ for extending the reach of Community law, he also critiques its timidity in the field of human rights protection, for which not even a hint of a legal basis can be found in the treaty (see pp. 403–4). From this evidence, an inference can be made that the Court has encountered low-level opposition because of the existence of a broad consensus around the values it wished to promote. This also implies, of course, that it is not so much the role assumed by the ECJ that has gained acceptance, but rather the values in the name of which it acted. The implications of this are considered later.

The second hypothesis is firmly linked to the nature of the judicial function and its role in the Community system. Recourse to a judicial organ is frequently motivated by the desire to resolve a conflict. Very often, this is not the only avenue of resolution; other means – mediation, arbitration, pressure of a more or less friendly nature, and so on – can be employed. Even in modern societies, one can still find traces of the consent of the parties to call in a judge which characterizes the judicial function in many primitive societies (Shapiro, 1981). If the choice is made to go to court, it is because certain advantages are seen to accrue from calling in a third party, who offers a guarantee of neutrality and who will impose his or her solution – or rather that of the judicial system to which he or she belongs. To put this another way, it could be said that the social role of courts confers on them a capital of legitimacy. Of course, this is neither absolute nor invariable. Above all, it depends on how the tribunals acquit themselves in performing their task: if they seem too contaminated by power, or if their impartiality is doubted, their prestige will suffer, thereby placing their authority at risk (Gibson, 1989). The legitimacy 'capital' possessed by courts explains the weight of authority which accompanies their judgments. Litigants tend to accept their decisions, even when they go against their own personal interests. The respect accorded to judicial decisions does not stem solely from acceptance of the rule of law; it also reflects a fairly extensive acceptance of the social role fulfilled by judicial organs in taking under their wing the resolution of conflicts. This attitude has benefited the ECJ just as it benefits its national counterparts.

As we have seen, the ECJ's powers far surpass those of other international jurisdictions. Why did national governments' representatives feel it necessary, at the time they drafted the Treaty of Rome, to be so generous with an institution which could limit their autonomy? The most plausible answer is that they had some interest in an independent jurisdiction being charged with ensuring the respect of Community-level engagements. The credibility of the Common Market would have been reduced if control of the application of Community law had rested in the hands of national governments, as is the rule at international level: each member state might have been tempted to believe that its genuine efforts found no echo in the other member states. Delegating to an independent umpire the task of controlling the behaviour of all states and of condemning any transgression of Community law which could occur contributed to the overall efficacy of the Community system (Garrett, 1992, p. 557). The principal players in this system thus had every interest in preserving the originality of the conflict resolution mechanisms, even if they resulted occasionally in decisions which went against their short-term interests.

All of these reasons help to explain why, both in the Community and the member states, the judicial function is perceived as an important social function and why the tradition of respect for judicial decisions has not been eroded. However, national experience suggests that judicial authority is linked to the perceived neutrality of the courts. Should a category of persons believe that judicial decisions tend systematically to be detrimental to their interests or should judges take decisions that hurt the feelings or the interests of a majority of citizens, they would place in danger the consent which underpins their societal role. As I shall try to demonstrate, the ECJ knew how to avoid both of these pitfalls.

The behaviour of the Court of Justice

The activist 'model'

While much ink has been spilt on judicial activism, no commonly shared definition of this phenomenon exists. This is partially due to the fact that the limits within which the judge must carry out his interpretative mission remain indistinct. However, the problem may also be apprehended from the other end, by focusing our attention on the reception given to judicial activities rather than on the action of judicial organs. Leaving normative considerations to one side and shifting to a more policy-orientated analysis, one could say that allegations of judicial activism are likely to appear when several conditions are met: when a court intervenes on an issue of some salience, when it seeks to impose its own opinions rather than 'apply the law', and when these views clash with those of elected government – the latter being generally able to claim greater legitimacy than the judicial organs when it comes to solving societal problems.

Each of these conditions is important in its own right and is linked to the standard perception of judicial offices. Having recourse to a judge, as we have said, means calling on an independent institution to resolve a conflict. Neutrality is one of the essential elements of the societal legitimacy of judges: if they become identified with the interests of one of the parties, they risk challenges to their position. In that respect, the fact that judges are seen to act as simple interpreters of a legal system and not as law-makers can be seen as an important guarantee for the parties. If judges were allowed to exercise discretionary power, the conflicting parties could fear that an arbitrary decision would favour their opponent's interests over their own. This, furthermore, explains the interest displayed by modern doctrine in techniques of interpretation and neutral principles which are supposed to guide the judiciary in their interpretive mission. The judiciary in turn are aware of the advantages for them in being perceived as mere interpreters; it is precisely for this reason that they generally present their decisions as the outcome of performing a deductive exercise on a legal rule (Shapiro, 1981, pp.7–8).

Naturally, the independence of the judiciary has a cost in terms of representativeness. All democratic societies rest on the principle that political choices proceed more or less directly from the general will. Yet, the legitimation of the judicial power is generally speaking very indirect: methods of judicial appointment and the irremovability often conceded to judges makes them weak representatives of the popular will. Their independence, which is one of the essential prerequisites of their office, explains why, in democratic societies, it is difficult for them to impose choices of a political nature. Going against the opinions of the political power is in fact equivalent to opposing the institutions which derive fairly directly from the popular will. It is precisely because it baulks at censuring the will of the representatives of the people that, in many Western European states, the judiciary has traditionally been extremely prudent in adjudicating the constitutionality of laws.

These conditions impose a quite precise model of behaviour on the judiciary: the judge is encharged with the application of the law and not with the imposition of his own solutions on the cases brought before him. As we stated earlier, insofar as this is a fiction, it is a fiction with a socially useful function, as it contributes to the legitimacy of the judicial function. Should a judge depart too overtly from this line of conduct, the judge would risk undermining the consensus upon which his office rests. The seriousness of this departure will depend in large part on the importance of the problem presented to the judge: if it is a marginal issue involving chiefly technical evaluations, any instance of judicial activism is likely to pass unobserved. On the other hand, when courts disagree with the political power on a sensitive issue, they leave themselves open to criticism. The conflict between the US Supreme Court and the Roosevelt administration figures among the most cited examples of judicial activism. This is no coincidence as, in this case, all the necessary elements were present: the court attempted to impose its reading of the Constitution on a political power capable of drawing on widespread popular support. Furthermore, the matter of contention was the intervention of public authorities in economic policy, an issue which was at the heart of political debate at that time. It is scarcely surprising, given these circumstances, that the Supreme Court's attitude was heavily criticized.

The Court as the interpreter of law

Having identified the conditions in which judicial decisions may elicit greater resistance, we are now in a better position to understand public perceptions of the ECJ. Several factors warrant singling out.

First, it is worth noting that the Court has always been careful to present its analyses – even the most audacious – as the outcome of interpretation of a rule of law. Clearly, it has favoured a teleological (and therefore extremely creative) interpretation of the Treaty of Rome by drawing on the preamble and the provisions relating to the objectives of the Community. However, even in the most extreme cases, it has always used the spirit of the treaty as the basis upon which to construct its legal arguments.

Van Gend & Loos, the cornerstone of its jurisprudential edifice, illustrates this perfectly. The ECJ refers to the objectives of the treaty as laid out in its preamble; it then deduces from the existence of certain institutions (Parliament, Economic and Social Committee) and procedures such as the preliminary reference procedure, a desire on the part of the authors of the treaty to create 'a new legal order…the subjects of which comprise not only Member States but also their nationals' (case 26/62, p. 23). The conclusion was revolutionary but it appeared that the Court did not stray from its role as interpreter of the law.

There is a seemingly inexhaustible supply of further examples. Even when the Court has chosen to go beyond what a simple reading of the treaty suggested, it has always been attentive to the need to bolster its interpretations by referring to the treaty system (case 6/64, *Costa* v. *ENEL*), to the necessity to ensure the effectiveness (*effet utile*) of its different provisions (case 22/70, *ERTA*) and so on. The Court speaks the language of law – one can only respond to it by putting forward competing interpretations of Community law. One may, of course, condemn its more daring decisions, but it never appears to depart from its task as interpreter of the law – to such an extent that it has sometimes been accused of ignoring the socio-economic effects of its judgments (Rasmussen, 1986). Because of this, it becomes more difficult to accuse it of wishing to play a political role: it is the treaty which seems to legitimate all its decisions.

Technical problems…

The ECJ has been greatly assisted in its task by the highly technical nature of the problems it has had to consider. This largely derives from the resolutely functionalist approach which, from the outset, has characterized European integration. The emphasis had been placed on co-operation in technical areas, rather than on grand political projects, in the hope that this would foster solidarity among those participating in the experience. This approach was inevitably reflected in the work of the Court. As the overriding objective was the creation of a common market, the questions it has had to examine relate principally to the field of economic integration: abolition of customs duties and quantitative restrictions, the elimination of non-tariff barriers to trade. These are not exactly crowd-pulling issues, and the act of pouring potentially conflictual elements into the apparently neutral mould of law has helped to mask any political implications of the ECJ's decisions (Burley and Mattli, 1993, pp.72–3). *Van Gend & Loos* came before the Court as a problem of tariff classification. *In Costa* v. *ENEL*, the payment of a derisory sum of money was at stake. It is true that the latter case raised the very delicate question of the compatibility of nationalizations with the Treaty of Rome, but the division of labour set out in Article 177 [234] allowed the Court to focus on the question of the supremacy of Community law, leaving it to the national judge to resolve the substantive issues at stake.

As a general rule, the preponderance of technical issues has let the ground-breaking decisions of the Court pass by largely unnoticed. Even today, in most European countries, except perhaps the UK, it is rare for media attention to turn to the activities of the ECJ. It is by far the least-known Community institution: according to an opinion poll carried out in September 1992, when the battle over the ratification of the Maastricht Treaty was raging, hardly more than a third of the European population had heard of the Court's existence (Gibson and Caldreira, 1993, pp. 210–13). This lack of fame provides significant benefits: as many neofunctionalist analyses have argued, integration is most likely to progress in technical, non-controversial areas where the political importance of the decisions taken is not readily perceived (see, for example, Haas, 1968). The relative indifference which has surrounded the ECJ's activities has permitted it to carry out an ambitious programme without coming up against systematic resistance (Stein, 1981). There are, however, limits: this 'state of grace' can only be preserved if the Court stays away from potentially inflammatory issues and if it sticks to a 'technical' vision of its own role: 'judges who would advance a pro-integration agenda are likely to be maximally effective only to the extend that they remain within the apparent bounds of the law' (Burley and Mattli, 1993, p. 57).

and a political void

As I mentioned earlier, judicial activism is at its height when the courts venture to impose their views on the political power. In such circumstances, the judges' activities, going against the will of a power which derives its legitimacy from the popular will, appear anti-democratic. Party political cleavages merely inflame these tensions (Holland, 1991, p. 9). The players in the set-piece conflicts which come to mind when the spectre of judicial activism is invoked are an active political power energetically going about its business and judicial organs trying to rein it in. I have already referred to the conflict between the Supreme Court and the Roosevelt administration; the French Constitutional Council – which has often dampened the ardour of both left-wing and right-wing majorities, which in their turn have lashed out against what seemed to them the first stirrings of 'government by judges' – could also serve as an example. The outcry provoked in 1993 by the Constitutional Council's decision on the right of asylum is but an illustration of a broader phenomenon which has been developing since the number of MPs needed to bring a matter before the *Conseil* was lowered (Stone, 1992). Yet, if we transpose this framework of analysis to Community level, one cannot but be struck by the absence of such a pattern of conflict.

Why? There are numerous reasons. In the first place, the Community political power can only draw on a relatively weak account of democratic legitimacy. The Council of Ministers, being composed of members of national governments, can only claim an indirect link with the electorate; it is also poorly representative as large countries are grossly under-represented therein. Moreover, until the Maastricht Treaty, the designation of Commissioners was within the exclusive competence of national governments. Given this scenario, it was difficult to claim that in censuring these institutions, the Court was defying the popular will (Volcansek, 1992, pp. 117–18).

Secondly, the Community decision-making process has always been something of a lumbering beast. The Treaty of Rome anticipated that a significant number of decisions would be taken by the Council of Ministers. However, the renunciation of majority voting, imposed *de facto* by France on its recalcitrant partners in what was subsequently dubbed the 'Luxembourg Compromise' impeded the functioning of this institutional mechanism. This relative weakness on the part of the legislature put the ECJ in the position of having to play an atypical role. Far from seeking to rein in the legislative powers through its decisions, it was instead propelled on several occasions to make up for its shortcomings. Thus, in *Reyners* (case 2/74), in allowing the partial direct effect of Article 52 [43], the Court got around the difficulties created by Council inactivity, which had not adopted the directives necessary to make freedom of establishment operational. This was a daring interpretation, inasmuch as it went beyond the apparent meaning of the provision in question, but it could not be said that it directly opposed the Council's will.

Rather, it clearly achieved – albeit in a roundabout way – the result desired by the treaty's authors.

Thirdly, the Community decision-making process is clearly less politicized than its national equivalent. All political institutions are characterized by a fair degree of pluralism, as they include representatives of all the major political groupings – and the decision-making process is largely consensual, since even the qualified majority specified in the treaty requires at least two-thirds of the votes cast in the Council. As a result, when the Court has intervened in inter-institutional disputes, it rarely finds itself, unlike its national counterparts, in the jaws of a majority-opposition dispute. In the majority of cases, institutional issues are at the forefront of the litigation. This is clearly the case in disputes relating to the legal basis of Community acts which came into being in the wake of the SEA.

The *Commission* v. *Council* (*Titanium Dioxide*) judgment (case C-300/89), for example, concerned a conflict between these two institutions about a directive dealing with the reduction of pollution provoked by waste from the titanium dioxide industry. The tensions between priorities of an economic nature (the elimination of distortions in competition) and environmental protection were at the heart of the dispute. However, though one might have expected to find here a confrontation between hard-line free marketeers and environmentalists, the main legal dispute was of a different nature. The Commission, supported by the Parliament, claimed that the Directive in question should have been adopted on the basis of Article 100a [95]. This provision, which aims at the achievement of the internal market, lays down recourse to a co-operation procedure, within which both the Commission and the Parliament dispose of much greater powers than when the Council decides unanimously. The Council, on the other hand, always keen to maximize member state prerogatives, wished to employ Article 130s [175], which provides for a unanimous Council decision.

On the facts, the ECJ decided in favour of the Commission. However, the ripples this decision created did not go beyond those 'in the know' as, given the lack of politicization of the debate, the Court could confine itself to arbitrating the institutional conflict. This kind of situation singularly facilitates its task as the decisions it hands down, even if they go against the institutional interests of one of the parties, are not subjected to the barrage of criticism that they would be if the political stakes emerged more clearly.

The judge and the political power

So far, my comments have focused on the environment in which the ECJ has had to operate. But the Court's attitude must also be mentioned, as it has displayed remarkable political flair. Generally, when it has had to take decisions about the activities of political organs it has displayed remarkable restraint.

In this respect, the case law dealing with proportionality is particularly indicative. This principle, laying down as it does a generic rule that the Community should not exceed 'what is necessary to attain the objectives of the Treaty' (Article 3b [5]) hands an enterprising judicial organ a powerful instrument for supervising the actions of political organs. Yet the ECJ has made very limited use of this possibility. In the areas where the treaty endows the Community legislature with a substantial discretionary power, the Court has contented itself with ensuring that the measures taken were not 'obviously inappropriate for the realisation of the desired objective' (case 40/72, *Schroeder* v. *Germany*). This would seem to indicate that, apart from clearly flagrant breaches, the Court, aware of the difficulties surrounding any attempts to evaluate efficacy of public policy, has been reluctant to substitute its evaluation for that of the Community legislature.

The ECJ has exhibited a similar reticence on other occasions. In case 276/80 (*Ferriera Padana* v. *Commission*), it had to decide whether, in establishing quotas in order to combat the crisis in the iron and steel industry at the end of the 1970s, the Commission had violated Article 58(I) of the European Coal and Steel Treaty, which states that quotas may only be used as a last resort. The plaintiff considered that Article 57, which invites the Commission to privilege 'indirect means of action at its disposal, such as … co-operation with governments to regularize or influence general consumption', or interventions on prices, provided sufficient adequate means for combating the crisis. In other words, the Court was confronted with a classic subsidiarity issue. In its judgment, it stated simply:

> in the event of a manifest crisis Article 58 of the ECSC Treaty confers upon the Commission a wide power of appraisal which it

> exercised in adopting Decision No 2794/80/ECSC. The Commission has set out the reasons for which it considered that the means of action provided for in Article 57 were not sufficient to deal with the crisis. It considered that it could not take steps to influence general consumption in the present economic situation. [...] The Commission accordingly concluded that the indirect means of action at its disposal had proved insufficient and that it was necessary to intervene directly in order to restore the balance between supply and demand. In arriving at that conclusion the Commission did not exceed the limits of its powers of appraisal. (p. 540)

Thus, the ECJ seems to have considered that, to the extent that the Commission had satisfied the formal conditions to which its actions were subject – in this case a detailing of reasons which had motivated its decision – the Court itself could only, as to the substance, ensure that the Commission had acted within the limits of its powers. A similar reasoning process was explicitly developed in a case where the Court was asked to rule on the legality of a Community regulation which modified financial subsidies due to the temporary withdrawal of the French Franc from the 'European currency snake' :

> As the evaluation of a complex monetary situation is involved, the Commission and the Management Committee enjoy, in this respect, a wide measure of discretion. In reviewing the legality of the exercise of such discretion, the Court must confine itself to examining whether or not it constitutes a manifest error or constitutes a misuse of power or whether the authority did not clearly exceed the bounds of its discretion. (case 29/77, *Roquette* v. *France*)

This reasoning suggests that when the treaty leaves a margin of discretion to the Community political institutions, the Court is not tempted to substitute its own interpretation for theirs.

Clearly, the situation changes radically when one moves from Community level to national level. Bent on ensuring the effectiveness of Community law, the Court has shown no hesitation in subjecting to strict scrutiny the actions of national authorities. It has constructed an extremely sophisticated jurisprudential apparatus to encase its activities in this area. However, even here, it would be unjust to attach an activist label, as is often done, to the Court's activities.

On several occasions, when the Court has had to decide issues opening up opportunities for intervention in sensitive matters, it has taken the abstentionist option. We have seen that in *Costa* v. *ENEL* (6/64) it confined its remarks to general statements concerning the Community legal order. More recently, it did the same in a case where the conformity of Irish abortion law with Community law was at issue. One of the arguments urged on the Court by the defendant was that the prohibition of the diffusion of information on overseas abortion services contravened freedom of expression. The Court limited itself to declaring that, in the context of a preliminary reference, it only furnishes

> all the elements of interpretation which are necessary in order to enable it to assess the compatibility of that legislation with the fundamental rights, the observance of which the Court ensures. However the Court has no such jurisdiction with regard to national legislation lying outside the scope of Community law. (case 159/90, *SPUC* v. *Grogan*)

More generally, in cases where the conformity of national measures with Community law is placed in doubt, the ECJ tends to leave the national judge with a much wider margin of discretion than when it is pronouncing merely on a simple interpretation of Community law (Weiler, 1992, pp. 120–1). This prudence would seem to suggest that the Court is aware that it benefits from a favourable environment, which it is anxious to preserve.

Splitting the difference: the ECJ as mediator

The judicial function is often perceived as a dichotomous conflict resolution procedure: in stating the law, the judge determines who is in the right and who is in the wrong, who is the winner and who is the loser. Reality, however, is often much more complex: it is not unusual to see judicial organs endeavouring to find a happy medium between the claims of both parties. In these cases, their role aligns itself more closely with that of a mediator, whose task is to privilege an equitable compromise between the parties rather than to impose on them preconceived rules. This low profile contributes to the acceptability of their decisions, in that each of the parties sees at least some of their claims vindicated (Shapiro, 1981, pp. 3–4).

The judges have not let the value of this kind of technique escape them. On several occasions, in fact, they have made use of it in key decisions: when the Court has enunciated principles clearly favourable to integration, it has relied on *ad hoc* considerations, often of a procedural nature, to hand in a ruling more favourable to states' interests in the litigation at hand.

In *ERTA* (case 22/70), for example, the Commission attacked a resolution in which the Council had laid down the rules of conduct for member states in negotiations relating to the modification of an agreement on road [long-distance lorry] transport concluded under the aegis of the UN Economic Commission for Europe. As we saw earlier (Chapter 2), the Commission maintained that this resolution encroached upon the competences of the Community. Although the treaty does not lay down a general competence for the Community to conclude international agreements, the Commission claimed that competence in this field derived from Article 75 [71], which confers extensive competences on the Community in the field of transport policy. The *effet utile* of this provision would thus be compromised if the Community was denied the opportunity to conclude international agreements in this sphere. The Council, for its part, invoked the principle of attribution of competences and emphasized the fact that Article 75 makes explicit reference only to the internal competences of the Community.

So far as the principle at issue was concerned, the ECJ essentially accepted the contentions of the Commission. However, on the facts of the case, it considered that the conditions necessary to find against the Council were not present: although the resolution at issue was adopted after the Community had acquired the competence to conclude international agreements dealing with transport matters, the negotiations had commenced while the member states were still in charge; they were therefore at liberty to conclude the agreement, provided they were acting in the interests of the Community. Therefore, while the Commission triumphed so far as the principle was concerned, its claim was rejected.

Another example of this technique was provided shortly after the SEA, when the UK government challenged a directive dealing with the hormone content of meat. The legal basis used to introduce the directive was Article 43 [37], concerning agricultural policy. The UK government alleged that as the directive in question aimed to harmonize national legislation, it should have had a dual legal basis, Article 43 and Article 100 [94]. The interest of the dispute was purely institutional: the choice of Article 43 by the Council led to a qualified majority vote, while legal bases advocated by the UK required a unanimous decision. The Court, by and large, accepted the former Council's arguments, which had the effect of simplifying decision-making at Community level. Simultaneously, however, going against the Advocate General's opinion, it annulled the contested directive on the grounds of a breach of procedural rules (case 68/86, *UK* v. *Council*). Thus, the UK won the battle in obtaining the annulment of the directive, but lost the war as the integrationist legal base argument held sway.

Many other examples of employment of this technique could be given. Mention has already been made of the possibility for the ECJ to resort to prospective rulings, and declare that its interpretations will be applicable for the future only, except for those plaintiffs who have already filed a suit. This technique was inaugurated with the *Defrenne II* case, in response to fears voiced by some governments, which had claimed that the attribution of direct effect to the principle of equal pay contained in Article 119 [141] would have had dramatic consequences for their economy (case 43/75). Techniques of this type, which of course require a fair deal of political skills, enable courts to exert considerable influence without putting their authority at risk. On the one hand, the principles enunciated in their rulings will shape long-term action by political actors. On the other hand, they do not provoke inflamed reactions, as the short-term costs for defeated parties are kept low.

The ECJ has clearly perceived the advantages of such an approach. It has regularly combined the affirmation of audacious principles and restrained concrete decisions in order to make its jurisprudential constructions acceptable (Hartley, 1994, pp. 78–9). Undoubtedly, this approach has been dictated by the singular position occupied by the Court. Possessing neither the power to annul laws in the member states nor the power to quash national court decisions, it can only make Community law prevail by eliciting voluntary compliance. In the absence of the power to simply impose its views, it must know how to convince (Jacqué, 1991, p. 127).

If we set these comments beside those made earlier on the ECJ's relationship with the Community's political institutions, it is clear that the ECJ has made considerable efforts to ensure that its judgments would not cause too much outcry. Allegations of activism should therefore be nuanced. That the Court has undertaken an ambitious reading of the treaty is indubitable; this, however, does not mean that it has not paid careful attention to how its decisions will be perceived. On the contrary, it has largely behaved as a political actor, aware of the implications of its judicial choices on its relationships with other political actors.

The Court and its interlocutors

Although the behaviour of the ECJ is a key variable in understanding the reception of its case law, one must add to the picture another series of actors who might have made greater resistance to the Court's rulings but, for a variety of reasons, have chosen not to do so. National courts and governments were directly affected by decisions taken in Luxembourg; the general public might have reacted against the pro-integration zeal of European judges. Yet, for decades the ECJ's main interlocutors responded without hostility to the development of its influence (Weiler, 1994).

National courts

It has already been indicated that, by and large, national judges have given a warm welcome to ECJ jurisprudence. Although there have been instances when a national court has openly refused to comply with ECJ rulings, the dominant pattern is clearly one of compliance with the ECJ judgments. Remarkably, there may even be striking contrasts between the position of domestic courts and that of their government. While the Conservative governments in power in the UK from 1979 to 1997 displayed systematic hostility to the development of social policy at European level, British courts have generally given European directives their full application, often by way of express reference to the guidance issued by the ECJ (Davies, 1997).

Several factors underpin this co-operative pattern. The first is of a functional nature. Since the coming into force of the Treaty of

Rome, the national judges have been confronted with a corpus of Community rules, which did not always correspond to national traditions, and with which they had, at best, only a passing familiarity. The Article 177 [234] preliminary reference procedure was conceived of to respond to the problems this situation was bound to pose, by giving national courts the opportunity to refer problems of interpretation which arose in national litigation to the ECJ. In this way, the Article 177 procedure establishes a real division of labour between the ECJ and the national courts: the former deals with problems of interpretation of the Community norm; to the latter falls the task of applying the norm in question.

This carving up of judicial responsibilities promotes the authority of the ECJ. By definition, Article 177 proceedings are triggered by national judges seeking to unravel a problem they have before them. The very fact that the judge has referred means that he is aware of the importance of Community law in the case before him. He will thus be naturally predisposed to follow the directions given as a result of the reference. In practice, it is not unusual to find national judges who are content to reproduce at length in their final judgment the conclusions of the ECJ. Furthermore, an examination of decisions made by national courts following a reference to the ECJ has revealed that respect for ECJ decisions tends to *increase* when the latter are completely unambiguous: while the percentage of decisions conforming to the preliminary reference where the Court left some margin of appreciation to the national court was 56 per cent, it soared to 88 per cent where the Court left no margin for national manoeuvre (Weiler, 1992, pp.116–17). This surprising finding seems to confirm the hypothesis that the national judges are pleased to be able to utilize the Court's decision when they are confronted with difficulties concerning Community law interpretation. Their willingness to align themselves with ECJ judgments is reinforced by the fact that, even if the Court looks at questions quite far removed from the daily preoccupations of the national judges, it speaks a language which is comfortingly familiar and which invites compliance: the language of law.

Secondly, the ECJ has often demonstrated the importance it attaches to its dialogue with the national courts. On paper, Article 177 preliminary references, which are the main avenue for this judicial dialogue, could have given rise to two distinct models of relationships: a hierarchical model, in which the ECJ would have tried to affirm its own superiority, or a co-operative model, based on goodwill and mutual respect (Lecourt, 1976, p. 272). Yet, one element clearly militated in favour of the co-operative model, namely the fact that Article 177 [234] is entirely dependent on the goodwill of national courts. As noted by Mancini and Keeling:

> It is true that the third paragraph of Article 177 *obliges* national courts against whose decisions there is no judicial remedy under domestic law, to seek a preliminary ruling from the Court of Justice whenever a question concerning the interpretation or validity of Community law is raised before them. That paragraph, however, lays down an obligation of a special kind: the litigant... whose plea for a 'compulsory' reference falls on deaf ears in the national court of last instance, has no direct access to the Court of Justice in Luxembourg and finds himself in the unfortunate position of possessing a right without a remedy. (Mancini and Keeling, 1991, p. 1, emphasis in original)

Given this situation, it is hardly surprising that the ECJ opted in favour of a co-operative partnership with domestic courts.

This choice is apparent in a number of rulings concerning the structure of Article 177 proceedings. Thus, the ECJ has adopted a broad definition of the concept of 'national court'. It has, for instance, accepted that an appeals committee established by the Dutch doctors' society could be regarded as a court or tribunal within the meaning of Article 177, even though it is not considered as a court under Dutch law (case 246/80, *Broekmeulen* v. *Huisarts Registratie Commissie*). As early as 1963, it indicated that the 'considerations which may have led a national court or tribunal to its choice of questions as well as to the relevance which it attributes to such questions in the context of a case before it are excluded from review by the Court of Justice' (case 26/62, *Van Gend & Loos*). Parties themselves are confined to a secondary role: they can take no initiative (see, for example, case 44/65, *Singer*) nor force domestic courts to refer a case to Luxembourg. The emphasis has therefore been clearly laid on the court-to-court dialogue. In general, the ECJ tends to reject allegations by domestic governments that the questions put to it are inadmissible (see, for example, case 20/64, *Albatros*). Although it has recently laid down stricter criteria to define the kind of questions which can be referred (see joined cases C-320–322/90, *Telemarsicabbruzzo*), this open-door policy *vis-à-vis* domestic judges seems naturally conducive to a form of judicial partnership in which governmental intrusion is resented.

The ECJ has also hinted that national courts were to be treated as responsible partners. Thus, national courts of last instance may, if they so wish, refer to Luxembourg questions identical to those answered earlier by the ECJ (joined cases 28–30/62, *Da Costa* v. *Nederlandse Belastingadministratie*). Endorsing the '*acte clair*' theory proposed by the French Council of State, the ECJ has indicated that courts of last instance may even refrain from referring questions which they deem irrelevant, although it hurried to add that this exception to the third paragraph of Article 177 [234] was possible only if the correct application of Community law is 'so obvious as to leave no scope for any reasonable doubt as to the manner in which the questions raised is to be resolved'. It then defined obviousness so narrowly that it is difficult to see when such a case could arise (case 283/81, *CILFIT* v. *Ministry of Health*). Although this show of trust in national courts was made almost obligatory by the absence of any instrument of coercion, the ECJ clearly hoped that it would be paid back by voluntary compliance to the fairly strict conditions it had set. While the evidence on the degree of compliance to ECJ rulings displayed by higher courts is scarce, the steady growth of Article 177 [234] references suggests that the risk was a calculated one, and that this ruling has not condemned the Court to irrelevance.

Defining its own jurisdiction in a way that appealed to domestic courts was but one factor in the success of the ECJ. A spirit of partnership has also pervaded its treatment of the questions raised by national judges. On several occasions, the Court itself has had to identify the relevant questions of Community law, where the national judge had simply transmitted the file to Luxembourg without explicitly formulating suitable questions to help him or her solve the case (see, for example, case 28/68, *Torrekens*). When national courts invite it to rule on the compatibility of national law with Community law, the ECJ will on its own motion reformulate in an abstract fashion the relevant questions, so as to avoid ruling them inadmissible. In regrouping and reformulating the questions in the reference, the better to respond to the issues raised in the case, and in carefully setting out the reasons for its decisions, it has often made considerable efforts to painstakingly lay out the path it would like the national judge to adopt (Mancini, 1989). All of this has undoubtedly contributed to the respect given to its decisions, in particular by lower courts.

The ECJ's awareness of the strategic importance of the partnership with its national counterparts has also led it to try to multiply personal contacts with national judges. In his account of the emergence of a 'Europe of Judges', former ECJ President Robert Lecourt, who was one of the chief architects of this policy, has told how the ECJ responded to the first preliminary references by developing a public relations policy of its own. Since 1965, the Court has organized in Luxembourg meetings of the Presidents of the higher national jurisdictions; it also sponsors at regular intervals judicial conferences bringing together dozens of judges from throughout the Community (Table 5.1). To these must also be added visits held each year to the seats of the most important national jurisdictions, lectures given by judges and Advocates General in a variety of domestic fora, the efforts undertaken by the Court to disseminate information about its case law. The declared objective of this policy is simple: to promote mutual knowledge and trust between national and Community judges, so as to guarantee smooth co-operation between the two levels (Lecourt, 1976, pp. 274–6).

TABLE 5.1

Study visits to the Court of Justice and the Court of First Instance, 1990–5

Description	*1990*	*1991*	*1992*	*1993*	*1994*	*1995*
National judges	543	999	897	537	739	831
Lawyers, legal advisers, trainees	1 518	1 394	1 250	1 064	1 423	1 631
Professors in Community law, teachers	206	152	140	537	170	382
Diplomats, Parliamentarians, political groups, national civil servants	845	1 176	832	2 042	755	871
Students, EEC/EP	5 799	5 453	6 158	5 465	5 464	5 158
Members of professional associations	399	226	170	603	815	264
Others	616	760	744	446	1 080	837
Total	*9 926*	*10 160*	*10 191*	*10 894*	*10 446*	*9 974*

Finally, any assessment of the relationship between the ECJ and national courts must take account of the fact that Community jurisprudence holds a number of attractive features for the latter (Weiler, 1994, p. 523). It is not difficult to imagine that a judge in a rural backwater may find something gratifying in having a direct line to one of the highest European courts. The sharing out of responsibilities delineated in Article 177 [234] gives the allure of a dialogue between equals to the relationship between the ECJ and the national courts – an impression scarcely banished by the deference with which the Court treats its national counterparts. Evidently, this happy equilibrium would not exist if a hierarchical pattern of relations had emerged, and if the ECJ had acted as an appeal court for national court decisions. Moreover, ECJ jurisprudence has not infrequently consolidated institutional prerogatives of domestic judges *vis-à-vis* other kinds of actors. In order to ensure the supremacy of Community law, the national judge has had to monitor the action of the legislature; a power which in many member states goes beyond the powers they possess in national law. Thus, a Dutch or an English court may have to examine the conformity of a national law with Community law, while, in the national legal order, the same court has no power to adjudicate on the constitutionality of laws. Similarly, and still in the name of supremacy, in countries such as Germany and Italy, where constitutional control is fairly developed, the ordinary courts may – or rather must – take on the task of setting aside national laws which contravene Community norms, despite the fact that their constitutions in principle reserve this power to the Constitutional Court.

In some cases, preliminary references to the ECJ have enabled national courts to obtain results which could not be achieved at domestic level. British courts, for instance had long been annoyed by the absence of interim injunctions: that is, orders suspending administrative action pending the decision of a court. Arrogating such a right to themselves would have been incompatible with the doctrine of precedent, which plays a central role in the British legal system. However, European litigation offered a cheaper opportunity for a change. In the *Factortame* case, the House of Lords was requested to issue such an interim injunction to give effect to EC law. Asked to confirm that domestic laws barring courts from granting interim relief had to be set aside if this was necessary to give effect to Community law, the ECJ had no difficulty in giving a positive reply. Having thus secured a European blessing for this assertion of power, the House of Lords could then move to phase two of its strategy: only three years after *Factortame*, it ruled that interim relief was available even where EC law was not involved (*M.* v. *Home Office*). The result was completely logical, for it would have been difficult to admit that procedural rights under EC law were greater than in purely 'domestic' proceedings. Yet it is doubtful that such a result could have been attained without the assistance of the ECJ (Harlow, 1995). Even when ECJ jurisprudence is not a source of institutional innovations, lower courts may use Article 177 [234] proceedings to 'appeal' before the ECJ against decisions of higher courts, whenever they are dissatisfied with their substance. Many of them have not been shy in referring matters to Luxembourg (see, for example, Rawlings, 1993, p. 32). It is tempting to believe that the additional powers this possibility gave to lower courts has smoothed the path of judicial acceptance of Community jurisprudence.

One might summarize the situation by saying that compliance with Community law has implied clear rewards for many a domestic court. Whereas on the international plane implementation often looks like a zero-sum game (if a state complies with rulings of international courts, it reduces its margin of manoeuvre), things are different when domestic courts have to implement EC law. There, implementation may often look like a positive-sum game, in which compliance will actually increase the powers of domestic jurisdictions with respect to other domestic actors, mostly the legislature. This hypothesis is given some credit by the fact that where a line of resistance to ECJ rulings has emerged, it was often due to higher courts, which have adopted a more confrontational stance. A constitutional court, like the *Bundesverfassungsgericht* which enjoys much influence in Germany, including on the political plane, has little to gain, and possibly much to lose, from the growing penetration of EC law; hence its insistence on the fact that there must be limits to the erosion of constitutional guarantees. In contrast, for UK courts, which are denied the right to review primary legislation, the acceptance of EC law supremacy has coincided with a greater readiness to challenge orthodoxy and to subject legislation to greater scrutiny (Craig, 1995). The two processes appear to have reinforced each other. This seems to confirm that the integration process does not offer the same incentives to all courts (Alter, 1995).

The Court of Justice and national governments

By and large, national administrations have seen their prerogatives reduced – sometimes considerably – by the ECJ's jurisprudence, to the benefit of the Community and of domestic courts. Yet, even if one cannot find evidence of an unqualified acceptance of Community law there has been no concerted resistance to the Court's jurisprudence. True, political leaders have occasionally rebelled against the supremacy of Community law. Some French MPs have tried every now and then to reassert the supremacy of Parliament (Alter, 1995, pp. 13–14). Yet, none of these attempts have succeeded, and the dominant pattern is one of acceptance of ECJ rulings. How can one explain this apparent acquiescence to an evolution which has clearly limited the authority of national administrations?

Many of the general reasons outlined earlier – the technical nature of the vast majority of Community decisions, the weakness of party political divisions – are particularly resonant for national governments. It is also important not to forget that running in parallel with the constitutionalization of the Community legal order by the ECJ, the member states have ensured for themselves control of the decision-making apparatus, most notably in reshaping the powers of the Commission. Developments such as the Luxembourg Accord, comitology and the setting up of the European Council which have punctuated this evolution are well-known and need not be recalled here. The essential point is the temporal coincidence between the assertion of authority by the Court and the national governments. This coincidence may have facilitated the acceptance of Community jurisprudence by national administrations: in developing the twin concepts of direct effect and supremacy, the Court was largely ensuring the efficacy of the decisions taken by national representatives at European level (Weiler, 1981). Expanding this kind of reasoning, it can even be argued that the existence of a strong judiciary at European level is consistent with the interests of Member States. It offers a solution to one of the problems that undermines the efficiency of international relations, namely the problem of monitoring the implementation of international agreements (Garrett, 1992, pp. 556–7).

Given the multitude of interactions that take place daily in the European Community, it is impossible for governments to know whether their counterparts duly respect their commitments. This uncertainty may have negative implications for the overall stability of the system. If they believe that their competitors will break the rules, states will have few incentives to abide by them. In contrast, the intervention of an impartial arbiter, easily accessible and entrusted with ensuring that each member state respects its Community obligations, is an essential component of the stability of the Community system, as it ensures that governments are not forced to have recourse to the destructive arsenal of countermeasures laid down in international law. Thus, it could be argued that in insisting on compliance with Community law, the Court was acting in the member states' objective interests, even when its rulings have adverse consequences for some of them.

One example may illustrate this. We have already seen that the concept of mutual recognition of national legislation, developed by the ECJ in *Cassis de Dijon* (case 120/78), played a central role in the relaunching of European integration in the mid-1980s. The Commission in fact used the idea of mutual recognition as a launching pad for its subsequent development of the completion of the internal market programme. Thus, the Court's intervention was instrumental in allowing the circumvention of the stumbling block of harmonization, which, due to its unwieldiness as a technique, had substantially delayed progress towards an internal market (see Chapter 3).

It has been claimed that this judgment was simply dictated by the immediate interests of the larger member states which had most to gain from a larger market (see Garrett, 1992, p. 557). This, however, is stretching the point. The German government, whose legislation was challenged in the case, heavily criticized the concept of mutual recognition, seeing therein a threat to its consumer protection policies. More generally, *Cassis de Dijon*, in affirming a rule of equivalence, considerably limited member states' opportunities to use technical rules for protectionist purposes. Yet, notwithstanding the inroads this judgment made on state sovereignty, it neither provoked rejection in the defendant member state nor, apparently, did it weaken the authority of the Court.

One of the reasons for this is that the ECJ enjoys a 'legitimacy capital' of its own (Gibson and Caldreira, 1993): member states, because they have a structural interest in the existence of a judicial umpire, will generally prefer to follow its decisions even when they happen to be detrimental to their immediate interest in a given area. The contrast between these two levels may at times be a source of ambivalence for national authorities. Thus, for instance, the UK, which has rarely displayed much enthusiasm for integration, let alone judicial integration, has, however, been a regular supporter of initiatives aimed at strengthening the monitoring of the application of Community law. It even took the lead in proposing that the ECJ be given the power to impose financial penalties against states, which resulted in the adoption of new Article 171 [228] in the Maastricht Treaty. The distinction between structural (systemic) interests and the interests that may be affected by a given decision is crucial to an understanding of behaviour which might otherwise appear contradictory.

Cassis de Dijon also points to another important role of the ECJ: mitigating the problems of incomplete contracting confronting EC member states (Garrett, 1992, p. 557). In a system where decision-making is by consensus, it is impossible for actors to make exhaustive agreements and anticipate every dispute that may arise between them. Hence the necessity to make broad agreements, and then delegate to a credible enforcer the authority to apply them to specific cases. This is what the founding fathers of the EC did when they entrusted the ECJ with the implementation of the broad principles set out in the Treaty of Rome.

Likewise, the existence of a strong judiciary was a precondition to the successful implementation of the single market programme. It is difficult to imagine a system of mutual recognition functioning in the absence of an impartial judicial body encharged with overseeing its application. Can we really conceive of a country such as Germany accepting products coming from another member state, if it were not convinced that the legislation of that state was in full compliance with the essential requirements laid down in Community law. And is it feasible to suppose that states will subject their enterprises to foreign competition in the absence of guarantees of reciprocity? In fact, for the system of mutual recognition set out in the White Paper to have any chance of success, mutual trust between the member states was indispensable. The ECJ has helped to build up this trust by ensuring the effectiveness of Community law, and national governments are fully aware of this. In so doing, it has made it possible for administrations to accept their confinement to harmonizing essential health and safety requirements, and to relying more

heavily on mutual recognition, as proposed in the Commission's 1985 White Paper.

This overall contribution of the ECJ to the effectiveness of the Community system explains why, despite occasional irritation with some of the Court's decisions, member states have not made serious attempts to redraft their role in the Community context. However, this did not imply that they were prepared to accept willingly judicial interference with their policy choices, as they made clear with the Maastricht Treaty (see Chapter 6).

Public opinion

Why was the public reaction to the activism displayed by the ECJ not more negative? Ignorance is one answer: as we have seen, its activities have slipped by largely unnoticed for many years. Furthermore, it has been able to count on the support of a certain number of important actors in informed circles. The very broad interpretation of the concept of direct effect sustained by the ECJ has in effect conferred on private persons a substantial number of individual rights, which the preliminary reference procedure has allowed them to effectively enjoy. This evolution, reported by specialists of Community law who were generally very favourable to European integration (Burley and Mattli, 1993, pp. 59–65), has had a considerable impact. It has allowed individuals to play a role in the Community system which is unparalleled with their role in other international systems.

As was seen in Chapter 4, some categories of actors have learnt how to exploit this potential to advance their own interests. Naturally, these groups include those – producers, importers, nationals of a member state residing in another member state – who wish to make the most of the freedoms guaranteed by the treaty. But, more unexpectedly, a number of groups have realized that, in certain areas, Community law is more advanced than national law in some member states. Thus, as we have seen, women have utilized the equal pay principle contained in Article 119 [141]; environmentalists have learnt the value of making national authorities comply with the impact studies required by Community law; consumer protection groups have claimed the right to take legal proceedings to ensure that the product quality requirements laid down in Community directives are respected, and so on.

For all these groups, ensuring that Community obligations are respected – whether this be through the Article 177 [234] channel or, more indirectly, through a complaint to the Commission – is merely an additional means of promoting a particular cause. Article 177 proceedings have thus become a means of subjecting national authorities' actions to review: almost 85 per cent of the cases which come before the ECJ via this route concern individuals in dispute with a public body (Weiler, 1992, p. 37). This has allowed the Court to be portrayed as a useful ally in the struggle against bureaucracy which characterizes modern societies (Rasmussen, 1986, p. 245). All of these factors have clearly assisted in the bolstering of the social legitimacy of the Court's jurisprudence.

Conclusion: environmental factors as a determinant of judicial behaviour

Given the traditional perception of the role of courts, the multi-faceted contribution of the ECJ to the integration process should have exposed it to much criticism and caused it to come up against considerable resistance. Yet, until the late 1980s, the evidence suggests that this was not the case. The dominant pattern was one of compliance with ECJ rulings, and its authority was not seriously challenged. The above analysis suggests that this unexpected acceptance of the Court's assertive role is due to a combination of factors.

First, ECJ jurisprudence has offered a number of functional benefits to some of its key interlocutors. The existence of a strong judiciary, endowed with the task of monitoring the implementation of Community law, has conferred on the latter a degree of effectiveness which is rarely achieved at international level. This has ensured the credibility of commitments undertaken by national governments, which had the upper hand in the European policy-making process. Community law as interpreted by the ECJ also empowered many domestic courts to play a much more incisive role than is usually the case at national level. It has also enabled various categories of private actors to secure advantages which otherwise would have been out of their reach. In other words, judicial decisions contained various incentives to compliance.

Secondly, the ECJ itself seems to have been aware that its legitimacy capital was in part due to a series of contingent factors, such as the technical character of the questions it had to handle or the absence of a strong political power at European level. It has often displayed evidence of political sensitivity, which has led it to act as a mediator between contrasting interests or to avoid unnecessary interferences in the policy choices of other institutions. As noted by Martin Shapiro, 'Bold establishment but modest application of the tenets of constitutional review seems to have been the pattern of the Court' (1992, p. 128).

It is of course tempting to relate the calculated boldness of the ECJ and the rather benevolent acceptance of its jurisprudence by its direct interlocutors. Reasoning backwards, one might argue that judicial behaviour may have been influenced by judges' perception of the environment in which they had to operate. Even if one does not subscribe to the deterministic view of those who hold that the ECJ is a mere servant of national interests, it seems likely that the reactions (if any) expected from its interlocutors can exert an influence on its decisions. How much of an influence is, of course, open to question.

At any rate, the linkage between judicial behaviour and environmental factors will be all the more plausible if changes at the level of the latter (for example, a shift in the ECJ's functions or more hostile reactions) coincide with a shift in its jurisprudence. Luckily for analysts of the ECJ, this is precisely what seems to have happened in the 1990s, as we shall now see.

6

The Structural Roots of Judicial Self-Restraint

Since the late 1980s, the ECJ has exercised ever greater caution in challenging member states' interests. Heralded by a series of rulings dealing with delicate issues such as tax matters (see for example case 81/87, *Daily Mail*) or Sunday trading (case 145/88, *Torfaen* v. *B & Q*, discussed in Chapter 4), this process has developed parallel to a growth in reactions against what appeared as a ceaseless Europeanization process. One should of course avoid over-simplification: the hundreds of rulings delivered each year by the ECJ cannot be squeezed into a single analytical mould. Yet, on the whole, the Court now appears to exercise greater restraint in most of its activities. It is more sensitive to the need to preserve member states' capacity to conduct their own public policies, even when this may entail (limited) costs in terms of market unity; it seems reluctant to expand the scope of Community competences against the wishes of national governments; and it has indicated on several occasions that it cannot substitute its own views for those of Community institutions when the latter enjoy discretionary power.

A retreat from activism?

The decision in the *Wallonian Waste Ban* case (case C-2/90, *Commission* v. *Belgium*), taken only a few months after the signing of the Maastricht Treaty and while difficult ratification campaigns were under way in several countries, is symptomatic of the ECJ's new line

(Shaw, 1995). The Belgian region of Wallonia had adopted a temporary ban on certain kinds of waste originating from other countries. Although the Court had in the past accepted that non-discriminatory measures, applicable equally to imported and non-imported goods, could justify derogations to the principle of free movement of goods on environmental grounds (see case 302/86, *Commission* v. *Denmark* [*Danish Bottles*]), the Wallonian measures were patently discriminatory. Yet, in a surprisingly generous ruling, the Court indicated that, given the special nature of waste and the necessity of having waste materials eliminated as closely as possible to their site of production, a temporary ban was admissible.

One year later, in the *Keck* case (C-267 and 268/91), the ECJ reconsidered its earlier approach to free movement of goods under Article 30 [28]. As indicated above, its earlier line, in particular the far-reaching definition of 'measures of equivalent effect' to a quantitative restriction, had opened the door to widespread challenges against national trading rules (see Chapter 4). It increasingly appeared that this had negative implications of two kinds: not only did free movement of goods cases place a substantial load on an already overburdened court but, more importantly, they often required the Luxembourg judges to oversee policy choices made by national authorities. This unavoidably exposed them to greater public attention, and occasionally to the reproach of activism.

The ECJ's fluctuating case law on the limits of Article 30 was indicative of a certain uneasiness. *Keck* provided it with a good opportunity to steer a new course. The case was brought by two traders who were prosecuted in application of the French law prohibiting selling at a loss. In their defence they argued that this legislation, to the extent that it affected imported goods, infringed Article 30. While admitting that the legislation in question might restrict the volume of sales of products from other member states, the Court noted that the purpose of such legislation was clearly not to regulate trade in goods between member states. It then added that:

> [i]n view of the increasing tendency for traders to involve Article 30 [28]...as a means of challenging any rules whose effect is to limit their commercial freedom even when such rules are not aimed at products from other Member States, the Court

> considers it necessary to re-examine and clarify its case law on this matter....
>
> [C]ontrary to what has previously been decided, the application to products from other Member States of national provisions restricting or prohibiting certain selling arrangements is not such as to hinder directly or indirectly, actually or potentially, trade between the Member States within the meaning of the *Dassonville* judgment... provided that those provisions apply to all affected traders operating within the national territory and provided that they affect in some manner, in law or in fact, the marketing of domestic products and of those from other Member States. (joined cases C-267 and C-268/91, *Keck and Mithouard*)

Through this rare example of overruling, the ECJ clearly intended to signal that a large number of national regulations – those governing the marketing of goods – should a priori not be subject to its control ex Article 30 [28], unless one could argue that they were discriminatory against imported goods. While governments welcomed a decision that preserved their regulatory autonomy, commentators were generally more critical of what one of them termed the 'November revolution' (Reich, 1994). They deplored what appeared to them a clear retreat from the scope of free movement principles (Chalmers, 1994), which would jeopardize the unity of the single market (Mattera, 1994). Be that as it may, everyone agreed on one point: *Keck* was inspired by the ECJ's eagerness not to disrupt unnecessarily member states' economic regulations. This was made abundantly clear by one member of the Court, the late Judge René Joliet, in a strong defence of the Court's new line:

> It may well be that certain regulations are unreasonable or vexatious. If economic actors cannot accommodate themselves to these regulations, it is up to them to lobby their national governments and national parliaments to get the regulations repealed. If it seems to them essential that the conditions of competition be uniform throughout the Member States of the European Community, they will have to turn to the Commission and the Council and try to convince these institutions of the need to harmonize directives... Harmonization of laws of the Member States is a function that belongs to the legislature and not to the Court. (Joliet, 1995, p. 451)

This concern for member states' prerogatives was also apparent in rulings on the scope of Community competences. Opinion 1/94, dealing with the conclusion of the agreement establishing the World Trade Organization and its annexes, bears evidence of this new trend. Although the agreement marked the end of the Uruguay Round, negotiations of which were characterized by tensions between the Commission, which negotiated on behalf of the Community, and some national governments, the dispute related to the position of the member states in the new organization. While the Commission accepted that the member states should become members of the WTO alongside the Community, it claimed that the entire WTO agreement was covered by exclusive Community competence, primarily under the common commercial policy, so that matters dealt with by the new organization would come under Community discipline. Unexpectedly, despite Commission reassurances that it was not attempting to evict them from the WTO (Kuyper, 1995), most member states disagreed with this interpretation. They insisted that the agreements on services (GATS) and on trade-related aspects of intellectual property (TRIPS) were largely within member states' competence.

In its earlier jurisprudence on the external relations of the Community, the ECJ had repeatedly supported a unitary approach at European level. In Opinion 1/75 (*re the Draft Understanding on a Local Cost Standard*), it had held that the concept of commercial policy is identical whether it is applied in the context of the international action of a state or in that of the Community. In Opinion 1/78 (*re the Natural Rubber Agreement*), it had underlined the evolutive nature of the common commercial policy. Many therefore expected the Court to give a sympathetic ear to the Commission's claims. The very fact that virtually all states had agreed on trade liberalization in the areas of services and intellectual property was perceived as a reflection of the fundamental changes under way in international economic relations, and the growing importance of those immaterial aspects. Could this evolution not be reflected in the scope of the common commercial policy? Besides, the new treaty itself indicated that all the agreements concluded as part of the 1994 WTO Agreement were to be regarded as a 'single undertaking'. On the other hand, the Council, eight of the twelve member states, and the European Parliament stood against the Commission. In its written observations, the UK defined this last's position as extravagant. The ECJ, consulted under the Article 228(6) [300 (6)] procedure, was therefore set to arbitrate a delicate political dispute (Hilf, 1995).

As is often the case in such situations, the Court's response can be best defined as Solomon-like. On the one hand, it declared that the Community had sole competence, pursuant to Article 113 [133] of the EC Treaty, to conclude the multilateral agreements on trade in goods, thereby resolving long-standing issues on coal and steel and agricultural products in favour of the Community. On the other hand, it did not accept the Commission's contention that GATS and TRIPS fell entirely within Community competences, either as part of the Commercial policy or as implied external powers under the *ERTA* jurisprudence (see Chapter 2). As a result, the WTO Agreement had to be concluded jointly by the Community and its member states. To compensate somewhat for this outcome, the ECJ added that in the name of 'unity in the international representation of the Community', member states and Community institutions were required to co-operate in the negotiation and conclusion of the agreement, as well as in its implementation (Opinion 1/94, *re the WTO Agreement* at para. 108). It is however doubtful that such an exhortation will suffice to ensure a smooth co-operation.

Opinion 1/94 is widely regarded as a step backwards with respect to previous case law (see Bourgeois, 1995; Kuilwijk, 1996, p. 74). The ECJ's refusal to accept that its decision would create serious risks of cacophony among the Commission and the member states in the WTO is in sharp contrast with bold teleological constructions *à la ERTA*. Yet given the fierce opposition which the Commission's claim met among national governments, the outcome of the dispute was hardly a surprise (Hilf, 1995). It is symptomatic of the current trend, in which the Court, aware of the political implications of its rulings, appears to have reverted to a more moderate course and to be more mindful of states' sensitivity to certain issues. In spite of repeated invitations from several Advocates General, it has declined to recognize the so-called 'horizontal direct effect' of directives: that is, the fact that these instruments can directly create obligations for private persons (see, for example, case C-91/92, *Faccini Dori* v. *Recreb*). Similarly, when states' interests are in conflict, and the legality of Community legislation is challenged before the ECJ, the latter has appeared reluctant to go against the views of a majority of member states (see, for example, cases C-280/93,

Germany v. *Council* or C-84/94, *United Kingdom* v. *Council*, discussed below).

Insiders have themselves emphasized the shift to a line of self-restraint in the Court's recent case law. ECJ President Rodriguez Iglesias has underscored that its task was to act as a guardian of the Constitution, rather than as a 'motor of integration' (Rodriguez Iglesias, 1996, p. 11). Mancini and Keeling have suggested that recent case law is

> not only distinguished by restraint, but also increasingly revisionist and not averse to blunting the conquests made in the previous decades. Much as generalizations are dangerous in dealing with changes of culture and mood, one is tempted to conclude that the Court has undergone a process of secularization. Realism is no longer a balance to passion; it has superseded passion and has become a synonym of minimalism. (Mancini and Keeling, 1995, p. 406)

Yet the picture is perhaps more complex than reactions to the cases mentioned here might lead one to believe. Cases like *Factortame* or *Francovich*, which date back to the early 1990s, added important elements to the construction of the Community legal orders, by introducing the possibility of interim relief or of financial liability in cases of violation of EC law (see Chapter 2). Even in recent years, the ECJ has shown that it can be bold when the fundamental principles underlying the European Community's legal architecture are at stake. *Brasserie du Pêcheur* (joined cases C-46/93 and C-48/93, discussed in Chapter 2) is certainly a good example of creative jurisprudence, in which the ECJ accepted the risk of strong reactions from powerful governments in order to ensure the effectiveness of Community law.

The ECJ's current line may be best described as conservative, rather than as reactionary: it attempts to consolidate the Community legal system, while at the same time avoiding – to the extent that this is possible – unnecessary frictions with national governments (see Hilf, 1995, for a similar assessment in relation to the WTO opinion). Why the Court has opted for this more cautious line can be understood only by reference to the transformations under way in the functions it performs and in the environment in which it operates.

A new institutional context

To understand the shift in the ECJ's judicial policy, it is necessary to return to the revival of European integration which took place around the mid-1980s. Weakened from the mid-1960s onwards by internal tensions and then recession, European integration enjoyed a new dynamism during the 1980s. The starting point of this movement was the programme for the completion of the internal market presented by the Commission in 1985, in which the first reference was made to the now mythical date of 31 December 1992. It is no exaggeration to say that this apparently modest programme changed the course of history – or at least the history of European integration. Not only did it bring a breath of fresh air to a Community which had gone rather stale, but it brought about a profound transformation of the European institutional landscape. Although most analyses examining this transformation have focused on the political institutions composed of the Commission–Parliament–Council trio, the Court was not immune to this transformation; in this new institutional context, its role was bound to be different.

In the wake of the internal market programme, the SEA introduced a series of modifications to the Community's institutional system. Among these, the move to majority voting in the Council of Ministers held a pole position, since it concerned a large number – around two-thirds – of the measures set out in the Commission's White Paper. We saw earlier how the ECJ contributed to this transformation (see Chapter 3). It is worth pausing to examine the effects of these institutional changes, in so far as they also entail consequences for the Court.

The internal market programme was chiefly of a legislative nature: the Commission's White Paper listed almost 300 measures which the Council had to adopt before the fateful date of 31 December 1992. Moreover, its primary objective was the elimination of non-tariff barriers to trade. Divergent national policies in areas such as health, consumer protection and the environment could lead to considerable difficulties in intra-Community trade. To diminish these difficulties, the White Paper proposed a harmonization programme of basic norms relating to the protection of health and safety.

The implementation of this programme profoundly modified the institutional balance of the Community in three principal ways:

- There was a dramatic intensification of legislative activity: the number of measures adopted each year by the Council, which hovered around 555 for the period 1981–4, shot up to 645 in the years 1985–92 (General Report of Activities of the EC, 1981 to 1992).
- There was an enlargement of the Community's activities: in order to eliminate legislative obstacles to trade, their focus widened to include areas ranging from health to environmental protection which went far beyond the framework of activities – primarily economic – with which the Community had previously dealt.
- The implementation was at times accompanied by a deepening of Community action: in several areas, the solutions contemplated at Community level were often more advanced than those in the majority of member states and at times went further than even the most exacting standards in any of the member states (Majone, 1993).

All of these factors have inevitably had repercussions on intra-institutional relations at Community level. Several zones of friction have emerged (Weiler, 1993). The first of these took the form of a new type of conflict: over the legal basis of Community measures. While the spirit of the 1966 Luxembourg 'Accords' reigned, following the crisis of the empty chair, this question was of merely academic interest: as putting proposals to the vote in the Council was rare, the legal basis on which the final decision was taken mattered little. This, however, was to change with the SEA, which provided for a vote in certain instances and also gave the Parliament a larger role in the framework of the new co-operation procedure. Following these changes, the legal basis issue was to take on considerable importance. Given that a choice now existed, each of the institutions was to make efforts to privilege the procedure which maximized their power: majority voting for the Commission, the co-operation procedure for the Parliament, unanimity for the member states. On several occasions, as we have already seen, the ECJ was called upon to arbitrate conflicts of this nature. Was the adoption of a system of generalized preferences in favour of products originating from developing countries part of a commercial policy or was it necessary to employ Article 235 [308] which gives a general authorization to the Council to act 'to attain...one of the objectives of the

Community'? (case 45/86, *Commission* v. *Council*). Did a measure relating to the use of hormones in meat fall under agricultural policy or consumer protection? (case 68/86, *UK* v. *Council*).

Figure 6.1 illustrates the increase in the volume of institutional conflicts. If we take as an indicator the number of annulment actions and the number of actions for failure to act introduced by the member states or the Community institutions we see that from an average of 10 cases per year in the period 1981–4, the number of cases per year went up to 27 in the period 1985–8 and to 28 in the period 1989–92. To an increasing extent, therefore, the ECJ was called upon to act as an arbitrator in institutional disputes, just like any constitutional court (Rodriguez Iglesias, 1996, p. 11).

The enlargement of Community competences created another site of conflict and tension. The trend is hardly new: at the 1972 Paris Summit, the Heads of State and of Government had expressed their desire to see Community intervention expand into areas such as social policy, the environment and consumer protection, using the textual possibilities offered by Article 235 [308] of the Treaty of Rome as the basis for these interventions. This proactive stance is not really surprising: Article 235, like Article 100 [94] which covers

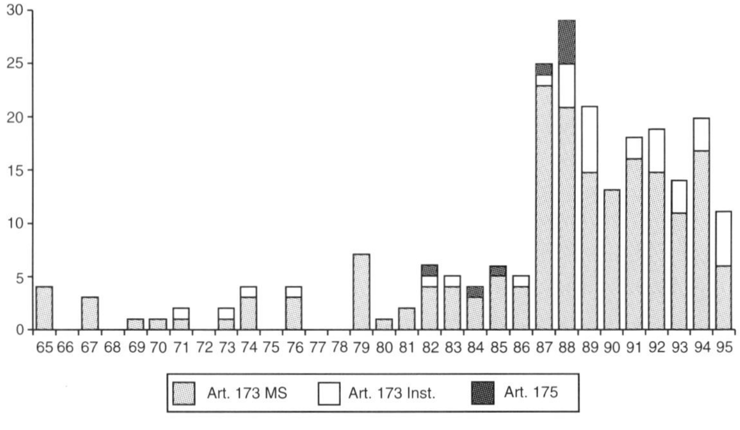

FIGURE 6.1 The development of interinstitutional litigation (cases brought before the ECJ by member states (MS) and European institutions (Inst), 1965–96)

Source: *EC General Reports of Activities for Art.173 and CELEX for Art.175.*

the harmonization of legislation, makes Community intervention subject to a unanimous Council decision. In other words, the Community can only use these legal bases when all the member states have agreed to both the principle and the means of application of the intervention. So long as any enlargement of Community competences took place under these conditions, it constituted a relatively neutral development for the member states; while they retained the power to control what was decided in Brussels, they did not feel that each Community decision involved dispossessing them of previously held powers.

Article 100a [95], added to the Treaty of Rome by the SEA, radically altered the contours of this issue. This provision allows the use of qualified majority voting in the Council for the adoption of measures to complete the single market. Henceforth, the objection of one, or even several, member states, no longer necessarily presents an insurmountable obstacle to the adoption of a measure. While the decision-making process still remained firmly based on consensus – one is still a long way from voting as often as the treaty authorizes – this new situation profoundly modified the way in which national governments perceived the expansion of Community competences. The loss of their right of veto gave some credit to the threat of a drift towards the centre feared by some member states.

The ECJ did not remain on the sidelines of this new debate. In the years following the SEA, several member states went before the Court claiming that the Commission had exceeded the limits of its competence (joined cases 281, 283–5 and 287/85, *Germany and Others* v. *Commission*; Case C-303/90, *France* v. *Commission*).

The insertion in the Maastricht Treaty of the principle of subsidiarity gave evidence of the member states' eagerness to assign clearer limits to the growth of Community powers:

> The Community shall act within the limits of the powers conferred upon it by this Treaty and of the objectives assigned to it therein.
>
> In areas which do not fall within its exclusive competence, the Community shall take action, in accordance with the principle of subsidiarity, only if and in so far as the objectives of the proposed action cannot be sufficiently achieved by the Member States and can therefore, by reason of the scale or effects of the proposed action, be better achieved by the Community.

> Any action of the Community shall not go beyond what is necessary to achieve the objectives of this Treaty. (Article 3bis [5])

National authorities seem to expect the ECJ to play an important role in the application of the subsidiarity principle by regulating the use made of it by the Community institutions. What is more, in a much-noticed judgment on constitutionality of the Maastricht Treaty, the Karlsruhe Constitutional Court clearly declared that the German Constitution only allowed limited and clearly-circumscribed transfers of competence to the European Union. While noting that the EU Treaty in its current form responded to this requirement, it recalled that development of EU competences beyond current limits would require a treaty amendment, which would have to be approved by Parliament. Furthermore, it stressed in unambiguous terms that there were to be limits to the expansion of EC competences on the basis of existing provisions of the treaty:

> Hitherto any dynamic extension of the existing Treaties has been based on a liberal application of Article 235 [308] of the EEC Treaty, along the lines of a 'competence to perfect the Treaty', on the idea of the inherent competencies of the European Communities ('implied powers') and on an interpretation of the Treaty as implying the fullest possible utilisation of Community powers (*effet utile*) (cf. Zuleeg, von der Groeben/ Thissing/Elhermann, *EWG Vertrag*, 4th ed. 1991, Article 2 marginal number 3). In future, however, when Community institutions and bodies interpret rules conferring competence, it will have to be borne in mind that the Union Treaty draws a fundamental distinction between the exercise of a sovereign power granted on a limited basis and amendment of the Treaty. Any interpretation of that Treaty must not, therefore, in effect amount to an extension of it. Such an interpretation of rules conferring competence would not give rise to any binding effect for Germany. (cases BvR 2134 and 2159/92, 12 October 1993)

This declaration constituted a barely veiled threat to question the supremacy of Community law. The reference to Professor Zuleeg, then a judge at the European Court of Justice, was widely perceived as a declaration that the Karlsruhe Court intended to monitor closely ECJ rulings on the scope of Community competences in order to be able to respond effectively to any centralist tendencies.

The ECJ responded by adopting a rather restrictive interpretation of Article 235 [308] in its Opinion 2/94. Pursuant to Article 228(6) [300 (6)] of the EC Treaty, it had been asked by the Council to declare whether the accession of the Community to the European Convention for Protection of Human Rights would be compatible with the treaty. The resort to the ECJ was intended to provide an answer to a vexed question over which the Council itself was divided: in the absence of specific provisions conferring upon the Community any power in the field of human rights, was it competent to adhere to the Convention? Several member states, noting that there were references to the respect for human rights in the preamble and in various provisions of the Maastricht Treaty, had suggested that this would suffice to regard human rights protection as an objective of the Community within the meaning of Article 235.

The ECJ rejected this interpretation. Interestingly, it chose to do so in terms that echo those of the *Bundesverfassungsgericht*:

> Article 235 is designed to fill the gap where no specific provisions of the Treaty confer on Community institutions express or implied powers to act, if such powers appear none the less to be necessary to enable the Community to carry out its functions with a view to attaining one of the objectives laid down by the Treaty. That provision, being an integral part of an institutional system based on the principle of conferred powers, cannot serve as a basis for widening the scope of Community powers beyond the general framework created by the provisions of the Treaty as a whole ... On any view, Article 235 cannot be used as a basis for the adoption of provisions whose effect would, in substance, be to amend the Treaty without following the procedure which it provides for that purpose....
>
> Accession to the Convention would...entail a substantial change in the present Community system for the protection of human rights in that it would entail the entry of the Community into a distinct international institutional system as well as integration of all the provisions of the Convention into the Community legal order.
>
> Such a modification of the system for the protection of human rights in the Community...would be of constitutional

> significance and would therefore be such as to go beyond the scope of Article 235 [308]. It could therefore be brought about only by way of Treaty amendments. (Opinion 2/94, *re the Accession of the Community to the European Human Rights Convention*, at paras 29–30 and 34–5)

In this opinion, the ECJ was clearly attempting to give evidence of its willingness to prevent an uncontrolled expansion of Community competences. The contrast with earlier rulings is quite remarkable, even though it is true that the Court had never been asked to rule that the Community had exceeded the powers it enjoys by virtue of Article 235 (Rodriguez Iglesias, 1996, p. 15). The least one can say is that it has been far less restrictive in its interpretations of the provisions governing the competences of the Community, not to mention its jurisprudence on the protection of fundamental rights (see Chapter 2). Opinion 2/94 appears to have been strongly influenced by the growing pressures to which Community institutions, and the ECJ in particular, are exposed in relation to the competence issue.

The ECJ has also been called upon to play an increasing role on another front – the implementation of Community law. In many respects, this is a structural problem which has been aggravated by Community development in recent years. Most of the measures adopted by the Council as part of the single market programme were directives, which must subsequently be legislatively transposed in each of the member states. Furthermore, the task of applying Community measures on the ground generally falls to the national administration in each member state. This system of decentralized implementation is naturally riddled with instances of dysfunction. To make matters worse, the acceleration of the decision-making process has exacerbated the problem: in a number of areas, an avalanche of Community measures has descended on national administrations which have not always been able to cope. The result, amply illustrated by the Commission's annual reports on the application of Community law, is a growing 'application deficit' (Commission, 1997).

The Court's attention has been drawn to this development in several different ways. The first – and most obvious – is the taking of infringement proceedings. Figure 6.2 shows that the number of actions taken by the Commission against member states has

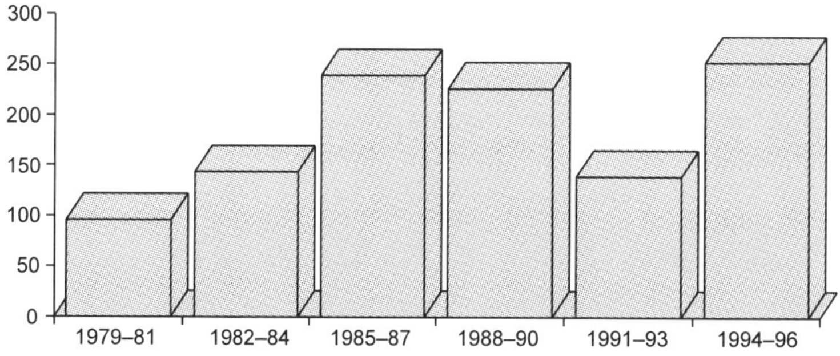

FIGURE 6.2 Article 169 [226] cases brought before the ECJ, 1979–96
Source: *EC General Reports of Activities.*

noticeably increased in the wake of the single market. From an average of 44 per year in 1980–4, they went up to 83 per year in 1985–9, to subsequently fall back to 63 per year in 1990–3. The Commission's activism has shown itself to be a double-edged sword, as the number of rulings resulting from infringement proceedings which have been ignored by member states has conspicuously increased, thus diminishing their persuasive power.

To confront this new challenge, the Maastricht Treaty gave the ECJ acting on the Commission's request, the power to impose pecuniary sanctions on member states which have not conformed with a prior judgment (Article 171, para. 2 [228, para. 2]). The preliminary reference procedure has also brought before the Court a large number of issues relating to the application of Community law. The ECJ has used these opportunities to define the powers with which national authorities are endowed when they implement Community law, and the effects which flow from inexecution of Community law. One may think that the boldness displayed by the ECJ in cases such as *Factortame* (case C-213/89) or *Francovich* (cases C-6 and 9/90) and their progeny was largely influenced by its awareness of the limited effectiveness of Article 169 [226] proceedings.

Lastly, the 1992 programme has also had a notable impact on public opinion. The idea of the 'big market' captured the public imagination, giving rise to often confused but none the less very real expectations. Ignored by the media for most of their existence, the European institutions suddenly found themselves in the full glare of media attention. People from all walks of life discovered that EC decisions affected their daily existence. This new-found notoriety has also been reflected in the activities of the Court, as illustrated in Figure 6.3. The average number of cases registered each year increased by 23 per cent from an average of 311 for the period 1980–4 to an average of 385 for the period 1985–90 (ECJ, 1991, p.111).

Thus the 1980s relaunch of the EC has affected the whole range of the ECJ's activities. These changes are not just quantitative. The rekindling of institutional dynamism has led to an augmentation of constitutional issues in EC jurisprudence. The arbitration of institutional conflicts and the delimitation of the respective competences of the Community and its member states occupy an ever-expanding position in the Court's activities, bringing it closer to a federal constitutional model. But the changes do not stop here: the Court's perception of its own role in the Community system was bound to be affected by this transformed environment.

Maastricht and the threat of political overruling

When discussing the conditions that have made possible the development of the ECJ's assertive judicial policy, mention has been made of the fact that for many years governments had put up little resistance to its rulings, apparently accepting the gradual construction of the *acquis communautaire*. In recent years, confronted with the increasing importance of the integration process, national authorities have shown growing signs of annoyance. The ECJ could not, and did not, remain immune to this trend.

There is perhaps no better indicator of the member states' unwillingness to sit idly by and accept uncritically the Court's rulings than the Maastricht Treaty itself. Like all complex multilateral agreements negotiated under the shadow of a veto (unanimity being required for any modification of the EC Treaties), the Maastricht Treaty, concluded in February 1992, was rich in ambiguities, not least with respect to the Court.

On the one hand, several treaty provisions can be read as a sign of trust and faith in the ECJ's work. Thus, Article 173 [230] has been modified to incorporate almost textually the Court's decisions in

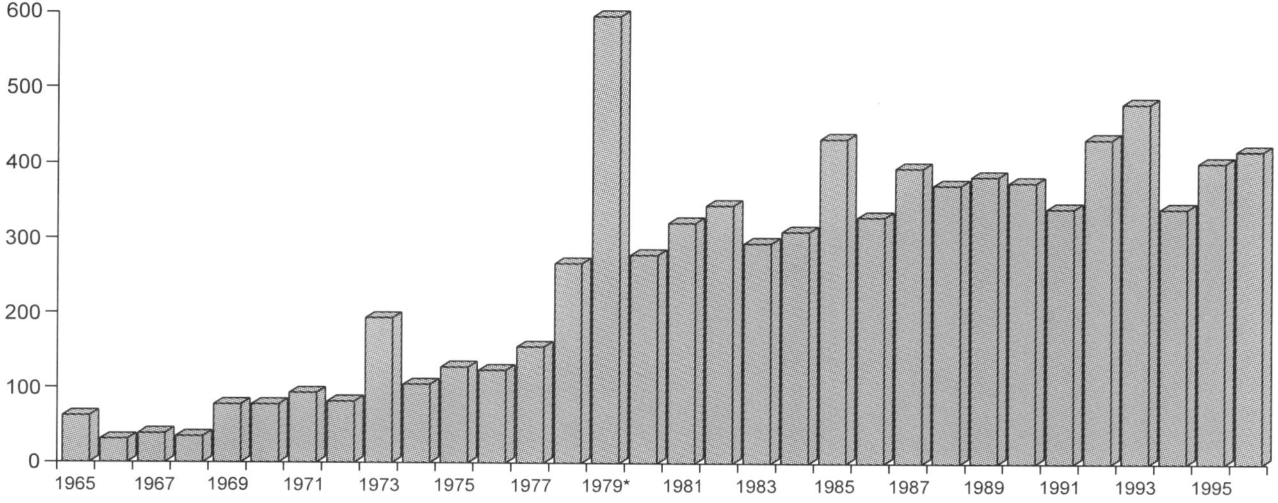

FIGURE 6.3 Cases brought before the ECJ, 1965–96

Source: *ECJ Report of Proceedings* 1992–4, p. 258, for years 1980–94 and *EC General Reports of Activites* for years 1995–6.

*For 1979 the actual number of cases brought before the ECJ was 1322 (of which 1163 proceedings by staff of the institutions).

Les Verts (case 294/83) and *Chernobyl* (case 70/88). Likewise, the Court has been granted the power to impose pecuniary sanctions on states which fail to comply with a judgment establishing that they are in breach of the obligations (Article 171, para. 2 [228 (para. 2)]).

Yet, in contrast with this line of consolidation of the *acquis communautaire*, the treaty contains a series of powerful messages for the ECJ. Confirming a solution which had been sketched in the SEA, the drafters of the treaty excluded entire areas of EU activities from the jurisdiction of the Court. This was in particular the case for sections covering EU foreign and security policies, as well as for what is known as the 'third pillar' of the Maastricht Treaty, namely cooperation in the fields of justice and home affairs, mostly in relation to immigration and security matters. Evidently, national governments, which were aware of the crucial part taken by the ECJ in the development of the European Community, did not want similar dynamics to develop in areas perceived as belonging to the hard core of national sovereignty. Even more significantly, several protocols have been added to the treaty which curtail the effects of the Court's rulings.

In *Barber* (case C-262/88), for instance, the ECJ had held that the equal pay principle of Article 119 [141] applied to benefits paid under private pension schemes. Considering the potential financial consequences of this ruling for the pension funds, the Court limited its retroactive effect, but it failed to indicate clearly the situations covered by the principle of equal treatment: should it apply to all pension *payments* made after the date of the ruling or only to benefits attributed in relation to a *period of employment* subsequent to that date? In a typical example of judicial dialogue, several national courts asked the ECJ to clarify this point. Before it could react, however, member states, alarmed by the powerful British and Dutch pension fund lobbies, and fearing the financial implications of the *Barber* judgment, imposed their own 'interpretation' of Article 119: Protocol No. 2 stated that benefits under occupational security schemes would not be considered remuneration if they were attributable to periods of employment anterior to the *Barber* ruling, except for those workers who had initiated legal proceedings before that date.

This reaction, which limited the ECJ's ability to interpret one of its earlier decisions, was widely perceived by the legal community as a not-so-veiled invitation for the ECJ to show greater deference to member states' interests (Curtin, 1993; Mancini and Keeling, 1995). But the *Barber* protocol may also be seen as a direct response to judicial interference in the legislative process. In its *Barber* judgment, the ECJ had hinted that some derogation clauses contained in Directive 86/378 contravened the principle of equal treatment laid down in Article 119 [141]. The member states' response, by considerably limiting the temporal effect of the Court's ruling, restricted the possibility for it to go further along the same lines. It clearly suggested that national governments were no longer willing to accept all ECJ rulings without reacting, and might if necessary contemplate a treaty amendment to protect their own rights.

The impression of an attempt to 'hijack the *acquis communautaire*' (Curtin, 1993) was confirmed by another proposal, dealing with the abortion issue. It will be remembered that in *SPUC* v. *Grogan* (case C-159–90), the ECJ had been asked to rule on the compatibility with the treaty of Irish legislation prohibiting the advertising of possibilities of abortion abroad. Although the Court declined to treat the issue as a problem of freedom of expression and ultimately ruled that in the case at issue the Irish ban did not conflict with Community law, the fact that Community provisions on the freedom to provide services were held to be applicable to abortion was perceived as a potential threat by the Irish authorities. In order to protect itself from an erosion of its ability to deal with this most delicate matter, the Irish government asked, and obtained, that a special protocol be added to the treaty that would confirm that it did not contain anything affecting the prohibition of abortion contained in the Constitution of Ireland.

In a similar fashion, a further protocol adopted at Maastricht authorized Denmark to retain its legislation prohibiting the acquisition of second homes by foreigners, although this legislation runs counter to the freedom of establishment, one of the cornerstones of the EC Treaty. A few years before, in a litigation involving a similar legislation in Greece, the ECJ had indicated that provisions of this kind were contrary to the treaty (case 305/87, *Commission* v. *Greece*). Protocol No. 1 was basically conceived as a way to avoid ECJ scrutiny of the Danish second home legislation.

Last but not least, although the Maastricht Treaty has extended the scope of Community competences beyond the realm of economic integration, the way in which this has been done bears evidence of the member states' eagerness to prevent an uncontrolled expansion of Community activities. Taken at face value, provisions like new Articles 126 [149] and following may be seen as an expansion of Community competences to areas as diverse as education, public health or culture. Yet this extension is more apparent than real as legislative incursions into those areas had already taken place in the past, relying mostly on general heads of competence such as Articles 100 [94] or 235 [308]. Moreover, clear limits have been assigned to EC activities under these new provisions. Article 126, para. 1 explicitly invites the Community to respect 'the responsibility of the member states for the content of teaching and organization of education systems', whereas the Court had denied the existence of states' reserved powers in this area (see case 9/74, *Casagrande*, discussed in Chapter 2); more importantly, it is explicitly excluded that these provisions can be used as a legal basis for harmonizing the laws and regulations of the member states.

As regards education policy, the insertion of such an exclusion clause in Article 126 appears as a direct reaction to earlier ECJ judgments which had opened the door to the development of a fully-fledged European education policy by offering a broad construction of the concept of vocational training, (see, in particular, case 242/87, *Commission* v. *Council [ERASMUS]*; see also Chapter 3). The drafters of the Maastricht Treaty clearly did not intend to let this happen. Although they accepted the principle of Community intervention in education matters, the exclusion clause enshrined in Article 126 was conceived as a means to prevent any undue Community interference in the regulation of education structures or teaching programmes. Provisions of this kind clearly aim more at freezing the growth of Community competences than at facilitating it (Dehousse, 1994). Once again, the message to the ECJ seems clear: there are limits to what member states are willing to accept.

When viewed as a whole, the seemingly contradictory provisions of the Maastricht Treaty actually make much sense. On the one hand, member states have indicated that they still value the Court's role as a guarantor of faithful implementation of the decisions they take collectively at European level. Likewise, they accept the need for an umpire to adjudicate inter-institutional disputes – hence the new Article 173 [230]. In contrast, they have clearly indicated through various protocols that they were not prepared to accept ECJ interference in what they regard as delicate policy choices, which they intend to keep for themselves. Put together, these various elements make for a perfectly coherent message to the Court: stick to your job as guardian of the treaties, and do not meddle unnecessarily with policy matters.

The second part of the message has actually been confirmed on several occasions by prominent political leaders. Members of the German cabinet, including Chancellor Kohl, have strongly reacted against Court rulings on the social security rights of migrant workers (*Agence Europe*, 14 October 1992, no. 5835). Apparently, the German ministry for justice has toyed for some time with the idea of tabling a draft treaty amendment removing the right for lower jurisdictions to refer questions of Community law to the ECJ (Mancini and Keeling, 1995) – a solution which was actually adopted in the Amsterdam Treaty for those parts of the third pillar to which ECJ jurisdiction was extended (new Articles K7 [35] and 73p [68]). Had such a system been retained for all areas of Community competence, it would no doubt have had a devastating effect, given the part played by references from lower courts in the development of Community law, and the reluctance of some higher jurisdictions to enter into a dialogue with the Luxembourg court (see Chapter 2). Similarly, in the framework of the intergovernmental conference on the reform of the Maastricht Treaty, the UK government published a memorandum on the ECJ which displays the same kind of dichotomy as the treaty.

On the one hand, the memorandum proposed to set out in the treaty the criteria for state liability to pay damages developed by the Court in *Francovich* and *Brasserie du Pêcheur and Factortame III* (C-46 and C-48/93). This is hardly surprising, as in this later case the Court followed closely the submissions of the UK government. Yet, at the same time the memorandum proposed amendments to the EC Treaty designed to enable the Council to overrule more easily judgments of the Court which it deems to be in contradiction with the 'original intent' of the Community legislature. As indicated earlier (see Chapter 5), overruling ECJ decisions, when it is at all possible, is made difficult by specific features of the Community legislative process, such as the monopoly of legislative initiative enjoyed by the Commission. The UK memorandum suggested ways around this difficulty: one would be to dispense with the requirement of a Commission proposal to initiate the legislative process; another one would be to allow the Council to require the Commission to submit within three months an amendment giving effect to the Council's legislative policy. The message to the Court was once more very clear: stick to your role of ensuring the uniform application of Community law, and do not interfere in policy choices, lest the risk of political overruling. So defined, the Court's mission is quite in line with states' interests, which is to see their joint decisions duly implemented.

Although the UK proposals were eventually not accepted, the Treaty of Amsterdam has confirmed the member states' ambivalence *vis-à-vis* the ECJ. On the one hand, the Court's jurisdiction has been extended to the 'Third Pillar' of the EU, which was largely unexpected at the beginning of the intergovernmental conference. On the other hand, there are important qualifications on its normal powers, most strikingly in relation to preliminary rulings, both in the reformed third pillar (New Article K7 [35]), and in sectors such as visas, asylum or immigration which were brought under the Community pillar (New Article 73p. [68]). While the balance sheet is probably more positive than many in the ECJ believed, this complex compromise can be viewed as a confirmation of national governments' reluctance to accept a judicialization of delicate policy choices.

Recent writings by prominent members of the Court suggest that it is quite aware that the current climate is not favourable to bold initiatives (Mancini and Keeling, 1995; Rodriguez Iglesias, 1996). But the best evidence of the impact of environmental factors is the Court's recent case law, characterized as we have seen by a mix of greater deference for member states' policy choices and insistence on enhancing further the effectiveness of Community law.

Thus, in spite of their seemingly contradictory character the developments of the 1990s display a striking pattern of rationality. Member states have become more assertive and have insisted that the ECJ concentrate on the task which is structurally most important to them: ensuring the implementation of Community law. And the Court has understood that it must pay heed to their warnings. Both sets of actors seem to have a clear understanding of their institutional interests, and act accordingly. Once more, institutional self-interest seems to be one of the main variables underpinning the evolution of the dialogue between political institutions and the judiciary.

Judicial politics after Maastricht

When reviewing the elements which explain the important role the ECJ has played in the Community system, we have seen that its influence owes a great deal to the relatively favourable environment in which it has operated: the absence of party political cleavages, the technical nature of many of the issues placed before it, the relative indifference surrounding its activities; all of these factors are crucial to understanding the developments of the first three decades. Yet, this general frame of reference has undergone a radical transformation in recent years.

If, for many years, the Court has benefited immeasurably from the absence of commotion which has greeted its rulings, several factors may combine to make it difficult for it to stay out of the spotlight of public opinion for much longer. The more the Community enlarges its sphere of activity, and the more it moves away from considering the economic issues which previously almost completely dominated the EC, the greater are the risks for the Court that it will be called upon to decide on delicate societal issues. Conflicts between economic imperatives and the qualitative necessity to protect the environment, the rights of immigrants, social protection: this is the stuff which makes up the – sometimes fraught – agenda of debate in European society today, and which the ECJ has already, if only tangentially, had to confront. Not only are national governments likely to have strong views on these questions, but, given their political salience in many countries, ECJ rulings are more likely to attract media attention. The days when it could benefit from the 'benign neglect' of governments and the general public now seem to be gone – even though the ECJ is not infrequently mistaken for the European Court of Human Rights, which sits in Strasbourg and interprets the European Convention on human rights (*The Economist*, 7 October 1995).

This upsurge of public attention clearly makes the ECJ's task more arduous. Commenting upon its equality jurisprudence, for instance, Elisabeth Meehan has noted that

> [b]y making social policy more expensive . . . the Court may or may not have politicized itself but it has politicized the policy field: or at least it has moved from the realm of low politics, where according to all but the most recent analyses, agreements

> are easy to reach, to the realm of high politics where they are not. (Meehan, 1993, p. 140)

The enhanced attention which the Community has attracted since the mid-1980s seems to have encouraged plaintiffs to come forward. Hence the development of judicial politics noticed in recent years: with a little imagination, one can find a problematic European angle, and thus an issue for the ECJ, in almost anything. We have already seen how often Article 30 [28] has been invoked to challenge domestic economic regulations. Abortion came to Luxembourg as a free movement of services issue (case C-159/90, *Grogan*); other sensitive issues could come before the ECJ through the channel of human rights protection, which lends itself to a multitude of possible uses.

The SEA has also lent greater dynamism to the political process. Majority voting has made it possible to ignore the opposition of some member states to proposed decisions. This has in turn enlarged the Commission's role in the decision-making process, as it can use its right of initiative to shape coalitions in the Council of Ministers. This reinvigorated political process has not only had consequences over the volume and structure of the ECJ's workload; it has also affected the margin of manoeuvre enjoyed by the Court. It was one thing to bypass a stalled Council of Ministers to give effect to principles contained in the treaty as the Court did on many occasions; it is quite another to reverse a decision taken by political institutions.

In the past, the ECJ has displayed the utmost caution when confronted with sensitive issues. Unfortunately, it is not always easy to maintain a neutral position. If the Court decides to make an explicit decision, it will anger one side or the other; if it adopts the cautious non-committal approach, it will be condemned by those wishing to get rid of the *status quo*. In either case, it will have to face more critical attention than it has in the past.

Consider, for instance, the Court's position in relation to the working time directive. The UK government was very vocal in claiming that by adopting that directive, the Council of Ministers had exceeded its powers under Article 118a [138]. It even threatened to table an amendment restricting the scope of that provision at the ongoing IGC, if its appeal were to fail. Yet all other governments had endorsed the resort to Article 118a. The ECJ found itself on the horns of a dilemma. Whatever its decision, it was sure to be confronted with strong reactions: if it annulled the directive for lack of competence, it would antagonize a large majority of member states; if it did not, it would be under heavy fire from London.

The Court did its best to steer a middle course: although it held that the directive was properly based on Article 118a, it annulled the Sunday rest provision on the grounds that the Council had failed to explain 'why Sunday . . . is more closely connected with the health and safety of workers than any other day of the week' (case C-84/94, *United Kingdom* v. *Council*, at para. 37). This attempt to split the difference was not sufficient to deflect criticism: the UK prime minister threatened to block the reform of the Maastricht Treaty if the ruling was not overturned (*The Times*, 13 October 1996).

The ECJ found itself in an equally difficult situation in a litigation involving the common market organization for bananas. After protracted negotiations, Regulation 404/93 established a regime which clearly favoured growers from ACP countries, traditionally attached to the EC, to the detriment of 'third country' (mostly Central American) growers. The regulation hit particularly hard German importers, who had long-standing ties with these countries. Not only did it establish tariffs which made those imports more expensive, but a share of the quota for 'third country' bananas was reserved to traders who had marketed EC and ACP bananas in the past, which gave rise to allegations that importers of 'third country' bananas would be driven out of business (Kuilwijk, 1996).

Germany, who had fiercely opposed the Commission proposal and was overruled, decided to seek the annulment of Regulation 404/93 before the ECJ, arguing *inter alia* that it breached the principles of non-discrimination and of proportionality, as well as the right of property and the freedom to pursue a trade.

What surprised most observers was less the fact that the Court of Justice dismissed the German arguments, than the high degree of deference that the Court showed for the views of the Community legislator (case C-280/93, *Germany* v. *Council*). While recognizing the importance of the right to property and the freedom to pursue a trade, it held that these rights were not absolute and had to be viewed in relation to their social function: in the case at issue, the regulation corresponded to 'objectives of general Community interest' and did not impair the substance of the traders rights to pursue their trade, even though it had a negative impact over their competitive position (paras 78–87). Likewise, recalling its well-established case law on the proportionality principle, it stressed that given the discretionary powers enjoyed by the Council of Ministers in the framework of the Common Agricultural Policy, the lawfulness of the regulation could be affected only if it was 'manifestly inappropriate' to the objectives pursued by the Council. It then added:

> While other means for achieving the desired result were indeed conceivable, the Court cannot substitute its assessment for that of the Council as to the appropriateness or otherwise of the measures adopted by the Community legislature if those measures have not been proved to be manifestly inappropriate for achieving the objective pursued (para. 94).

This judgment was the subject of much criticism in Germany, not least by courts, as will become apparent below. The Court of Justice was blamed for what was regarded as a cursory treatment of the fundamental rights issues and for refusing to consider the possibility of an infringement of GATT provisions (Kuilwijk, 1996). Yet, the difficulty of its position must be recognized. Although it had strongly negative implications for importers of 'third country' bananas, the regulation at issue had been adopted by a large majority of member states. Had the Court censured them, the latter would have been likely to protest strongly against what would certainly have appeared to them as an undue interference in their powers of political appraisal.

Cases of this kind illustrate the difficulties now faced increasingly by the ECJ as a result of the revival of the Community's political process. The growing politicization of the policy process and emergence of a pattern of majoritarian politics do not only make it more likely that the Court will be asked to arbitrate political disputes, but also that it runs serious risks of being dragged into conflicts in which it has much to lose: if it stands on the majority side, it will be blamed for ignoring its duty to protect rights granted by the treaty; if it opts for the minority side, it will be accused by the majority of unwanted judicial activism. The very development of judicial politics thus renders the ECJ's position much more difficult than in the past, as it can no longer shield itself behind the 'mask' of law (Burley and Mattli, 1993).

Integration as disintegration

As any law student knows, legal systems generally view themselves as a coherent set of norms, rooted in national traditions and structured by dogmatic principles. Legal reasoning is an exercise in interpreting these norms in the light of underlying principles, with a view to applying them to concrete situations. The coherence of the whole system is a central element of its legitimacy: lacking this, judges' and lawyers' choices are likely to be perceived as arbitrary.

These basic elements are recalled here because they are necessary to stress an element which is vital to an understanding of national reactions to the development of European integration. From the standpoint of a national lawyer, European law is often a source of disruption. It injects into the national legal system rules which are alien to its traditions and which may affect its deeper structure, thereby threatening its coherence. It may also be a source of arbitrary distinctions between similar situations. As Christian Joerges has noted, although the intervention of national parliaments is at times resented as an unwelcome intrusion by specialists in a given field, at least

> [l]egislative acts of national parliaments remain rooted in [traditional] contexts, even when they are perceived as destructive interventions. Moreover, they are still subject to control by case law, which is formulated with the objective of maintaining coherence. (Joerges, 1995, p. 183)

Not so with European law, over whose interpretation domestic courts have no direct influence. Thus, what appears as integration at European level is often perceived as a source of disintegration from the perspective of national legal systems.

Although the ECJ is not the only source of EC law, its law-making role has been considerable. Moreover, preliminary references are one of the central elements in the interface between Community law and national law. The ECJ is therefore perceived as the central agent in a process of perforation of national sovereignty.

We have already seen many examples of Community law's disruptive effect in the first part of this book. In *Simmenthal* (case 106/77), the Court held that in order to protect rights conferred by the Treaty on individuals, national courts were under a duty to set aside any conflicting legislation, even if they do not enjoy a power of judicial review of legislation in the domestic legal order. *Factortame I* (case 213/89) contained a similar invitation to disregard national law in the event of a claim for interim relief: the Court held that the full effectiveness of Community law would be impaired if a rule of national law could prevent a court from granting interim relief in cases where this is necessary to preserve rights claimed under Community law. *Marshall II* (case 271/91) invalidated a statutory limitation on damages in gender discrimination cases.

As noted earlier, the rights based logic inherent in these rulings ended up magnifying the powers of the judiciary, which certainly facilitated their acceptance. However, they introduced serious inconsistencies into domestic legal systems. The powers of courts are larger when they are seized of a dispute governed by EC law than when they have to rule in a purely domestic litigation. As a result, rights granted by Community law enjoy a better protection than those which derive from another source, which may be difficult to justify. EC law aside, it is not clear why sex discrimination ought to be treated any differently from, say, race discrimination.

Moreover, the ECJ emphasis on market unity and on the *effet utile* of the Community is often perceived as a threat to the consistency of entire sections of national legal systems. Areas like tax law, administrative or family law, are informed by national traditions and values. The Court's intermittent interventions in these areas has a clearly disruptive effect: it is far away from the parties and from the actual controversies; its decisions are influenced by abstract principles and look at the reality through the prism of market integration.

Since the beginning of the 1990s, the Court's case law has been the object of a growing number of critical comments. Interestingly, there seems to have been an evolution in the kind of criticism levelled at it. In addition to 'standard' attacks on judicial activism, where the ECJ is blamed for favouring a federal-type, purpose-orientated interpretation of the treaty, at times against the apparent meaning of the text – a view often voiced in the UK (see, for example, Neil, 1995; Hartley, 1996) – in various countries specialists from diverse branches of the law have accused the Court of paying insufficient attention to the specificities of their discipline, or to values which are deemed important in domestic legal systems (see Samara-Krispis and Steindorff, 1992; Simitis, 1997). Moreover, courts, which tend to regard themselves as being under a duty to uphold the national legal system and maintain its coherence, have shown increasing signs of impatience. Thus, UK courts, invoking the *acte clair* doctrine (see above, p. 138), have become experts in declining to refer cases to Luxembourg whenever they fear that the ECJ might be pressing too hard (Harlow, 1995). More diplomatically, German courts often choose to resubmit further questions to the ECJ when it has in their view failed to understand the legal background of the problem.

In the *Paletta* case (case C-45/90, *Paletta* v. *Brennet AG*), for instance, the ECJ held that German employers had to accept medical certificates from other member states. According to the certificate at issue, four members of the same family had fallen ill together during their summer holiday, as had already happened in the three previous years. To many German labour lawyers, the Court's decision appeared to exclude any effective means to prevent abuses of the right to paid sick leave. The Federal Labour Court shared this concern, and referred the case back to Luxembourg, stressing that the ruling of the ECJ violated the proportionality principle (Kokott, 1996, p. 45). Similarly, following the judgment of the ECJ in the *Banana* case (case C-280/93, *Germany* v. *Council*), several German courts referred to Luxembourg questions in which they stressed their disagreements with some of the most controversial aspects of that ruling (Reich, 1996).

The Maastricht ruling of the *Bundesverfassungsgericht*, already mentioned above, is another example of judicial reaction to the growing influence of the EC over domestic legal systems. The image of the German constitutional order which emerged from this judgment is very much that of a system whose coherence is endangered by the uncontrolled transfer of legislative powers to Community institutions, which lack democratic legitimacy and which will continue to do so in the foreseeable future (see Weiler, 1995 for a critique). The Karlsruhe court reacted by reasserting the basic primacy of German constitutional law and by recalling that the transfer of competence to the Community level was to be monitored in order to ensure that it would not alter the essence of the German constitutional order.

Reactions of this kind are symptomatic of a new trend in the relationships between the ECJ and two of its direct interlocutors: the national judiciary and the academic world, which both occupy a prominent position in national legal systems. Both have been staunch supporters of the Court in the first decades of existence of the Community. Yet, integration, because of its disruptive effects over national legal systems, is now breeding increasing resistance. Critiques of the ECJ, which were a rare event not so long ago, have become more commonplace. The Court is aware of this new mood, and it knows how dependent it is on its relations with its direct interlocutors. The retreat to a line of self-restraint is indicative of its willingness to accommodate itself to pressures emanating from national legal systems.

Conclusion

The developments of the last decade appear to lend credibility to the idea of a nexus between ECJ jurisprudence and the environment in which the Court operates.

Following the 1992 programme, the atypical equilibrium which had allowed the ECJ to act as a driving force in the integration process came to be significantly altered. From the mid-1980s on, it has been confronted with a much more dynamic political process. The growing reach of Community law has generated greater public attention to the deeds of European institutions, including of course the ECJ. This, combined with the development of inter-institutional litigation, has led the Court to be involved in disputes that had more of a political profile than was the case in the past.

At the same time, it has become clear that integration breeds ever greater resistance. The seemingly endless expansion of the EC's activities has come to be resented in a number of quarters. This trend has also affected the ECJ, whose rulings are often perceived as a source of disruption in national legal systems. Hence the growing number of critical voices heard in recent years among the Court's traditional interlocutors: domestic courts, national governments, academic circles.

As has been seen, this evolution has coincided with a shift in the jurisprudence of the Court, which appears anxious to avoid unnecessary clashes. The coincidence is so clear as to suggest that the two elements are related. Apparently, the Court has realized that the favourable constellation that allowed the constitutionalization of the Community Treaties is no longer there, and it has chosen to adapt itself to this new environment.

7

Conclusion: The ECJ as an Integration Catalyst

Unlike most international courts which are often confined to a somewhat obscure role, the ECJ has played a leading role in the development of European integration. Its influence has been felt at various levels, as has been seen throughout this book. It has utterly transformed the nature of the European Community and its relations with national legal systems, conferring upon Community law an authority akin to that enjoyed by federal law in federal systems. Its interpretations of the Treaty of Rome have had a decisive impact on the dynamics of integration. Its weight has been felt at all levels of the decision-making process, and its rights-based approach has on several occasions enabled the resolution of a stalemate that had prevented any decision from being taken. Results have been achieved that could not have been achieved were it not for the ECJ.

These remarkable accomplishments owe much to unexpected developments in the pattern of litigations that have come before the Court. Its rulings on direct effect and its willingness to let Article 177 [234] proceedings be used to review national legislation have opened the doors of the courtroom to private plaintiffs. As a result, individuals have played a role in the Community context without precedent on the international plane. More recently, Community institutions seem to have discovered that litigation can provide them additional means to pursue their policy objectives. These parallel developments have magnified the role of the ECJ, while also bringing about a notable juridification of the European policy process.

The importance of judge-led integration gives rise to two fundamental questions. How has the ECJ been able to play such an active role, which contrasts with the low profile normally expected from judicial bodies? Will the Court be able to play a similar role in the future?

The ECJ as a strategic actor

Understanding the factors that have enabled the ECJ to play such a prominent role in the integration process, requires an assessment of the relationships between judges and their legal and political environment.

Traditional perceptions of these relationships oscillate between two extreme poles. On the one hand, lawyers' views of courts often rest on a more or less implicit assumption of autonomy of the legal system. Judicial decisions are essentially regarded as an eminently rational exercise, in which general norms are applied to concrete cases. In this view, the outcome of judicial proceedings is (and ought to be) determined by the objective meaning of legal rules and by legal values rooted in each legal system. As indicated in the Introduction, many legal analyses of ECJ jurisprudence seem to be informed by this kind of view. At the opposite end of the scale, international relations analyses of the integration process often rule out any possibility of an autonomous action for the Court whose rulings are perceived to be determined by the anticipated reactions of national governments.

The analysis developed in this book suggests that there are elements of truth in both of these views, but that neither of them suffice to account for the behaviour of the Court.

A mere glance at the case law shows that it is difficult to regard ECJ rulings as a mere offspring of national governments' preferences. From *Van Gend & Loos* to *ERTA* or to *Cassis de Dijon*, there is no shortage of decisions taken in spite of the objections raised by powerful governments. The timing itself of some rulings is revealing: *Costa* v. *ENEL* was decided at the time when political tensions leading to the 1965–6 crisis were already looming; the *Cassis de Dijon* ruling was announced during an intensely difficult period marked by the conflict over the British contribution to the EC budget. In contrast, we have seen quite a few examples of cases in which the ultimate decision appears to have been shaped by legal values: the Court's interest in the protection of human rights was in part at least motivated by its eagerness to preserve the coherence of the Community legal system; the 'rule of law' concept clearly shaped its verdict in *Les Verts*, and so forth.

This, however, should not blind us to the fact that the ECJ has also given ample evidence of its sensitiveness to political constraints. Its reluctance to censure political institutions, its frequent attempts to identify a middle path when it has had to rule on a thorny political case clearly suggest its awareness that its authority can be challenged in the event of open conflicts with political actors. Moreover, both the flamboyant pro-integration approach of the 1960s and 1970s and the more recent shift towards a more cautious line appear to have been strongly influenced by the feedback received from its most direct interlocutors.

The ECJ must therefore be seen as a strategic actor, whose agenda is influenced by legal values, whether these be enshrined in the treaty or informed by judges' vision of their own role, but whose rulings are also informed by the knowledge that it must come to terms with reality in order to ensure compliance.

Looking at the future

Can the ECJ be expected to play in the years to come as important a role as it has in the past? The answer to this question will largely depend on its ability to respond to two challenges which have gained increasing importance in recent years. The first is the challenge of numbers: will the ECJ be able to cope with the seemingly endless growth of its workload? The second is more qualitative: as the constitutional profile of the ECJ has expanded in the post-SEA period, how will it adjust to the enhanced politicization which might develop as a result of recent institutional changes? Interestingly, both questions bear evidence of the Court's success as an institution: if its role was similar to that of most international courts, neither of these two problems would arise.

The challenge of numbers

As noted in Figure 6.3, the number of cases brought before the ECJ has been growing steadily. The creation of the Court of First

Instance, which was primarily motivated by the desire to reduce the ECJ's case-load, has not been sufficient even to slow down this trend. While the large number of cases referred to the ECJ has greatly contributed to the remarkable effectiveness of the integration process, as was seen in Chapter 2, this success has had its price. The number of cases undecided at the end of each year has grown at a steady pace: from 328 cases at the end of 1980, it jumped to 605 cases in 1988 (ECJ, 1991, p. 121), the year preceding the creation of the Court of First Instance. Figure 7.1 shows that each transfer of cases to the new court has had only temporary effects on the ECJ's backlog. The number of pending cases eased down for a while, but the increase resumed immediately afterwards. More importantly, the increase in the average length of proceedings does not seem to have been stopped by the creation of the court. For direct actions, it rose from 18.6 months in 1983 to 17.1 months in 1995, with peaks of above 25 months in 1990 and 1992. But the average duration of preliminary rulings which had been in the region of 18 months during 1987–94 (ECJ, 1991, p. 122; 1995, p. 241; 1996, p. 206), reached to 20.5 months in 1995 (ECJ, 1996, p. 206).

However, it must be kept in mind that preliminary references are interlocutory proceedings, which are preceded and normally followed by other proceedings before national courts. These data

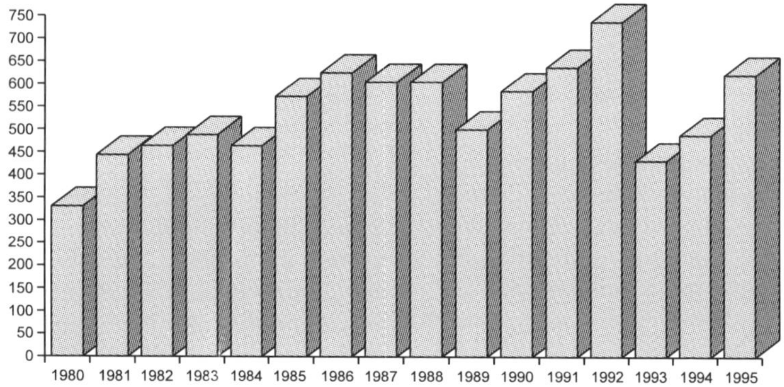

FIGURE 7.1 Cases pending on 31 December of each year
Source: *Synopsis of the work of the Court of Justice* for years 1980–91, *Report of Proceedings* for years 1992–4 and *Annual Report of the Court of Justice and CFI* for 1995.

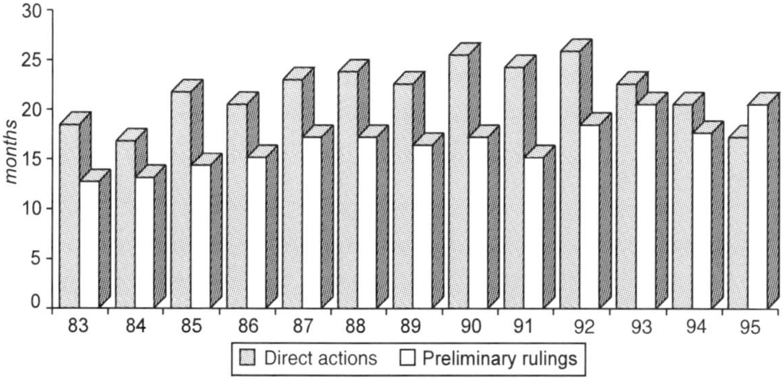

FIGURE 7.2 Average length of proceedings before the ECJ
Source: *Synopsis of the work of the Court of the Justice* for years 1980–91, *Report of Proceedings* for years 1992–4 and *Annual Report of the Court of Justice* for 1995.

clearly suggest that, in spite of the creation of the Court of First Instance, the EC's judicial system still faces great difficulties in handling the volume of complaints it receives. This is clearly a threat to the overall effectiveness of the Community, in that it may represent a disincentive to seek the courts' help in order to protect the rights granted in the treaty.

Various remedies have been suggested, ranging from the establishment of a mechanism of docket control, which would allow the Court to filter the cases and pick only the most important, as is the practice of the American Supreme Court (Rasmussen, 1986), to the establishment of regional courts which would relieve the Court of Justice of part of its burden (Jacqué and Weiler, 1990). Despite intense debate (see, for example, ECJ, 1996; Kapteyn, 1994; Koopmans, 1991, Van Gerven, 1996), none of these proposals has achieved a large consensus.

The prospect of an enlargement of the EU to incorporate Eastern European countries in a not-too-distant future adds considerable weight to these questions. With further increases in the number of cases and proceedings in several new languages, future expansions will undoubtedly complicate the work of the Court. It is far from clear that an increase in the number of judges would provide an adequate response to these difficulties. As the ECJ itself has pointed out,

> Any significant increase in the number of Judges might mean that the plenary session of the Court would cross the invisible boundary between a collegiate court and a deliberative assembly. Moreover, as the great majority of cases would be heard by Chambers, this increase could pose a threat to the consistency of the case law. (ECJ, 1996, p. 28)

At the same time, however, the presence of a judge from each member state enhances the legitimacy of the Court's decisions. Its submissions to the 1996–7 intergovernmental conference clearly suggest that there are contrasting views within it as to the way the enlargement challenge must be tackled (ibid.).

The growth of judicial politics and its implications

The last decade has been characterized by an increase in inter-institutional litigation. This trend may be exacerbated by changes introduced with the Maastricht and Amsterdam Treaties. motivated by the laudable desire to democratize the institutions, the member states have agreed to increase the power of the European Parliament in the procedure for selecting the Commission. Not only will it be consulted on the choice of the executive and the President, but the new Commission cannot begin to function until it has received a vote of confidence from the majority of the Parliament (new Article 158). Moreover, as the appointment of the Commission comes shortly after the European elections, the composition of the new executive could become one of the central issues in electoral campaigns in deciding which political tendencies and which personalities to favour. Perhaps the day will come when the European electorate, in throwing its support behind this or that party, will express a preference for a certain candidate as President of the Commission, just as German or British voters, in voting for the Christian Democrats or the Conservative Party, are voting for Mr Kohl or Mr Major.

Be that as it may, the new procedure for appointing the Commission is likely to reinforce the importance of party political cleavages at European level. This may bring about profound changes, particularly for the Commission, which in the past has known how to turn to its advantage its pluralistic – both in terms of nationality and political affiliation – character. What will happen in the future if a gulf separates majority and opposition? Undoubtedly, any developments in this direction will dramatically alter institutional equilibria in the Community system. If this is the case, what impact will these developments have on the ECJ's workload?

The conjunction of several factors make it likely that there will be a further increase in institutional conflicts before the ECJ, thereby strengthening its role as an umpire in institutional disputes. The grant to the Parliament of the right to take annulment proceedings against the other institutions when its prerogatives are threatened now permits it to have more frequent recourse to litigation as a means of asserting its own point of view. There is little reason to believe that it will not make use of this new right, inasmuch as the Maastricht Treaty has multiplied the range of procedures which can be employed. In areas such as the environment or research, no less than four different procedures are laid down, depending upon which type of measure is envisaged. This additional complexity is likely to lead to a further development of inter-institutional litigation.

This natural tendency could be prematurely activated by the politicization of decision-making. If different political balances dominate the Parliament and the Council, there will be an increased tendency to turn to the ECJ to arbitrate institutional conflicts and, this time around, pronounced political stakes are likely to peep through the institutional demands. It is also conceivable that member states which are marginalized in the Council will turn to the Court to correct the 'mistakes' of the majority, as has already happened in the past.

The temptation to do so will be reinforced by long-term developments in the jurisdiction of the ECJ. The need for a judicial protection of fundamental rights in the Community legal order, finally recognized in the Treaty of Amsterdam (new Article L [46]), has supplied the Court with an opportunity to control the Community political organs. And the member states, in conferring upon it the dubious honour of ensuring application of the subsidiarity principle, have acted, consciously or not, in the same direction. Human rights and subsidiarity: rules with very different origins and objectives but which both subscribe to the same logic – to ensure, in the name of higher principles, a measure of control over the actions of the political power. In responding to this invitation, however, the Court risks clashes with political organs which will now be able to claim much more political legitimacy than in days gone by.

Moreover, its position as a constitutional umpire is rendered particularly delicate by the heterogeneity of the EU. There are important divergences from country to country as to the degree of protection which specific human rights warrant – abortion being the most obvious example of a contentious area. A judicial response to this question is bound to meet with strong reactions, particularly if it emanates from a body like the ECJ, which will inevitably be denounced as alien to national traditions by those who object to its decision. A further development of judicial politics would therefore be likely to expose the Court to much more criticism than in the past.

The above elements suggest that the difficulties currently faced by the Court are not merely of a temporary nature. They bear evidence of deep-seated changes in the policy-making structure of the Community. Many of the factors which facilitated the ECJ's task by attenuating the impact of its case law are being side-lined, while new elements foreshadowing conflict between the judicial and political powers are moving into sharp focus in the Community institutional landscape. On the one hand, we have a court being called upon to rule on an growing number of socially sensitive issues and, on the other, we find a set of institutions within which party political cleavages seem destined to become increasingly significant. All of this at a time when public opinion is more and more attuned to European issues, and where consensus on the integration process is falling apart at the seams, as the debates surrounding ratification of the Maastricht Treaty clearly demonstrated. All the ingredients for conflict are present.

How will the Court react to a further development of judicial politics? Much will depend on how the judges conceive of their institutional mission. Here, it is worth noting that a significant number of former members of the ECJ have urged it to keep a low profile in order to avoid being dragged into political conflicts (Koopmans, 1986; Mackenzie Stuart, 1992; Mischo, 1990).

Be that as it may, whatever choice the ECJ does make, the political costs of its decisions could be much higher than in the past. The days when integrationist advances were given a favourable welcome by well-disposed elites and were ignored by the vast majority of the population are probably over. Paradoxical as it may seem, the stronger the links between the countries which make up the Community, the more the integration process seems to lose its value. Those for whom the union is an absolute value are increasingly rare, whilst social groups who feel that integration is desirable, but not at any price, are growing in number. Those making up this latter group will certainly disapprove if, as in the past, the ECJ continues to privilege institutional considerations. On the other hand, if it chooses to intervene more actively in contested issues, it risks coming up against institutions which have become much more politicized and which are endowed with a new legitimacy. In all probability, the conflict will be more acute than ever before, and the Court will be exposed – and this time with more reason – to the hostility of those who reject any idea of 'government by judges'.

The dangers of constitutionalization

If the above analysis is correct, the change in the ECJ's position in the institutional context of the EU is something of a paradox.

Now that the Community political system is moving away from the international model and closer to national models, perceptions of its principal actors tend to alter. The considerable influence enjoyed by the Court during a period when the Community was seen as a distant organization was atypical. Like all courts exercising constitutional jurisdiction, whenever it is called upon to rule on important political issues, the ECJ must come to terms with a stronger political power and more media attention. Thus, by a strange reversal of fortune, the ECJ, which worked so hard to constitutionalize Community law, seems to have lost ground in this process. Constitutional-type developments certainly complicate its own role and risk exposing it to growing criticism.

How should a rational judge react to such a transformation process? On paper, the answer would be: consolidate your own institutional position and the effectiveness of EC law, but do not get involved in political fights. This is exactly what the Court seems to be doing presently. That it was able to adapt to its new environment is hardly surprising: throughout its history, the ECJ has given ample evidence that it had a clear perception of its own institutional interest. Even in the 'golden decades' of the construction of the EC legal order, the Court displayed great caution in dealing with political actors (see Chapter 5). Its unwillingness to challenge national governments and EC institutions has become more obvious as opportunities for judicial review have increased. But it would be wrong to describe this evolution as a complete U-turn: the ECJ's current jurisprudence has remained a subtle blend of calculated boldness combined with caution, even if the respective doses of these two elements have changed.

Although this evolution might alarm traditional supporters of court-driven integration, it can also be seen as a sign of institutional maturity for the EU as a whole – a sign that in the European political system, as in 'normal' ones, political decisions tend to be left to the political process, with judges ensuring the fairness and the correct functioning of this process.

Appendix A: Table of Equivalence between the Former and the Renumbered Versions of the Treaty on European Union

Previous numbering	*New numbering*	*Previous numbering*	*New numbering*
Article A	Article 1	Article J 18	Article 28
Article B	Article 2	Article K.1	Article 29
Article C	Article 3	Article K.2	Article 30
Article D	Article 4	Article K.3	Article 31
Article E	Article 5	Article K.4	Article 32
Article F	Article 6	Article K.5	Article 33
Article F.1	Article 7	Article K.6	Article 34
Article G	Article 8	Article K.7	Article 35
Article H	Article 9	Article K.8	Article 36
Article I	Article 10	Article K.9	Article 37
Article J.1	Article 11	Article K.10	Article 38
Article J.2	Article 12	Article K.11	Article 39
Article J.3	Article 13	Article K.12	Article 40
Article J.4	Article 14	Article K.13	Article 41
Article J.5	Article 15	Article K.14	Article 42
Article J.6	Article 16	Article K.15	Article 43
Article J.7	Article 17	Article K.16	Article 44
Article J.8	Article 18	Article K.17	Article 45
Article J.9	Article 19	Article L	Article 46
Article J.10	Article 20	Article M	Article 47
Article J.11	Article 21	Article N	Article 48
Article J.12	Article 22	Article O	Article 49
Article J.13	Article 23	Article P	Article 50
Article J.14	Article 24	Article Q	Article 51
Article J.15	Article 25	Article R	Article 52
Article J.16	Article 26	Article S	Article 53
Article J.17	Article 27		

Appendix B: Table of Equivalence between the Former and the Renumbered Versions of the Treaty Establishing the European Community (The EC Treaty or Treaty of Rome)

Previous numbering	*New numbering*	*Previous numbering*	*New numbering*
Article 1	Article 1	Article 9	Article 23
Article 2	Article 2	Article 10	Article 24
Article 3	Article 3	Article 11 (repealed)	
Article 3a	Article 4	Article 12	Article 25
Article 3b	Article 5	Article 13 (repealed)	
Article 3c	Article 6	Article 14 (repealed)	
Article 4	Article 7	Article 15 (repealed)	
Article 4a	Article 8	Article 16 (repealed)	
Article 4b	Article 9	Article 17 (repealed)	
Article 5	Article 10	Article 18 (repealed)	
Article 5a	Article 11	Article 19 (repealed)	
Article 6	Article 12	Article 20 (repealed)	
Article 6a	Article 13	Article 21 (repealed)	
Article 7 (repealed)		Article 22 (repealed)	
Article 7a	Article 14	Article 23 (repealed)	
Article 7b (repealed)		Article 24 (repealed)	
Article 7c	Article 15	Article 25 (repealed)	
Article 7d	Article 16	Article 26 (repealed)	
Article 8	Article 17	Article 27 (repealed)	
Article 8a	Article 18	Article 28	Article 26
Article 8b	Article 19	Article 29	Article 27
Article 8c	Article 20	Article 30	Article 28
Article 8d	Article 21	Article 31 (repealed)	
Article 8e	Article 22	Article 32 (repealed)	

Previous Numbering	*New Numbering*	*Previous Numbering*	*New Numbering*
Article 33 (repealed)		Article 73d	Article 58
Article 34	Article 29	Article 73e (repealed)	
Article 35 (repealed)		Article 73f	Article 59
Article 36	Article 30	Article 73g	Article 60
Article 37	Article 31	Article 73h (repealed)	
Article 38	Article 32	Article 73i	Article 61
Article 39	Article 33	Article 73j	Article 62
Article 40	Article 34	Article 73k	Article 63
Article 41	Article 35	Article 73l	Article 64
Article 42	Article 36	Article 73m	Article 65
Article 43	Article 37	Article 73n	Article 66
Article 44 (repealed)		Article 73o	Article 67
Article 45 (repealed)		Article 73p	Article 68
Article 46	Article 38	Article 73q	Article 69
Article 47 (repealed)		Article 74	Article 70
Article 48	Article 39	Article 75	Article 71
Article 49	Article 40	Article 76	Article 72
Article 50	Article 41	Article 77	Article 73
Article 51	Article 42	Article 78	Article 74
Article 52	Article 43	Article 79	Article 75
Article 53 (repealed)		Article 80	Article 76
Article 54	Article 44	Article 81	Article 77
Article 55	Article 45	Article 82	Article 78
Article 56	Article 46	Article 83	Article 79
Article 57	Article 47	Article 84	Article 80
Article 58	Article 48	Article 85	Article 81
Article 59	Article 49	Article 86	Article 82
Article 60	Article 50	Article 87	Article 83
Article 61	Article 51	Article 88	Article 84
Article 62 (repealed)		Article 89	Article 85
Article 63	Article 52	Article 90	Article 86
Article 64	Article 53	Article 91 (repealed)	
Article 65	Article 54	Article 92	Article 87
Article 66	Article 55	Article 93	Article 88
Article 67 (repealed)		Article 94	Article 89
Article 68 (repealed)		Article 95	Article 90
Article 69 (repealed)		Article 96	Article 91
Article 70 (repealed)		Article 97 (repealed)	
Article 71 (repealed)		Article 98	Article 92
Article 72 (repealed)		Article 99	Article 93
Article 73 (repealed)		Article 100	Article 94
Article 73a (repealed)		Article 100a	Article 95
Article 73b	Article 56	Article 100b (repealed)	
Article 73c	Article 57	Article 100c (repealed)	

Previous Numbering	*New Numbering*	*Previous Numbering*	*New Numbering*
Article 100d (repealed)		Article 118	Article 137
Article 101	Article 96	Article 118a	Article 138
Article 102	Article 97	Article 118b	Article 139
Article 102a	Article 98	Article 118c	Article 140
Article 103	Article 99	Article 119	Article 141
Article 103a	Article 100	Article 119a	Article 142
Article 104	Article 101	Article 120	Article 143
Article 104a	Article 102	Article 121	Article 144
Article 104b	Article 103	Article 122	Article 145
Article 104c	Article 104	Article 123	Article 146
Article 105	Article 105	Article 124	Article 147
Article 105a	Article 106	Article 125	Article 148
Article 106	Article 107	Article 126	Article 149
Article 107	Article 108	Article 127	Article 150
Article 108	Article 109	Article 128	Article 151
Article 108a	Article 110	Article 129	Article 152
Article 109	Article 111	Article 129a	Article 153
Article 109a	Article 112	Article 129b	Article 154
Article 109b	Article 113	Article 129c	Article 155
Article 109c	Article 114	Article 129d	Article 156
Article 109d	Article 115	Article 130	Article 157
Article 109e	Article 116	Article 130a	Article 158
Article 109f	Article 117	Article 130b	Article 159
Article 109g	Article 118	Article 130c	Article 160
Article 109h	Article 119	Article 130d	Article 161
Article 109i	Article 120	Article 130e	Article 162
Article 109j	Article 121	Article 130f	Article 163
Article 109k	Article 122	Article 130g	Article 164
Article 109l	Article 123	Article 130h	Article 165
Article 109m	Article 124	Article 130i	Article 166
Article 109n	Article 125	Article 130j	Article 167
Article 109o	Article 126	Article 130k	Article 168
Article 109p	Article 127	Article 130l	Article 169
Article 109q	Article 128	Article 130m	Article 170
Article 109r	Article 129	Article 130n	Article 171
Article 109s	Article 130	Article 130o	Article 172
Article 110	Article 131	Article 130p	Article 173
Article 111 (repealed)		Article 130q (repealed)	
Article 112	Article 132	Article 130r	Article 174
Article 113	Article 133	Article 130s	Article 175
Article 114 (repealed)		Article 130t	Article 176
Article 115	Article 134	Article 130u	Article 177
Article 116	Article 135	Article 130v	Article 178
Article 117	Article 136	Article 130w	Article 179

Previous Numbering	*New Numbering*	*Previous Numbering*	*New Numbering*
Article 130x	Article 180	Article 168	Article 224
Article 130y	Article 181	Article 168a	Article 225
Article 131	Article 182	Article 169	Article 226
Article 132	Article 183	Article 170	Article 227
Article 133	Article 184	Article 171	Article 228
Article 134	Article 185	Article 172	Article 229
Article 135	Article 186	Article 173	Article 230
Article 136	Article 187	Article 174	Article 231
Article 136a	Article 188	Article 175	Article 232
Article 137	Article 189	Article 176	Article 233
Article 138	Article 190	Article 177	Article 234
Article 138a	Article 191	Article 178	Article 235
Article 138b	Article 192	Article 179	Article 236
Article 138c	Article 193	Article 180	Article 237
Article 138d	Article 194	Article 181	Article 238
Article 138e	Article 195	Article 182	Article 239
Article 139	Article 196	Article 183	Article 240
Article 140	Article 197	Article 184	Article 241
Article 141	Article 198	Article 185	Article 242
Article 142	Article 199	Article 186	Article 243
Article 143	Article 200	Article 187	Article 244
Article 144	Article 201	Article 188	Article 245
Article 145	Article 202	Article 188a	Article 246
Article 146	Article 203	Article 188b	Article 247
Article 147	Article 204	Article 188c	Article 248
Article 148	Article 205	Article 189	Article 249
Article 149 (repealed)		Article 189a	Article 250
Article 150	Article 206	Article 189b	Article 251
Article 151	Article 207	Article 189c	Article 252
Article 152	Article 208	Article 190	Article 253
Article 153	Article 209	Article 191	Article 254
Article 154	Article 210	Article 191a	Article 255
Article 155	Article 211	Article 192	Article 256
Article 156	Article 212	Article 193	Article 257
Article 157	Article 213	Article 194	Article 258
Article 158	Article 214	Article 195	Article 259
Article 159	Article 215	Article 196	Article 260
Article 160	Article 216	Article 197	Article 261
Article 161	Article 217	Article 198	Article 262
Article 162	Article 218	Article 198a	Article 263
Article 163	Article 219	Article 198b	Article 264
Article 164	Article 220	Article 198c	Article 265
Article 165	Article 221	Article 198d	Article 266
Article 166	Article 222	Article 198e	Article 267
Article 167	Article 223	Article 199	Article 268

Previous Numbering	*New Numbering*	*Previous Numbering*	*New Numbering*
Article 200 (repealed)		Article 222	Article 295
Article 201	Article 269	Article 223	Article 296
Article 201a	Article 270	Article 224	Article 297
Article 202	Article 271	Article 225	Article 298
Article 203	Article 272	Article 226 (repealed)	
Article 204	Article 273	Article 227	Article 299
Article 205	Article 274	Article 228	Article 300
Article 205a	Article 275	Article 228a	Article 301
Article 206	Article 276	Article 229	Article 302
Article 206a (repealed)		Article 230	Article 303
Article 207	Article 277	Article 231	Article 304
Article 208	Article 278	Article 232	Article 305
Article 209	Article 279	Article 233	Article 306
Article 209a	Article 280	Article 234	Article 307
Article 210	Article 281	Article 235	Article 308
Article 211	Article 282	Article 236	Article 309
Article 212	Article 283	Article 237 (repealed)	
Article 213	Article 284	Article 238	Article 310
Article 213a	Article 285	Article 239	Article 311
Article 213b	Article 286	Article 240	Article 312
Article 214	Article 287	Article 241 (repealed)	
Article 215	Article 288	Article 242 (repealed)	
Article 216	Article 289	Article 243 (repealed)	
Article 217	Article 290	Article 244 (repealed)	
Article 218	Article 291	Article 245 (repealed)	
Article 219	Article 292	Article 246 (repealed)	
Article 220	Article 293	Article 247	Article 313
Article 221	Article 294	Article 248	Article 314

Guide to Further Reading

Chapter 1

Detailed descriptions of the organization and the functioning of the ECJ can be found in Brown and Kennedy (1995) and in March Hunnings (1996). Schermers and Waelbroeck (1992) offer an exhaustive account of the various remedies established by the EC Treaty.

Chapter 2

As regards the 'constitutionalization' of the EC Treaty, the classics are Mancini (1989), Stein (1981) and Weiler (1991). Lecourt (1976) offers an account of the same process as seen from an insider's standpoint (the author was the President of the ECJ for a substantial part of the 'heroic' period). A review of the various routes that have been followed to ensure the effectiveness of EC law is provided in Snyder (1993).

Chapter 3

Surveys of the impact of the Court's case law are scarce and sectorial. Leibfried and Pierson (1996) document its influence on social policy, while Alter and Meunier-Aitsahalia (1994) focus on the *Cassis de Dijon* ruling and its impact on free movement of goods. Garrett (1992 and 1995) is very sceptical as to the possibility for the ECJ to exert an autonomous role in the integration process; see however Mattli and Slaughter (1995) for a rebuttal. The interaction between the ECJ and political institutions is discussed in Lenaerts (1992) and Shapiro (1992).

Chapter 4

Harlow and Rawlings (1992) and Rawlings (1993) have shown how private plaintiffs may resort to litigation at European level to achieve results that they were unable to achieve through the political process.

Chapter 5

Burley and Mattli (1993) and Weiler (1994) have offered insightful surveys of the interaction between the ECJ and its interlocutors. Their analysis is in sharp contrast with that of Rasmussen (1986), which is much more critical of the Court's work.

Chapter 6

Curtin (1993) has analyzed the reactions to ECJ jurisprudence contained in the Maastricht Treaty. Mancini and Keeling (1995) and Rodriguez Iglesias (1996) show various ways in which this has influenced post-Maastricht case law.

Bibliography

Allen, D. (1996) 'Cohesion and Structural Adjustment', in H. Wallace and W. Wallace (eds), *Policy Making in the European Union* (Oxford University Press).

Alter, K. (1995) 'Explaining National Court Acceptance of European Jurisprudence: A Critical Evaluation of Theories of Integration', EUI Working Paper RSC no. 95/27, European University Institute, Florence.

Alter, K. J. and S. Meunier-Aitsahalia (1994) 'Judicial Politics in the European Community: European Integration and the Pathbreaking *Cassis de Dijon* Decision', *Comparative Political Studies*, **26**: 535–61.

Barnard, C. (1995) 'A European Litigation Strategy: the Case of the Equal Opportunities Commission', in J. Shaw and G. Moore (eds), *New Legal Dynamics of European Union* (Oxford: Clarendon Press).

Berlin, D. (1992) 'Interactions between the Lawmaker and the Judiciary within the EC', *Legal Issues of European Integration*, **2**: 17–48.

Berman, G. A. (1995) 'Regulatory Decision-Making in the European Commission', *Columbia Journal of European Law*, **1**: 415–33.

Boulouis, J. (1974) 'A propos de la fonction normative de la jurisprudence – Remarques sur l'oeuvre jurisprudentielle de la Cour de Justice des Communautés européennes', *Mélanges offerts à Marcel Waline – Le Juge et le Droit public*, vol. 1 (Paris: Pichon et Durand-Auzias).

Bourgeois, J. (1995) 'The EC in the WTO and Advisory Opinion 1/94: An Echternach Procession', *Common Market Law Review*, **32**: 763.

Brown, L. N. and T. Kennedy (1995) *The Court of Justice of the European Communities*, 4th edn (London: Sweet & Maxwell).

Bulmer, S. (1994) 'Institutions and Policy Change in the European Communities: The Case of Merger Control', *Public Administration*, 423–44.

Burley, A.-M. and W. Mattli (1993) 'Europe Before the Court: A Political Theory of Legal Integration', *International Organization*, **47**: 41–76.

Caporaso, J. A. and J.T. S. Keeler (1993) 'The European Community and Regional Integration Theory', Paper presented at the International Conference of the European Studies Association, Washington DC, May.

Cappelletti, M. (1989) *The Judicial Process in Comparative Perspective* (Oxford: Clarendon Press).

Chalmers, D. (1994) 'Repackaging the Internal Market – The Ramification of the Keck Judgment', *European Law Review*, **19**: 385–403.

Close, G. (1978) 'Harmonisation of Laws: Use or Abuse of Powers under the EEC Treaty', *European Law Review*, **3**: 481–6.

Commission (1997) Fourteenth Annual Report on the Implementation of Community Law, COM(97) 299 final.

Corbett, R., F. Jacobs, and M. Shackleton (1995) *The European Parliament*, 3rd edn (London: Cartermill).
Craig, P. P. (1995) 'The European Court and National Courts – Doctrine and Jurisprudence, Legal Change in Its Social Context, Report on the United Kingdom', EUI Working Paper RSC 95/29.
Curtin, D. (1993) 'The Constitutional Structure at the Union: A Europe of Bits and Pieces', *Common Market Law Review,* **30**: 17–69.
Davies, P. L. (1997) 'The Relationship between the European Court of Justice and the British Courts over the Interpretation of Directive 77/187/EC', Working Paper Law no. 97/2, European University Institute, Florence.
Dehousse, R. (1990) *Europe After Maastricht – An Ever Closer Union?* (LBE München).
Dehousse, R. (1995) 'Constitutional Reform in the European Community: Are there Alternatives to the Majoritarian Avenue?', *West European Politics*, **18**: 118–36.
Dehousse, R. (1997) 'European Integration and the Nation-State', in M. Rhodes, P. Heywood and V. Wright (eds), *Developments in West European Politics* (London: Macmillan).
Dehousse, R. and G. Majone (1994) 'The Dynamics of Integration: From the Single European Act to the Maastricht Treaty', in S. Martin (ed.) *The Construction of Europe – Essays in Honor of Emile Noël* (Dordrecht: Kluwer) pp. 91–112.
Dehousse, R. and J. H. H. Weiler (1990) 'The Legal Dimension', in W. Wallace (ed.) *The Dynamics of European Integration* (London – New York: Pinter) pp. 242–60.
de Witte, B. (1984) 'Retour à Costa: la primauté du droit communautaire à la lumière du droit international', *Revue trimestrielle de droit européen*: 425–54.
Diez-Picazo, L. (1993) 'Reflexiones sobre la idea de Constitucion europea', *Revista de Istituciones Europeas*, **20**: 533–59.
European Court of Justice (1991, 1995) *Synopsis of the Work of the Court of Justice and the Court of First Instance of the European Community* (Luxembourg: Office for Official Publications).
European Court of Justice (1996) *Annual Report 1995* (Luxembourg: Office for Official Publications).
Everson, M. (1993) 'Laws in Conflict – A Rationally Integrated European Insurance Market?', PhD Thesis, European University Institute, Florence.
Galanter, M. (1974) 'Why the "Haves" Come Out Ahead: speculations on the limits of legal change', *Law and Society* (Fall 1974): 95–160.
Garrett, G. (1992) 'International Cooperation and Institutional Choice: The European Community's Internal Market', *International Organization*, **41**: 533–60.
Garrett, G. (1995) 'The Politics of Legal Integration in the European Union', *International Organization*, **49**: 171.

Gibson, J. G. (1989) 'Understandings of Justice: Institutional Legitimacy, Procedural Justice, and Political Tolerance', *Law and Society Review*, **23**: 469–96.

Gibson, J. G. and G. A. Caldreira (1993) 'The European Court of Justice: A Question of Legitimacy', *Zeitschrift für Rechtssoziologie*, **14**: 204–42.

Gibson, J. G. and G. A. Caldreira (1995) 'The Legitimacy of Transnational Legal Institutions: Compliance, Support and the European Court of Justice', *American Journal of Political Science*, **39**: 459–89.

Golub, J. (1996) 'Modelling Judicial Dialogue in the European Community: the Quantitative Basis of Preliminary References to ECJ', EUI Working Paper RSC no. 96/58, European University Institute, Florence.

Gormley, L. (1985) *Prohibiting Restrictions on Trade within the EEC* (Amsterdam: North Holland).

Green, A. W. (1969) *Political Integration by Jurisprudence* (Leyden: Sijthoff).

Haas, E. (1968) *The Uniting of Europe*, 2nd edn (Stanford: Stanford University Press).

Harding, C. (1992) 'Who Goes to Court in Europe? An Analysis of Litigation against the European Community', *European Law Review*, **17**: 104–25.

Harlow, C. (1992) 'A Community of Interests? Making the Most of European Law', *Modern Law Review*, **55**: 331–50.

Harlow, C. (1992) 'Towards a Theory of Access for the European Court of Justice', *Yearbook of European Law*, **12**: 213–48.

Harlow, C. (1995) 'The National Legal Order and the Court of Justice: Some Reflections on the case of the United Kingdom', *Rivista italiana di diritto pubblico comunitario*, **V**: 929–45.

Harlow, C. (1996) 'Francovich and the Problem of the Disobedient State', *European Law Journal*, **2**: 199–225.

Harlow, C. and R. Rawlings (1992) *Pressure Through Law* (New York: Routledge).

Hartley, T. C. (1996) 'The European Court, Judicial Objectivity and the Constitution of the European Union', *Law Quarterly Review*, **112**: 95–109.

Hartley, T. C. (1994) *The Foundations of European Community Law*, 3rd edn (Oxford: Clarendon Press).

Hilf, M. (1995) 'The ECJ's Opinion 1/94 on the WTO – No Surprise, but Wise?', *European Journal of International Law*, **6** (2): 245–59.

Holland, K. M. (1991) 'Introduction' in K. M. Holland (ed.) *Judicial Activism in Comparative Perspective* (London: Macmillan), pp. 1–11.

Jacqué, J.-P. and J.H.H. Weiler (1990) 'On the Road To European Union – A New Judicial Architecture', *Common Market Law Review*, **27**: 185.

Jacqué, J.-P. (1991) 'Le Rôle du droit dans l'intégration européenne', *Philosophie politique*, pp. 119–133.

Joerges, C. (1995) 'The Europeanization of Private Law as a Rationalization Process and as a Contest of Disciplines – An Analysis of the Directive on Unfair Terms in Consumer Contracts', *European Law Journal*, **2**(1).

Joliet, R. (1995) 'The Free Circulation of Goods: the Keck and Mithouard Decision and the New Directions in the Case Law', *Columbia Journal of European Law*, **1**: 437–51.

Kapteyn, P. J.G. (1994) 'The Court of Justice of the European Communities after the Year 2000', in D. Curtin and T. Heukels (eds), *Institutional Dynamics of European Integration* (Dardrecht: Nijhoff).

Keohane, R.O. and S. Hoffmann (1991) 'Institutional Change in Europe in the 1980s', in R. Keohane and S. Hoffmann (eds), *The New European Community* (Boudler: Westview), pp. 1–40.

Kilroy, B. (1996) 'Judicial Independence or Politically Constrained Courts. The Politics of Decision-making in the European Court of Justice', paper presented at the meeting of International Studies Association, San Diego, 16–20 April.

Kingdon, J.W. (1984) *Agendas, Alternatives and Public Policies* (Boston: Little, Brown).

Kokott, J. (1996) 'The European Court and the National Courts – Doctrine and Jurisprudence: Legal Change in its Social Context, Report on Germany', EUI Working Paper RSC no. 95/25, European University Institute, Florence.

Koopmans, T. (1986) 'The Role of Law in the Next Stage of European Integration', *International and Comparative Law Quarterly*, **34**: 925–31.

Koopmans, T. (1991) 'The Future of the Court of Justice of the European Communities', *Yearbook of European Law,* **11**: 15–32.

Kuilwijk, K.J. (1996) *The European Court of Justice and the GATT Dilemma: Public Interest versus Individual Rights?* (Beuningen: Nexed Editions).

Kuyper, P.J. (1995) 'The Conclusion and Implementation of the Uruguay Round Results by the European Community', in *European Journal of International Law*, **6** (2): 222–44.

Lagrange, M. (1979) 'La Cour de Justice des Communautés européennes du Plan Schuman à l'Union européenne', *Mélanges Fernand Dehousse*, vol. 2 (Paris and Brussels: Nathan-Labor) pp. 127–35.

Lecourt, R. (1976) *L'Europe des Juges* (Brussels: Bruylant).

Lecourt, R. (1991) 'Quel eut été le droit des communautés sans les ârrets de 1963 et 1964?' in *L'Europe et le Droit – Mélange en hommage à Jean Boulouis* (Paris: Dalloz).

Leibfried, S. and P. Piersòn (1996) 'Social Policy' in H. Wallace and W. Wallace (eds) *Policy-Making in the European Union*, 3rd edn, pp. 185–207.

Lenaerts, K. (1992) 'Some Thoughts about the Interaction between Judges and Politicians in the European Community', *Yearbook of European Law*, **12**: 1–34.

Louis, J.-V. (1990) *L'Ordre juridique communautaire*, 5th edn (Luxembourg: Office for Official Publications).

Mackenzie, Stuart Lord (1992) 'Subsidiarity: A Busted Flush?' in D. Curtin and D. O'Keeffe (eds), *Constitutional Adjudication in European Community and National Law – Essays for the Hon. Mr Justice T.F. O'Higgins* (Dublin: Butterworth) pp. 19–24.

Majone, G. (1993) 'The European Community between Social Policy and Social Regulation', *Journal of Common Market Studies*, **31**: 153–70.

Mancini, G.F. (1989) 'The Making of a Constitution for Europe', *Common Market Law Review*, **26**: 595–614.

Mancini, G.F. and D.T. Keeling (1995) 'From Cilfit to ERT: the Constitutional challenge facing the European Court', *Yearbook of European Law*, **11**:1–13.

Mancini, G.F. and D.T. Keeling (1995) 'Language, Culture and Politics in the Life of the European Court of Justice', *Columbia Journal of European Law*, **1**: 397–413.

Mandel, M. (1994) *The Charter of Rights and the Legalization of Politics in Canada*, 2nd edn (Toronto: Thompson Educational).

March Hunnings, N. (1996) *The European Courts* (London: Cartermill).

Mattera, A. (1994) 'De l'arrêt "Dassonville" à l'arrêt "Keck": l'obscure clarté d'une jurisprudence riche en effets novateurs et en contradictions', *Revue du marché unique européen*, **1**: 117–60.

Mattli, W. and A. -M. Slaughter (1995) 'Law and Politics in The European Union', *International Organization,* **49**: 183–90.

Meehan, E. (1993) *Citizenship and the European Community* (London: Sage).

Mischo, J. (1990) 'Un rôle nouveau pour la Cour de Justice?', *Revue du marché commun*, **342**: 681–6.

Moravcsik, A. (1993) 'Preferences and Power in the European Community: A Liberal Intergovernmentalist Approach' *Journal of Common Market Studies*, **31**: 473–524.

Neil, P. (1995) *The European Court of Justice: A Case Study, in Judicial Activism* (London: European Policy Forum).

Nicolaïdis, K. (1993) 'Legal Precedent and Political Innovation in the European Community: Explaining the Emergence of Managed Mutual Recognition', paper presented at the conference of European Community Studies Association, Washington, 27–29 May.

Oppenheimer, A. (1994) *The Relationship between European Community Law and National Law: The Cases* (Cambridge University Press).

Pellet, A. (1994) 'Le fondaments juridiques internationaux du droit communautaire', in Academy of European Law (ed.) *Collected Courses of the Academy of European Law* vol. V, bk 2 (The Hague: Kluwer Law International) pp. 173–271.

Pescatore, P. (1981a) 'Les Travaux du "groupe juridique" dans la négotiation des traités de Rome', *Studia Diplomatica*, **34**: 159–78.

Pescatore, P. (1981b) 'Aspects judiciaires de l'acquis communautaire', *Revue trimestrielle de droit européen*, 619.

Pescatore, P. (1983a) 'La Carence du législateur communautaire et le Devoir du juge', *Rechtsvergleihung, Europarecht, Staatsintegration – Gedächtnisschrift für L.-J. Constantinesco* (Cologne: Carl Heymanns Verlag) pp. 559–80.

Pescatore, P. (1983b) 'The Doctrine of "Direct Effect": An Infant Disease of Community Law', *European Law Review*, **8**: 155–77.

Pinder, J. (1968) 'Positive Integration and Negative Integration – Some Problems of Economic Union in the EEC', *The World Today*, **24**: 88–110.
Piris, J.C. (1994) 'After Maastricht, Are the Community Institutions More Efficacious, More Democratic and More Transparent?', *European Law Review*, **19**: 449–87.
Rasmussen, H. (1986) *On Law and Policy in the European Court of Justice – A Comparative Study* (Dordrecht: Nijhoff).
Rawlings, R. (1993) 'The Eurolaw Game: Some deductions from a saga', *Journal of Law and Society*, **20**: 309–40.
Reich, N. (1994) 'The November Revolution', *Common Market Law Review*, **31**: 459–92.
Reich, N. (1996) 'Judge-made "Europe à la carte": Some Remarks on Recent Conflicts between European and German Constitutional Law Provoked by the Banana Litigation', *European Journal of International Law*, **7**: 103–11.
Rodriguez Iglesias, G. C. (1996) 'Le pouvoir judiciaire de la Communauté européenne au stade actuel de l'évolution de l'Union', Jean Monnet Chair Papers, no. 41, Robert Schuman Centre at the European University Institute, Florence.
Rousseau, D. (1992) 'Constitution', in O. Duhamel and Y. Mény (eds) *Dictionnaire constitutionnel* (Paris) pp. 208–12.
Samara-Krispis, A. and E. Steindorff (1992) Case note, *Common Market Law Review*, **29**: 615.
Sandholz, W. and J. Zysman (1989) 'Recasting the European Bargain', *World Politics*, **42**: 95–128.
Scharpf, F. (1995) 'Negative and Positive Integration in the Political Economy of European Welfare States', Jean Monnet Chair Papers, no. 28, Robert Schuman Centre at the European University Institute, Florence.
Scheingold S.A. (1971) 'The Law in Political Integration: The Evolution and Integrative Implications of Regional Legal Processes in the European Community', Occasional Papers in International Affairs no. 27 (Cambridge, Mass.: Harvard University Center for International Affairs).
Schermers, H.G. (1980) *International Institutional Law*, 2nd edn (Alphen aan den Rijn: Sijthoff and Noordhof).
Schermers, H.G. and D. Waelbroeck (1992) *Judicial Protection in the European Communities*, 4th edn (Deventer: Kluwer).
Shapiro, M. (1980) 'Comparative Law and Comparative Politics', *Southern California Law Review*, **53**: 538.
Shapiro, M. (1981) *Courts – A Comparative and Political Analysis* (Chicago and London: University of Chicago Press).
Shapiro, M. (1992) 'The Giving Reasons Requirement', *The University of Chicago Legal Forum*, 179–220.
Shaw, J. (1995) 'European Union Legal Studies in Crisis? Towards a New Dynamics', EUI Working Paper RSC no. 95/23, European University Institute, Florence.

Simitis, S. (1997) 'Dismantling or Strengthening Labour Law: the Case of the European Court of Justice', *European Law Journal*, **3**(1): 156–76.
Simon, D. (1991) 'Les exigences de la primauté du Droit communautaire: continuité ou métamorphoses?', *L'Europe et le droit – Mélanges en hommáge à Jean Boulouis* (Paris: Dalloz) pp. 481–93.
Snyder, F. (1993) 'The Effectiveness of European Community Law: Institutions, Processes, Tools and Techniques', *Modern Law Review*, **56**: 19–54.
Stein, E. (1981) 'Lawyers, Judges, and the Making of a Transnational Constitution', *American Journal of International Law*, **75**: 1–27.
Stone, A. (1992) *The Birth of Judicial Politics in France: The Constitutional Council in Comparative Perspective* (Oxford University Press).
Stone Sweet, S.A. and J. Caporaso (1996) 'From Free Trade to Supranational Polity: The European Court and Integration', prepared for presentation at the conference *Supranational Governance: The Institutionalization of the European Union*, Berkeley, California, November.
Van Empel, M. (1992) 'The 1992 Programme: Interaction between Legislator and Judiciary', *Legal Issues of European Integration*, **2**: 1–16.
Van Gerven, W. (1996) 'The Role and Structure of the European Judiciary Now and in the Future' in J.A. Winter *et al.* (eds), *Reforming the Treaty on European Union – The Legal Debate* (The Hague: Kluwer).
Volcansek, M.L. (1992) 'The European Court of Justice: Supranational Policy-Making', *West European Politics*, **15**: 109–21.
Wallace, W. (1990) (ed.) *The Dynamics of European Integration* (London and New York: Pinter) pp. 242–60.
Weiler, J.H.H. (1981) 'The Community System: The Dual Character of Supranationalism', *Yearbook of European Law*, **1**: 267.
Weiler, J.H.H. (1982) 'Community, Member States and European Integration: Is the Law Relevant?', *Journal of Common Market Studies*, **20**: 399–56.
Weiler, J.H.H. (1986) 'Eurocracy and Distrust: Some Questions concerning the Role of the European Court of Justice in the Protection of Fundamental Human Rights within the Legal Order of the European Communities', *Washington Law Review*, **61**: 1103–42.
Weiler, J.H.H. (1992) 'Primus inter Pares: The European Court and National Courts – Thirty Years of Cooperation', unpublished manuscript.
Weiler, J.H.H. (1993) 'Journey to An Unknown Destination: A Retrospective and Prospective of the European Court of Justice in the Arena of Political Integration', *Journal of Common Market Studies*, **31**: 417.
Weiler, J.H.H. (1994) 'A Quiet Revolution – The European Court of Justice and its Interlocutors', *Comparative Political Studies*, **26**: 510–34.
Weiler, J.H.H. (1995) 'Does Europe Need a Constitution? Demos, Telos and the German Maastricht Decision', *European Law Journal*, **1** (3).
Weiler, J.H.H. and N.J.S. Lockhart (1995) '"*Taking Right Seriously*" Seriously: The European Court and its Fundamental Rights Jurisprudence', Parts I–II, *Common Market Law Review*, **32**: 51–94 and 579–627.

Index of Cases Cited*

European Court of Justice

*Cases are listed in chronological order.

National Jurisdication

France

Germany

United Kingdom

United States

General Index